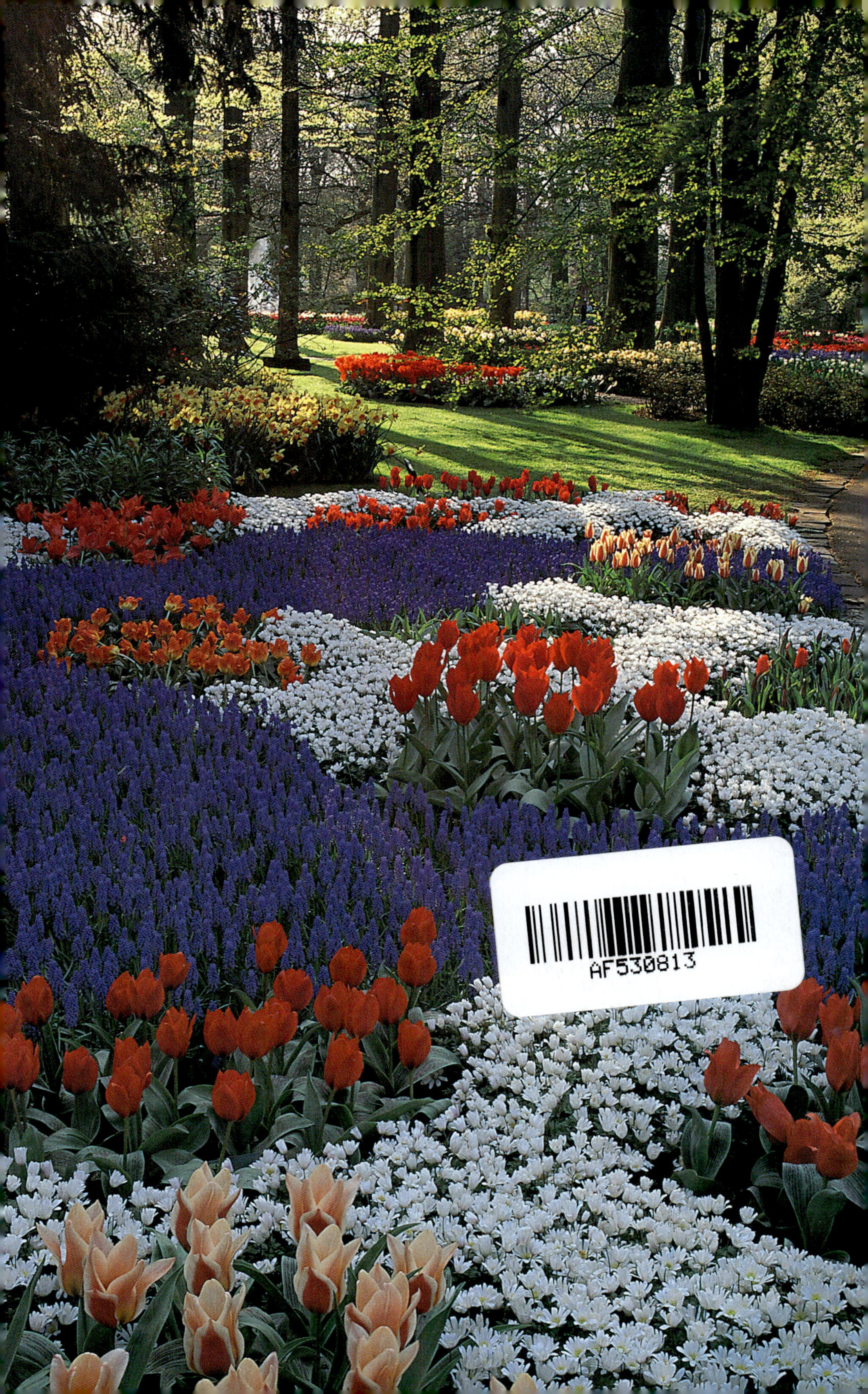

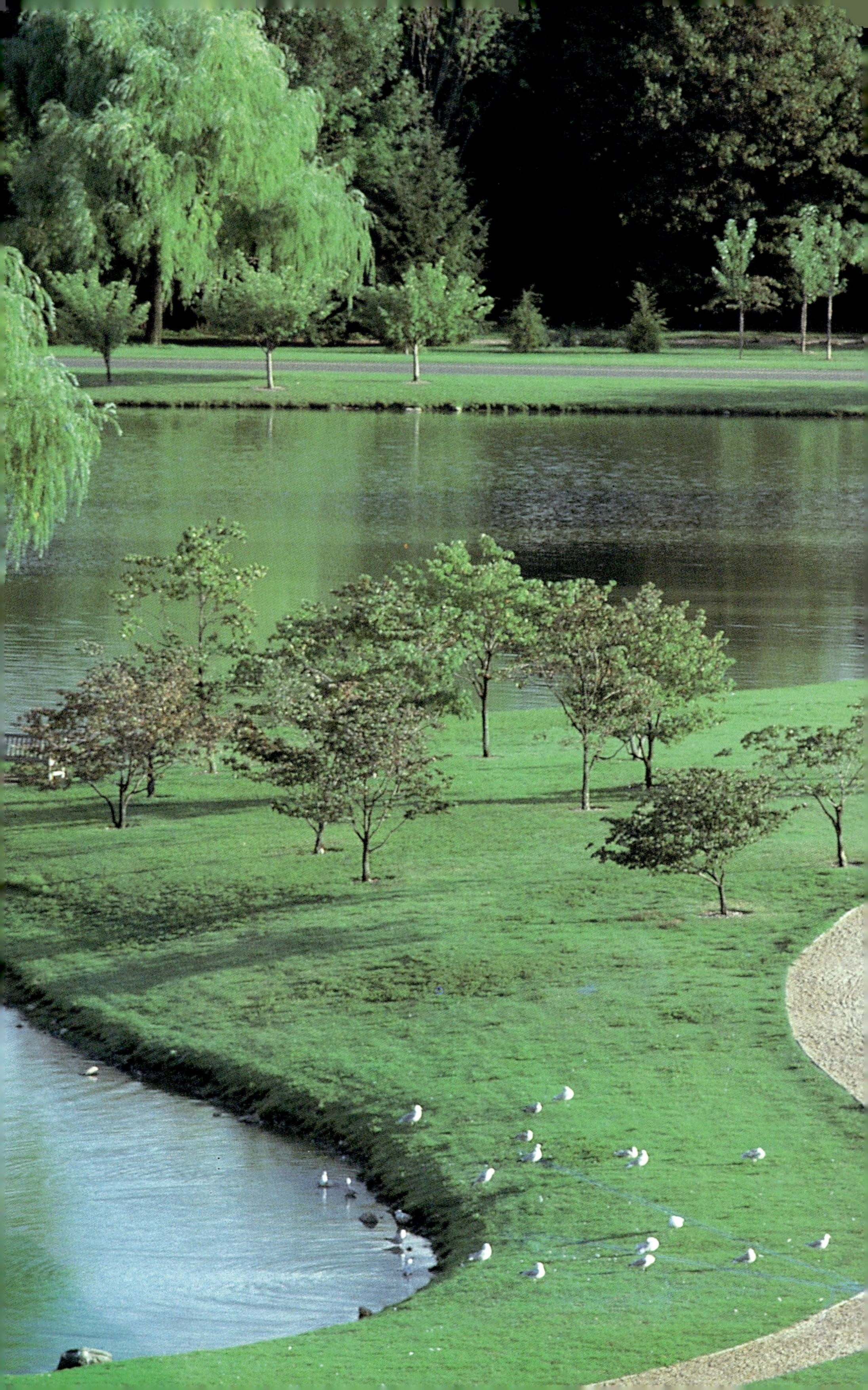

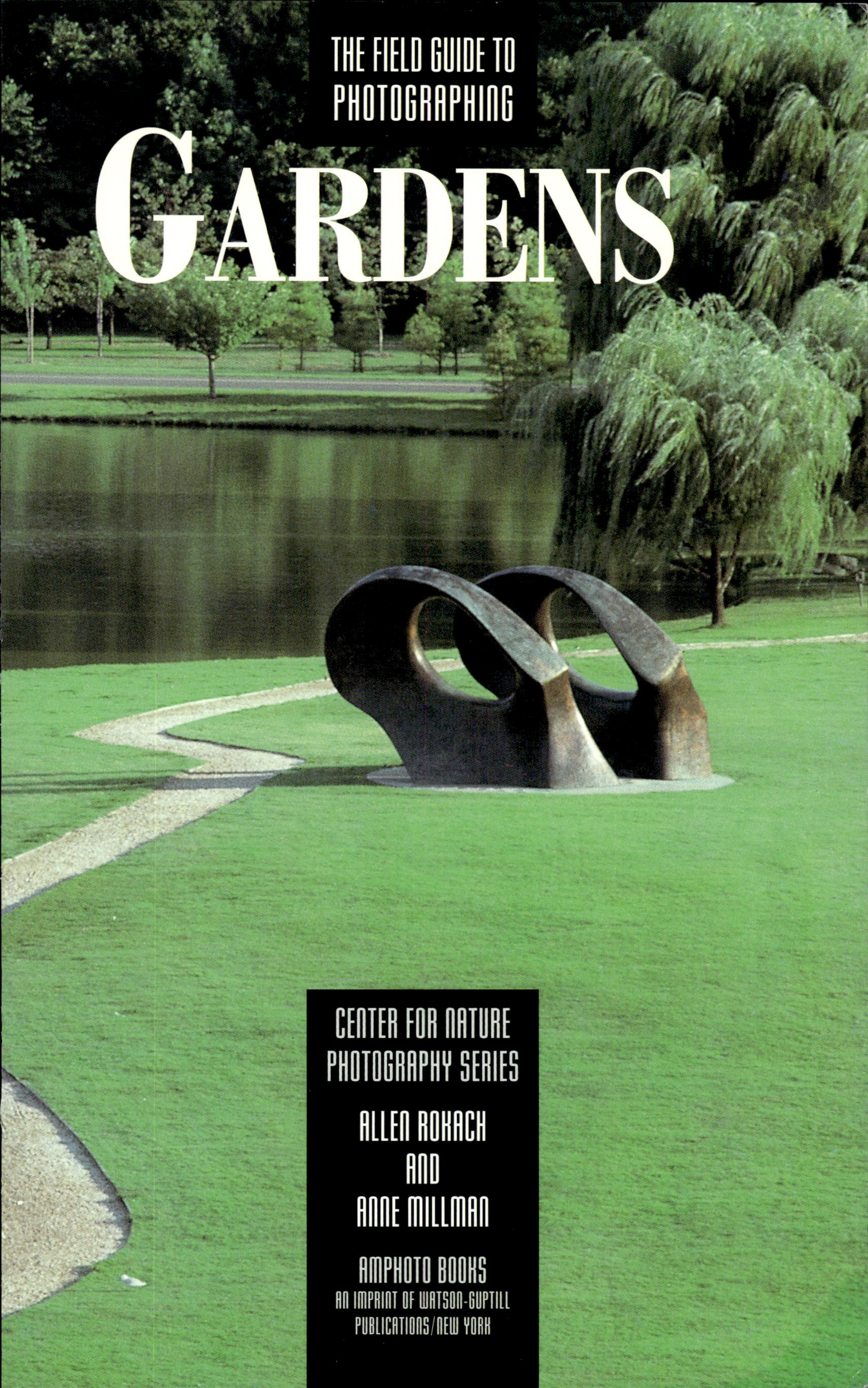

THE FIELD GUIDE TO PHOTOGRAPHING

GARDENS

CENTER FOR NATURE PHOTOGRAPHY SERIES

ALLEN ROKACH
AND
ANNE MILLMAN

AMPHOTO BOOKS
AN IMPRINT OF WATSON-GUPTILL PUBLICATIONS/NEW YORK

To Frank Kecko, for his invaluable help and for his infectious and tireless enthusiasm for gardens and photography.

PICTURE INFORMATION:
Page 1: Tulips, grape hyacinths, and other spring blooms. Holland's Keukenhof Garden.
Pages 2-3: Donald M. Kendall Sculpture Garden. PepsiCo World Headquarters, Purchase, New York.
Page 5: Abstract vignette. Holland's Keukenhof Garden.
Page 6: Small, private garden. Atlanta, Georgia.

Senior Editor: Robin Simmen
Editor: Liz Harvey
Designer: Bob Fillie, Graphiti Graphics
Graphic-production Manager: Hector Campbell

Text by Allen Rokach and Anne Millman,
co-founders of the Center for Nature Photography
(3916 Glenwood Avenue,
Birmingham, AL 35222; 205-595-5665)
Photographs by Allen Rokach

First published 1998 in New York by Amphoto Books,
an imprint of Watson-Guptill Publications,
a division of BPI Communications,
1515 Broadway, New York, NY 10036

Library of Congress Cataloging-in-Publication Data
Rokach, Allen.
The field guide to photographing gardens/ by Allen Rokach and Anne Millman.
p. cm.—(Center for Nature Photography series)
Includes index.
ISBN 0-8174-3876-9 (pbk.)
1. Photography of gardens—Handbooks, manuals, etc. I. Millman, Anne. II. Title. III. Series: Rokach, Allen. Center for Nature Photography series.
TR662.R65 1998
778.9'96359—dc21 97-46887
CIP

Manufactured in Singapore

1 2 3 4 5 6 7 8 9/06 05 04 03 02 01 00 99 98

ACKNOWLEDGMENTS:
We want to thank Mary Suffudy, who helped us launch this series of books when she was at Watson-Guptill; and Liz Harvey, our editor, for her patience and skill.

Years of photographing gardens would never have begun without the confidence and enthusiasm of Dr. James Hester, former president of the New York Botanical Garden, and Marge Lovero, the Director of Public Relations during his watch.

People at a variety of public gardens across the United States facilitated access at odd hours. Thanks go particularly to Meegan McCarthy of the Bilow-Chicago Botanic Garden in Illinois, Carl Suk of the Bernheim Arboretum in Kentucky, James W. Sutherland of the Cantigny Garden in Illinois, and William Radler of the Boerner Botanic Garden in Wisconsin.

We owe a special debt of gratitude for support from Olympus America, Inc., which generously provided equipment, technical advice, and funds to create nearly all the photographs in this book. In particular, we want to thank Marlene Hess, Manager, Public Relations; Dave Willard, Vice President, Marketing Communications; and John Lynch, Group Executive Vice President.

A number of organizations provided travel assistance to Holland. We want in particular to acknowledge Odette Fodor of KLM Royal Dutch Airlines, and Barbara Veldkamp and Eline van Bon of the Netherlands Board of Tourism.

We also want to thank John Floyd, editor at *Southern Living* magazine, for granting permission to reproduce images originally taken for that publication in this book.

A few people deserve mention for the lessons they taught and the backing they provided early on: Linda Wolfe, a friend and supporter from the New York Botanical Garden, who facilitated introductions to various private clients, including PepsiCo Inc., Marco Polo Stefano, Director of Horticulture at the Wave Hill Environmental Center and a masterful gardener, who showed how to appreciate the structure and beauty of plants as individuals, not just as parts of a whole; and the late Russell Page, the dean of landscape designers, who inspired an awareness of the interaction of plants and ornamental structures and demonstrated how to recognize and record good design in gardens, especially as they evolve over time.

Finally, many personal friends and work colleagues offered advice, reactions, and criticisms over the years that helped sharpen our abilities as photographer and writer. We truly appreciate their keen eyes and ears: Frank Kecko, David Ferguson, Ross Horowitz, Ted Spiegel, Ann Guilfoyle, Tom Page, Steve Bender, Mark Stith, Linda Askey, Susan Costello, and Nai Chang.

Contents

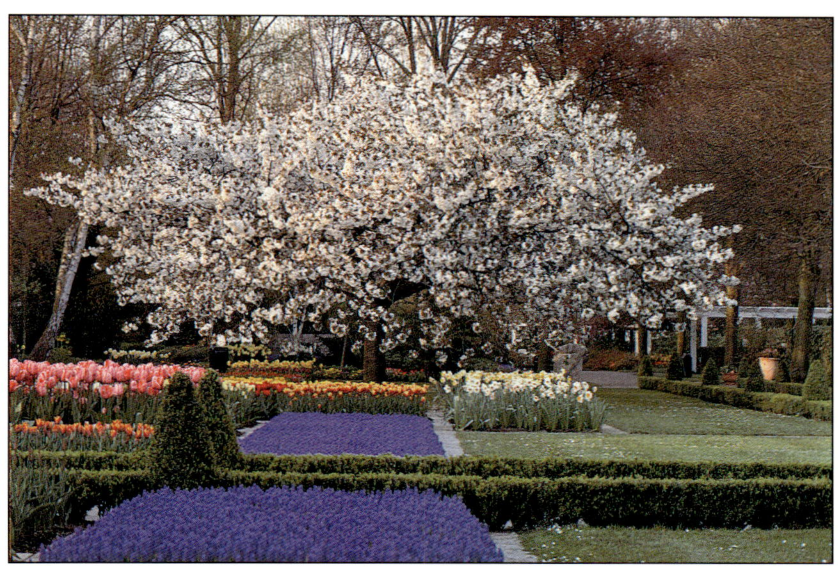

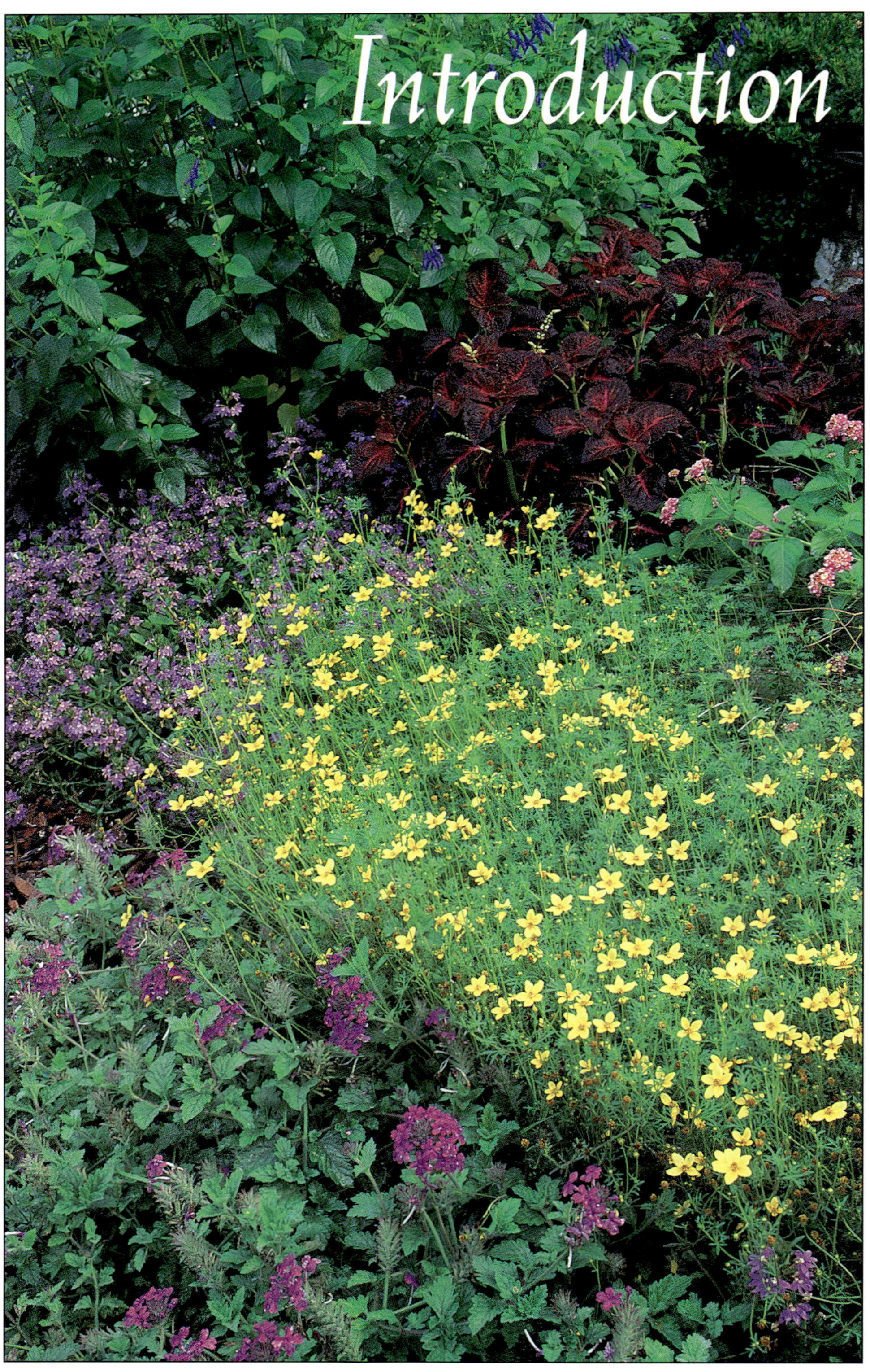

Introduction

I've looked at gardens all over the world. I've seen huge, magnificent estate gardens in England and France, tiny but artfully planned and pruned patches in Japan, and a host of family-style gardens in all parts of the United States. All that looking and photographing has taught me a few things.

First, gardens are a universal form of expression, though regional and national character helps shape them. Wherever they are, gardens humanize the environment, taking what is often dull, lifeless terrain, and, through imagination and toil, turning it into a delight for the eye. No wonder people of all ages take such pleasure in gardens. I still don't quite know what makes people plant and tend gardens, what the underlying impulse is, but I am certainly grateful for it.

Next, as a nature photographer as well as a photographer of gardens, I've come to appreciate the similarities and differences between the wild and tamed environment. Both are made of a mix of living materials, often the very same vegetation in nature and in gardens. After all, many garden specimens are varieties derived and adapted from wild plants. So photographically they entail some of the same issues regarding color, texture, and form. But the fact that gardens are planned—designed by the human mind and tended by human hands—makes all the difference. When I look at a garden, I see a kind of order that I rarely find in nature. I see the workings of human imagination, which adds a conscious dimension that stimulates my own thinking about how I want to portray a garden.

No matter how beautiful a garden might be, it has to be photogenic to produce a memorable image. The distinction between "beautiful" and "photogenic" isn't one all garden photographers keep clearly in mind, but they should. A garden scene or subject might look perfectly lovely to the eye, but it might have qualities that don't translate well on film. Perhaps the light isn't right for the scene, perhaps distracting background elements mar the effect, or, just possibly, perhaps the lens or film I have on hand won't enable me to capture what I want. With years of experience, I've learned to make the most of less than ideal situations. But it takes creative thinking and effort to overcome such difficulties.

On the other hand, a quite ordinary scene or subject might have the makings of a magnificent photograph. That is when the ability to recognize what is photogenic pays off. And this is why you might see a photographer focusing on something and wonder why he or she is bothering. Chances are that the photographer sees the visual potential that eludes those who are looking only at apparent beauty. The more skilled you become at identifying what is photogenic—and this book should help you do that—the more sensitive your eye will become and the more pleased you'll be with your photographic results.

Finally, everyone can benefit from a lesson I've learned: return to the same gardens often to increase your awareness of changes and to take advantage of seasonal variations. If you've ever photographed children who are close to you, you know that you see countless expressions that captivate you, even though to a stranger their faces might look more or less the same. This is true of gardens, too. They present a new face each time as new plants emerge and old ones wither, as the light shifts over the course of days and seasons, and as weather casts its spell over the landscape. Each time you go back to a garden, you'll discover something new. And this will help keep your photographs fresh and exciting.

I hope you find more ideas to inspire you as you read this book. Good luck!

ALLEN ROKACH

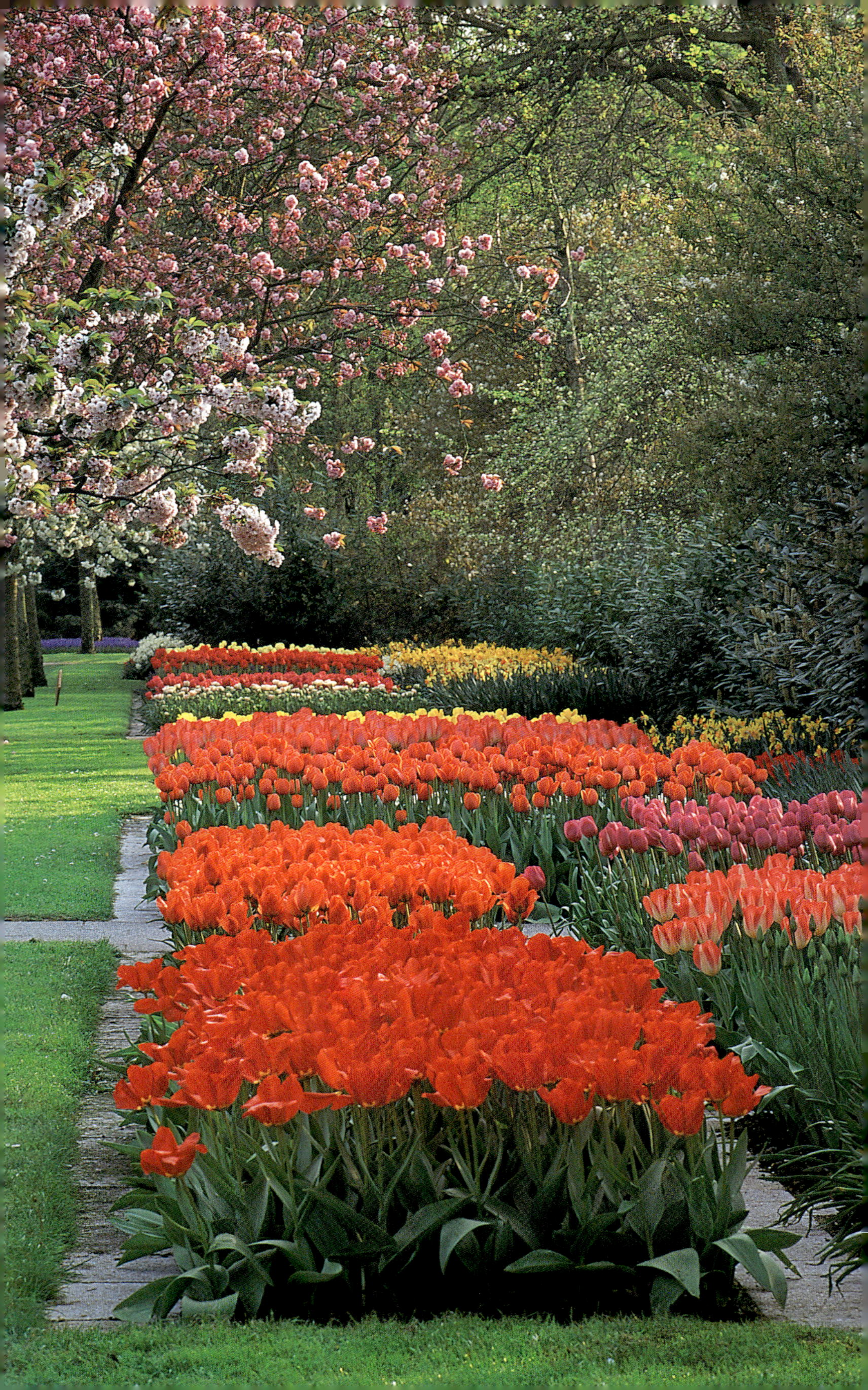

CHAPTER 1

Evoking a Sense of the Garden

Architectural elements in this overview help define the character of the garden at Villa Garzoni in Tuscany, Italy. To capture this image, I used a Zuiko 35mm lens and shot Fujichrome 100 for 1/15 sec. at *f*/16.

Orderly arrangements of colorful bulbs characterize Holland's Keukenhof Garden in the spring. This composition aligns the flower beds and concentrates the rich colors. Shooting with a Zuiko 50-250mm lens set at 200mm, I exposed Fujichrome Velvia for 1/30 sec. at *f*/16.

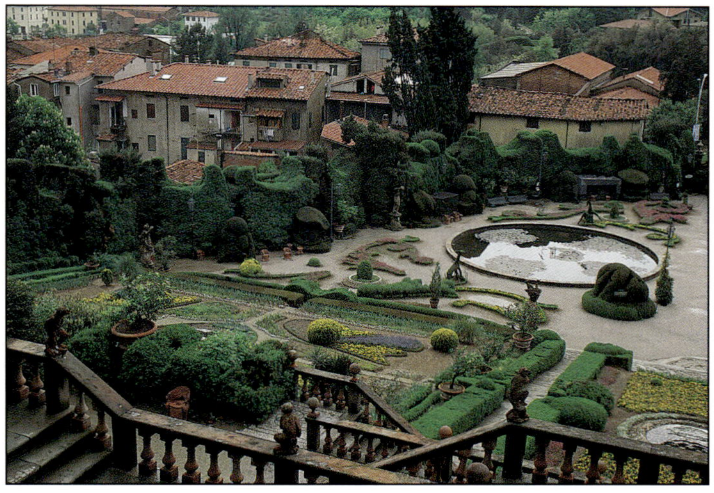

Walk into any famous public garden, and it won't surprise you to see many people with their cameras in hand. After all, a well-planned garden is a joy to the eye. What might be surprising is that few of those would-be photographers stand much of a chance of capturing on film the beauty they came to behold.

The classic grandeur of the Villa Garzoni estate garden comes across in its symmetrical organization of living and artificial materials cascading down the naturally terraced terrain. Working with a Zuiko 28mm lens, I exposed for 1/15 sec. at *f*/11 on Fujichrome 100.

This is because many shutterbugs tend to make a common mistake: they assume that what you see is what you get, that a thing of beauty is bound to produce a spectacular photograph. And what could be lovelier than a garden? (They might also believe that their camera equipment determines how good their photographs will be, which is only a half-truth.)

In fact, as in most photography, good results depend much more on the photographer's vision and technique than on an ideal subject. Most students of photography believe they can acquire technique. But they don't always realize that learning how to see with clarity and purpose is also something they can learn. That lesson, above all, has the potential to transform your photographs so they not only capture the experience of being in a magnificent garden, but surpass it. And that is the lesson of this first chapter.

UNDERSTANDING GARDEN DESIGN

The first step in developing vision for garden photography is to gain a basic understanding of garden design. Unlike purely natural environments, gardens are an amalgam of natural and artificial elements. They start with what famed twentieth-century British garden designer Russell Page called the "bones." These are the underlying topographical structures, such as hills and rock outcrops; permanent architectural features, such as buildings; and any natural bodies of water.

For the photographer, as for the garden designer, these skeletal rudiments provide the foundation for everything else in the garden. When you pay attention to these fundamental structures, your eye can better grasp the way in which the surface elements of the garden are planned. Specifically, notice whether the vegetation emphasizes or camouflages the underlying structure. Look at how the interplay of living and inorganic materials works. And see how the plantings contrast or harmonize with the structural foundations of the landscape.

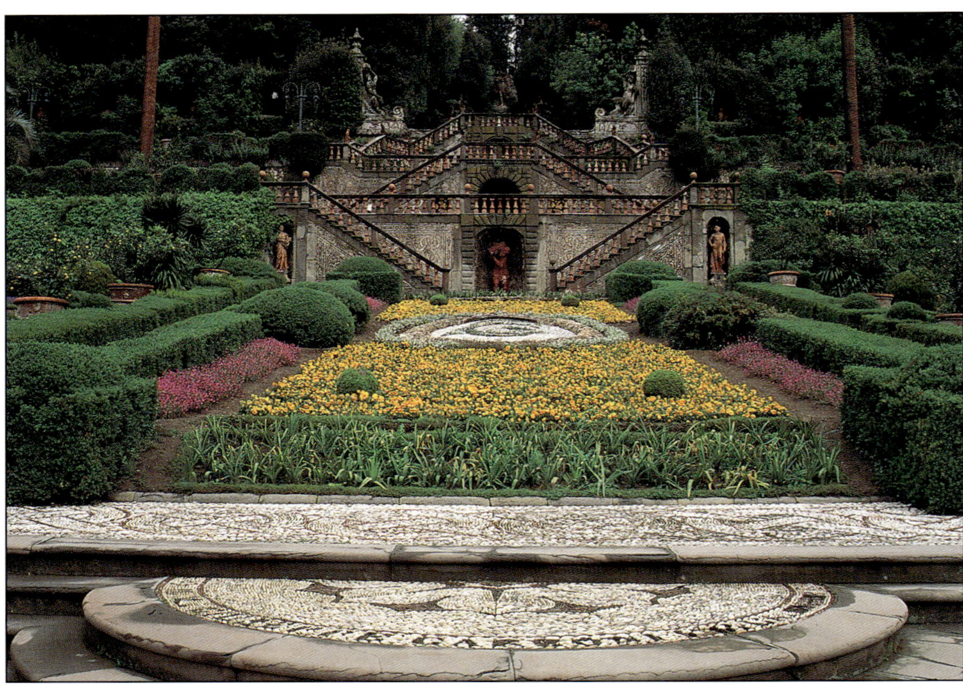

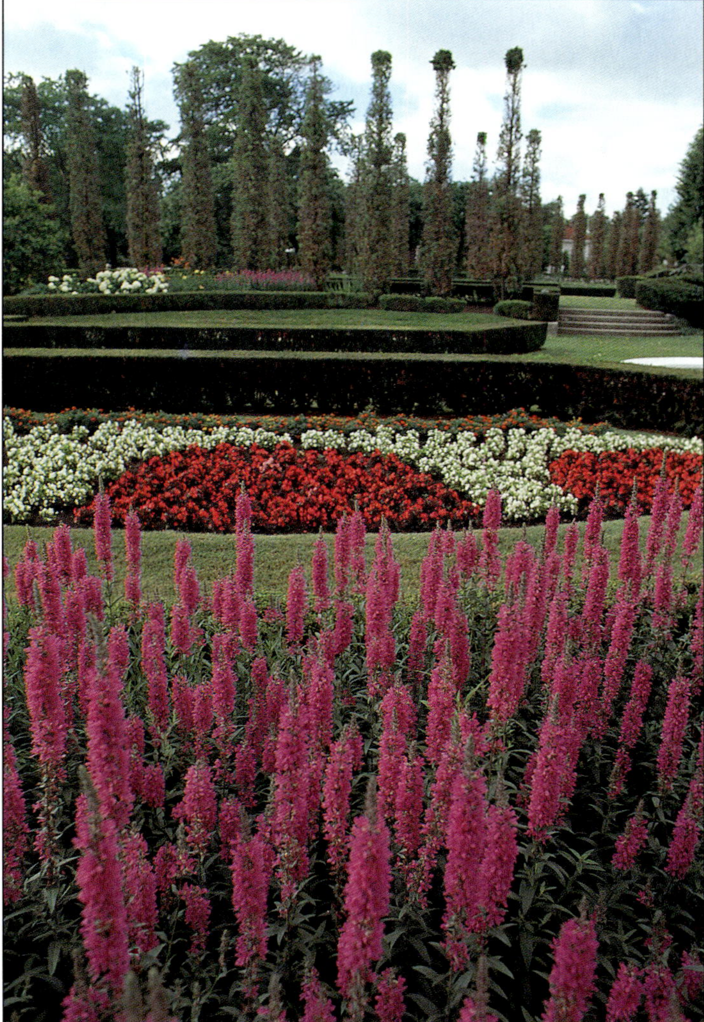

Vertical plant elements add stature to the flat midwestern landscape of Illinois' Bahai Temple Garden. I made this shot with a Zuiko 21mm lens and Ektachrome 100 EPZ, exposing for 1/30 sec. at *f*/16.

Beyond these basics, you can start to appreciate the different ways designers approach a particular garden. Formal garden designs tend to be more symmetrical and balanced, often with a clearly visible grid and a specific category of plantings in each section. Think of the magnificent vegetable gardens at some French chateaux, the sculpture gardens in many parts of Italy, and most English rose gardens. On the other hand, informal garden designs might aspire to a naturalistic look, with asymmetrical arrangements, winding paths, and a mix of compatible plantings. Think of an English perennial garden or a Japanese water garden.

Of course, whether gardens are formal or informal, they are never accidental. An effective casual look is in reality a kind of studied artifice: it might appear effortless, but it is actually the result of very careful planning. As a photographer, you need to train your eye to look for differences in design and find ways to underscore creative design elements in your images.

Because gardens are created for people to enjoy, their layouts generally include such structural elements as paths, benches, and statuary. Even

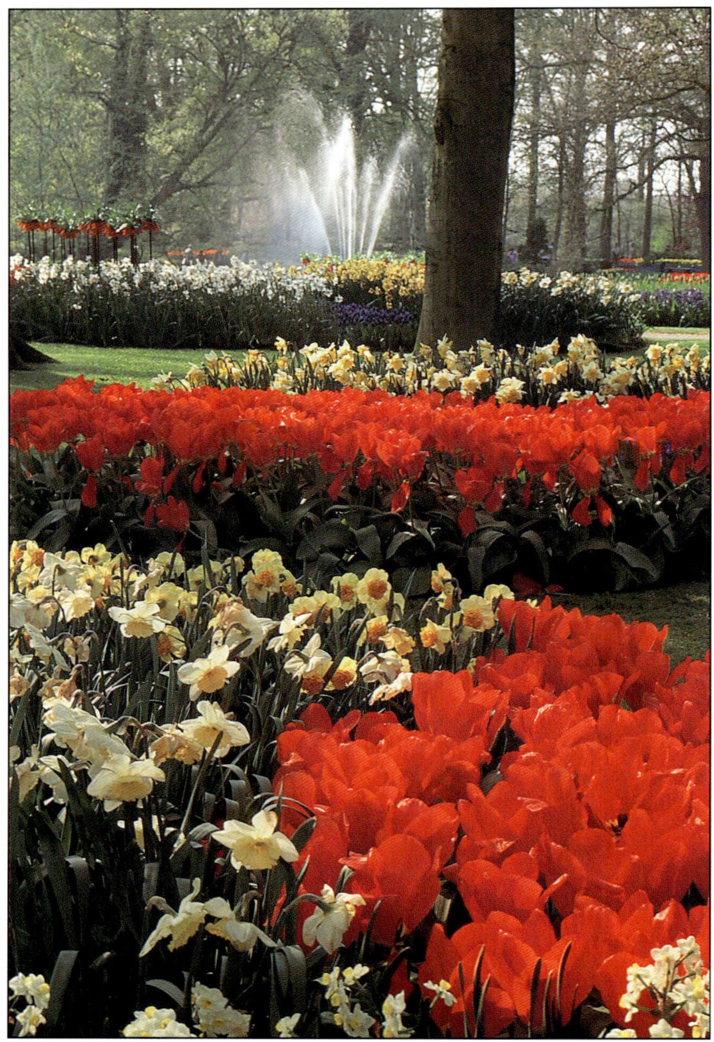

The casual aura of Holland's Keukenhof Garden relies on the careful integration of flowering bulbs, towering trees, and fan-like fountains. With a Zuiko 35-70mm zoom lens set at 35mm, I exposed for 1/8 sec. at *f*/16 on Ektachrome 100 EPZ.

small backyard gardens often incorporate nonplant fixtures, both for their utility and as visual focal points in the overall concept. A well-planned garden has a good balance between the plantings and these nonplant features. In fact, a bench, trellis, or gate can function, like a topographical feature, as part of the garden's underlying structure. The main difference is that these artificial elements can be placed wherever the designer wants them, so they play a key role in organizing the garden and, by extension, in helping you organize your photographs. As you look at a garden, you should consider how these nonplant elements work in the overall design, especially how they help define the arrangement of plants around them.

Finally, think of a garden design as the work of an artist whose medium happens to be living materials. Just as an artist plans a canvas in terms of scale, shape, line, color, and texture, so does a garden designer. As you survey any garden, notice how the design balances various visual aspects: large-scale plantings with smaller ones, vertical and horizontal planes, and assorted colors and textures.

As your understanding of garden design increases, your images will convey a clearer vision and purpose. Which design aspects you emphasize will depend to some degree on the kind of image you're trying to create: an overview, a vignette, or a detail.

SHOOTING THE OVERVIEW

A good place to begin your photography in any garden is with an overview shot. Unfortunately, this is the very sort of image many people tend to ignore. Instead, they home in on specific flower beds or even individual flowers when they shoot. As a result, they have no pictures that reveal the overall design of the garden—images that serve to identify the specific location. And at the very least, a good overview shot reminds you where it was taken.

But successful overviews aren't a snap to achieve. Pulling them off requires not only an appreciation of the garden's telling features, but also the determination to find a perspective that reveals those features and the ability to integrate them with aesthetic integrity. In other words, your overview should document the garden in a recognizable and beautiful way.

This kind of overview is almost impossible to get from a path or at ground level. For truly dramatic overviews, try getting a high perspective. Find a nearby hill, climb a ladder, shoot out of a window, get access to the roof, or stand on a bridge; do whatever works best so you can view the scene from above. If that isn't possible, you should at least try to stand on a bench.

If all else fails, achieve a sense of the garden's space, and include some identifying features. For example, choose an eye-catching feature, such as a fountain or trellis, as the focal point for the background, with a rich foreground leading up to it. Also, position yourself off the path so the line it creates leads the viewer's eye forward into the frame. And combine close plantings with more distant ones.

The diagonal line of the path, echoed in the row of flowering apple trees, leads the viewer's eye into the frame in this otherwise flat, ground-level overview of Holland's Keukenhof Garden. Shooting with a Zuiko 35-70mm zoom lens set at 35mm, I exposed for 1/30 sec. at *f*/16 on Fujichrome Velvia.

(Overleaf) From foreground details to more distant plantings, this high, wide-angle overview documents the symmetrical design of Mansfield, Ohio's Kingwood Center. Here, I used a Zuiko 21mm lens and exposed Ektachrome SW for 1/2 sec. at *f*/11.

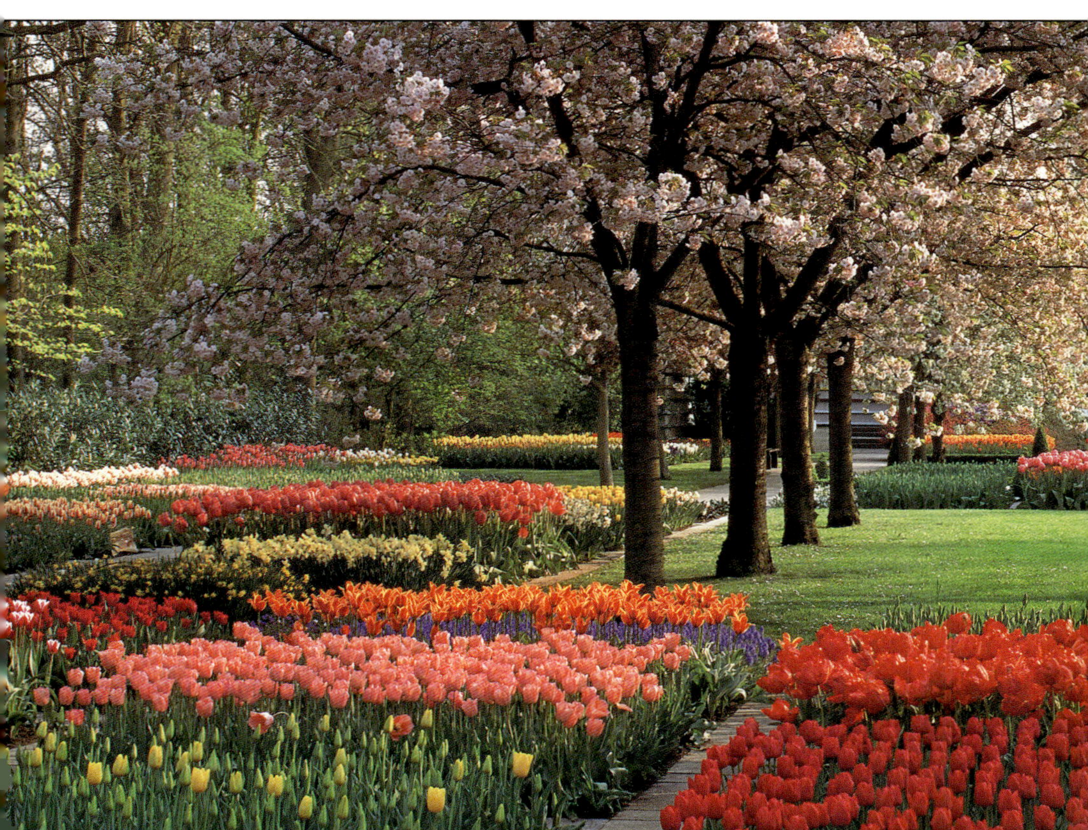

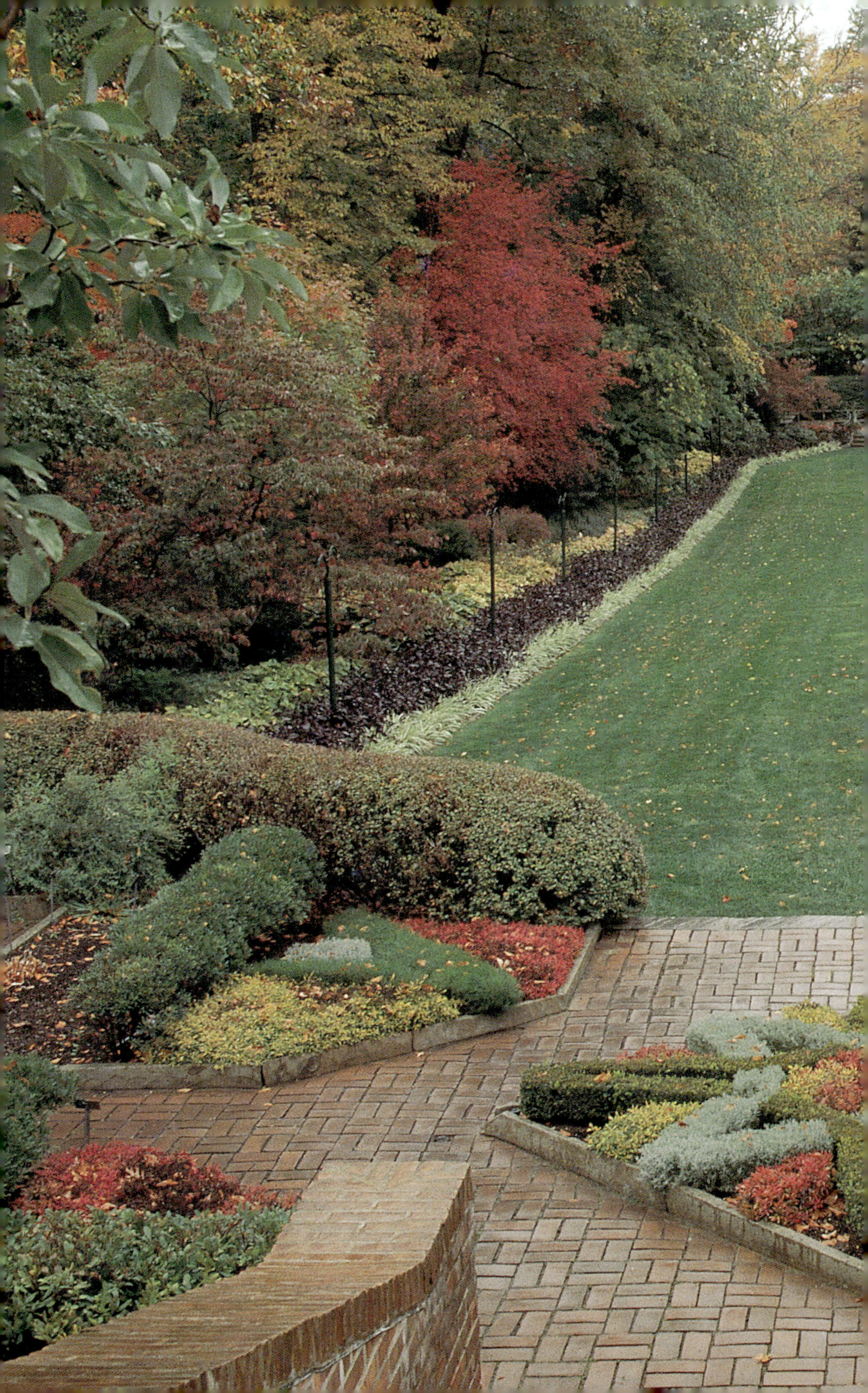

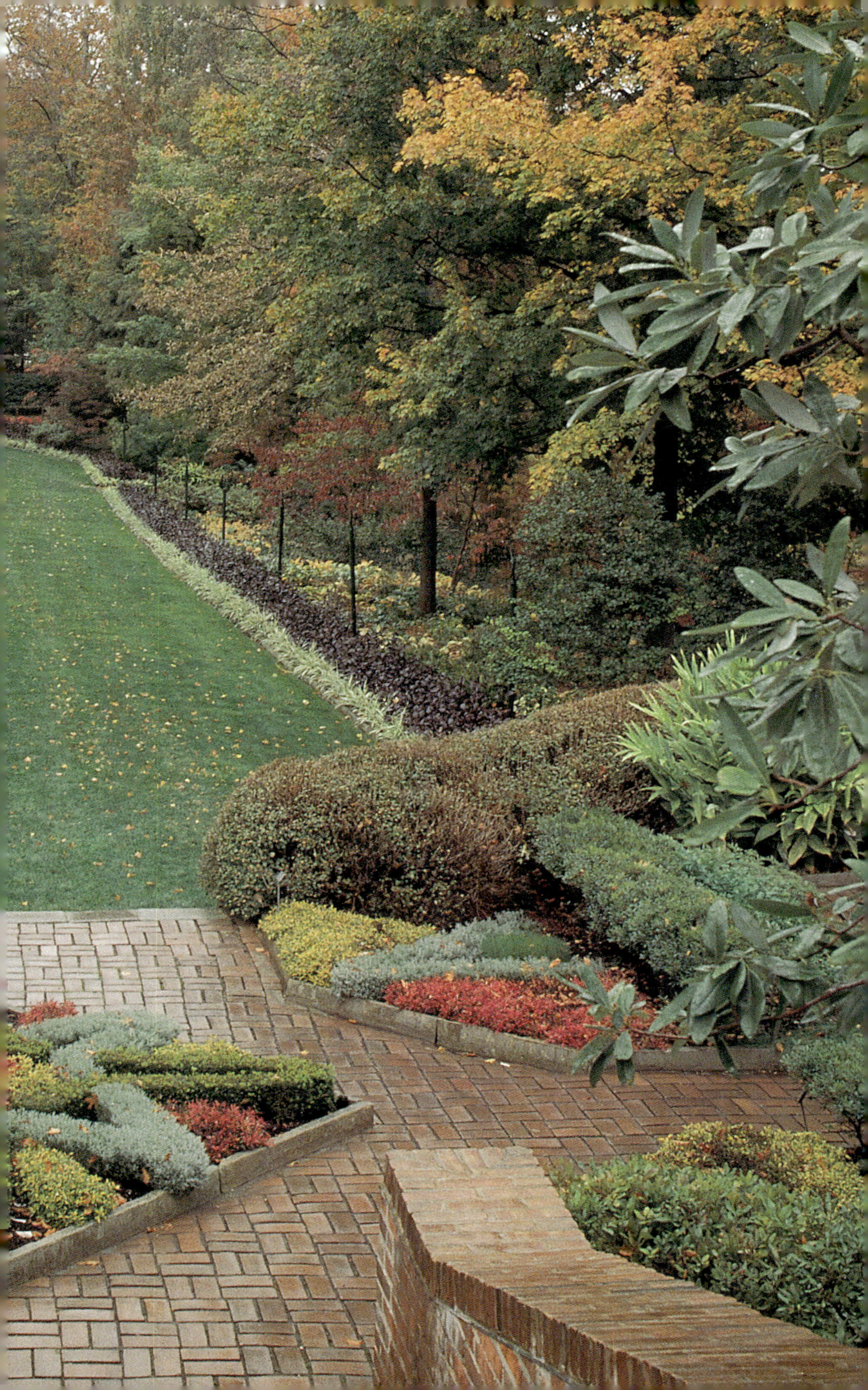

CAPTURING VIGNETTES

The bread and butter of great garden photography is the vignette, an image that portrays a discrete, coherent portion of the garden. Vignettes clarify the design of the garden on a small scale and draw the viewer closer to the particulars. Vignettes might not enable the viewer to identify a specific garden, but they'll leave no doubt about its character. In other words, these images encompass the essence of the garden in miniature or from an intimate perspective.

As you search for photogenic possibilities, look for the garden's distinctive elements, particularly those that reveal relationships of color, texture, and form. These will be quite different in a perennial border and a topiary garden, or a grass garden and a rose garden. As you look at how plants interact with one another, start to think of ways to arrange them into an aesthetically powerful composition that will enhance and strengthen the impact of the plantings. The better your composition, the more effective your attempt to convey the visual qualities of the garden.

Also, build your vignette around a focal point. This can be a tree, a bench, a trellis, or a garden statue. Without a clear focal point, the image will lack a visual center.

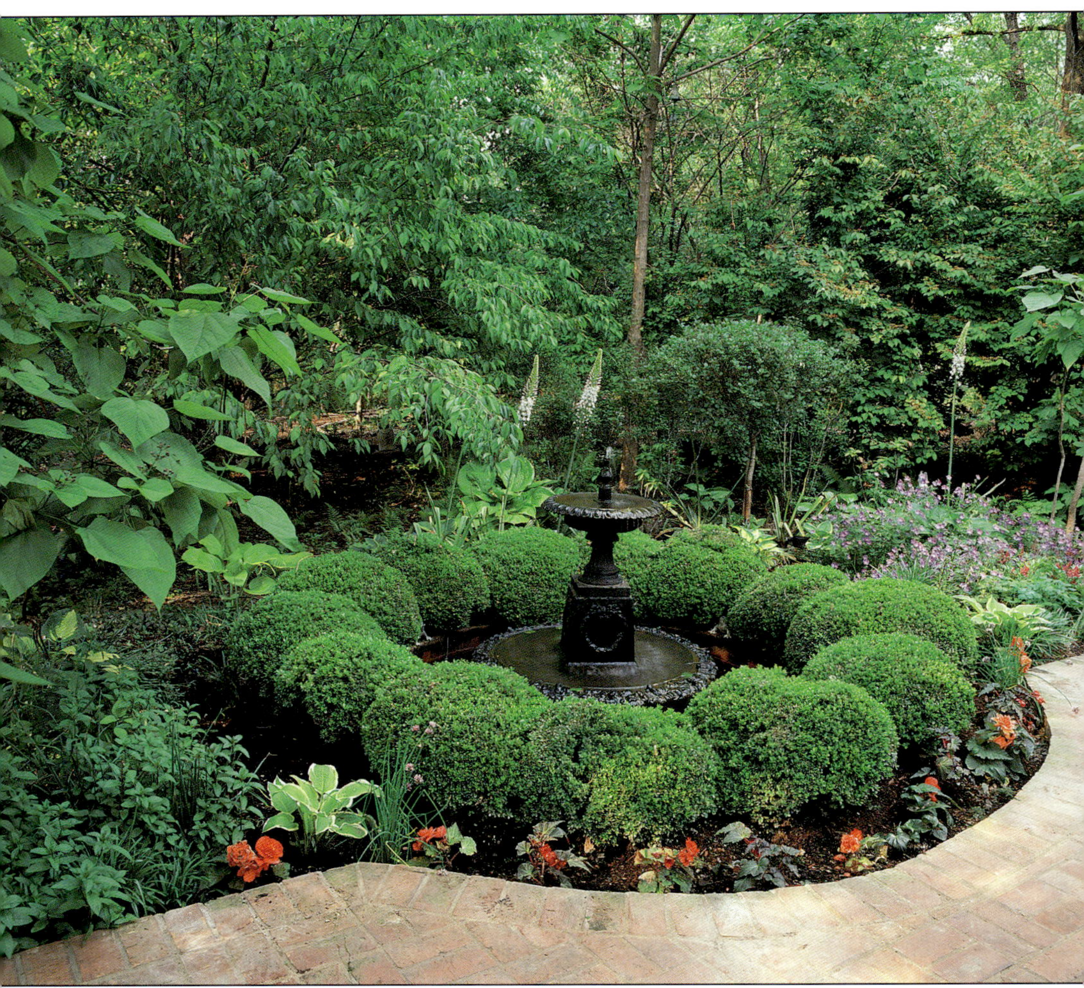

A ring of meticulously shaped box hedge contrasts in texture and form with the surrounding perennials, adding definition to this vignette of a private garden in St. Louis, Missouri. Here, I used a Mamiya 80mm lens and exposed at *f*/16 for 1/30 sec. on Fujichrome RVP.

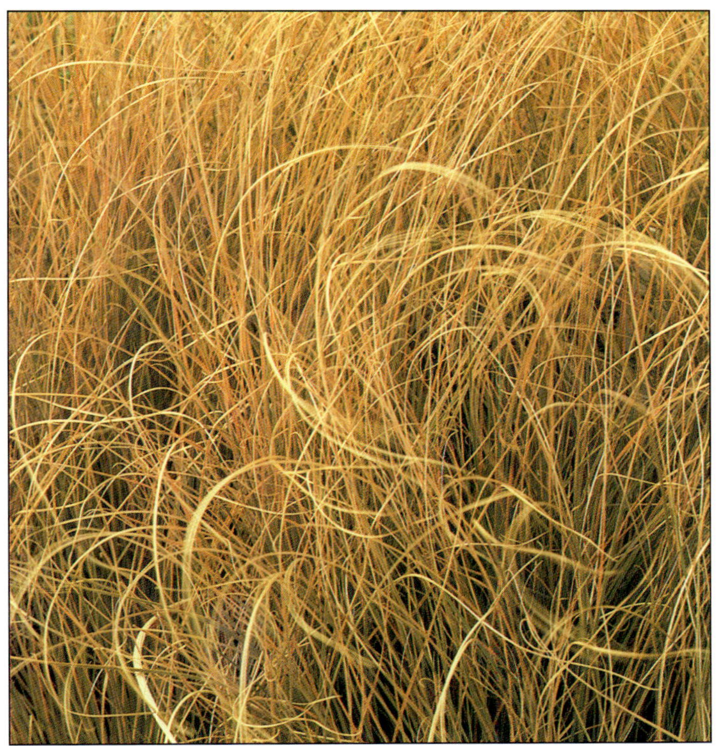

The swirling lines of autumn grasses provide texture, color, and movement in this abstract vignette taken at Becton Dickinson World Headquarters in New Jersey. I made this shot with a Sonnar 150mm lens, exposing for 1/8 sec. at *f*/11 on Ektachrome EPN.

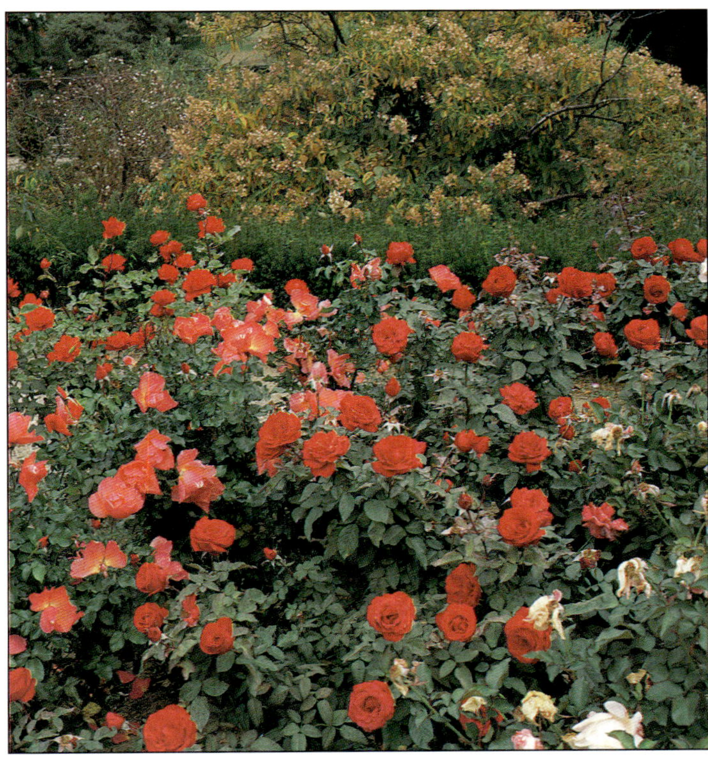

Instead of focusing on an individual rose, this vignette, photographed at the New York Botanical Garden in the Bronx, New York, masses brilliantly red roses across the entire frame. Here, I used a Sonnar 80mm lens and exposed Fujichrome RFP for 1/60 sec. at *f*/8.

Telling details like these bedding petals in a private natural garden in New York, so rich in subtle colors, textures, and light effects, reveal themselves to a sensitive eye. Working with a Zuiko 35-70mm zoom lens set at 50mm, I exposed for 1/8 sec. at *f*/11 on Ektachrome LLP.

A tight detail shot of ornamental cabbages in a vegetable garden at Cantigny in Wheaton, Illinois, builds an unusual image on repeated shapes and a near-monochromatic palette. I used a Zuiko 50-250mm lens set at 180mm and exposed Ektachrome SW for 1/4 sec. at *f*/11.

EXPERIMENTING WITH DETAILS

More than any other kind of image, garden photographers gravitate toward shooting details. Usually, the photographers aim their cameras at some fine specimen of a flower hoping for a brilliant floral portrait. This approach is all well and good, but it can become monotonous. Poet Gertrude Stein might have been right when she wrote, "A rose is a rose is a rose," but that is just the kind of repetition photographers hope to avoid. When all your results start to look alike, you'll appreciate that it is no small feat to maintain a high level of originality and newness in such closeups. That is not to say you should not shoot floral portraits. Just be sure to make them—and all your other detail shots—startling eye-openers, things most people see but don't notice.

Think of details as the telling minutiae, either the special and unique or the typical and characteristic building blocks of the garden. Look for pockets of interesting color or texture. Another possibility is to notice the quality of light illuminating a particular flower. Experiment with depth of field in order to create interesting images that combine sharp

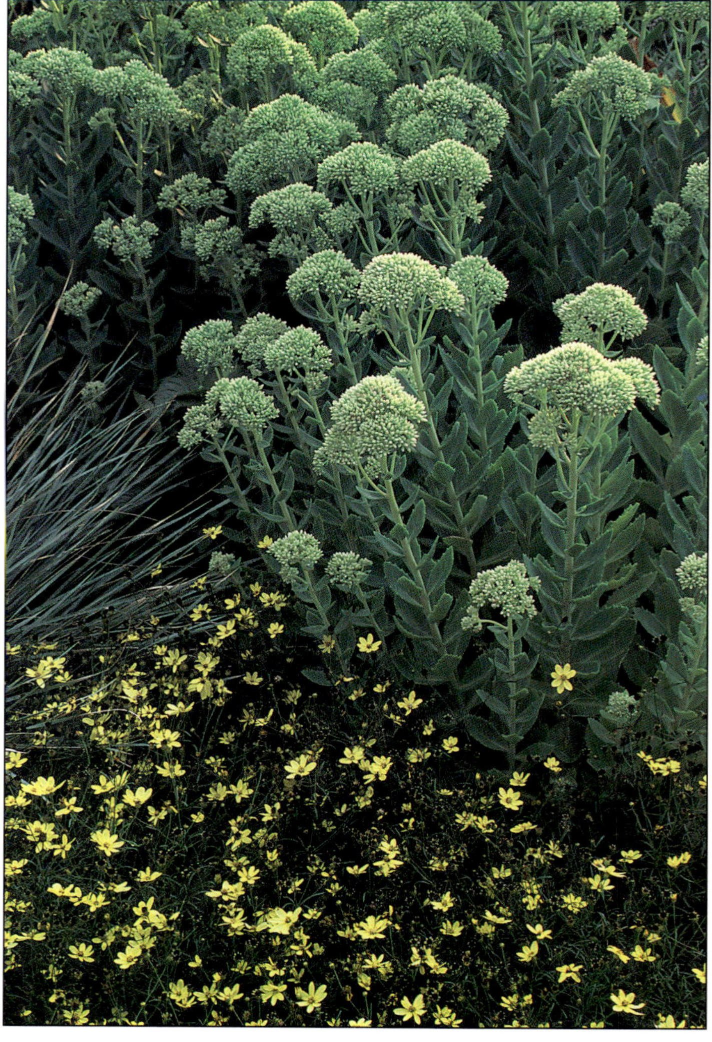

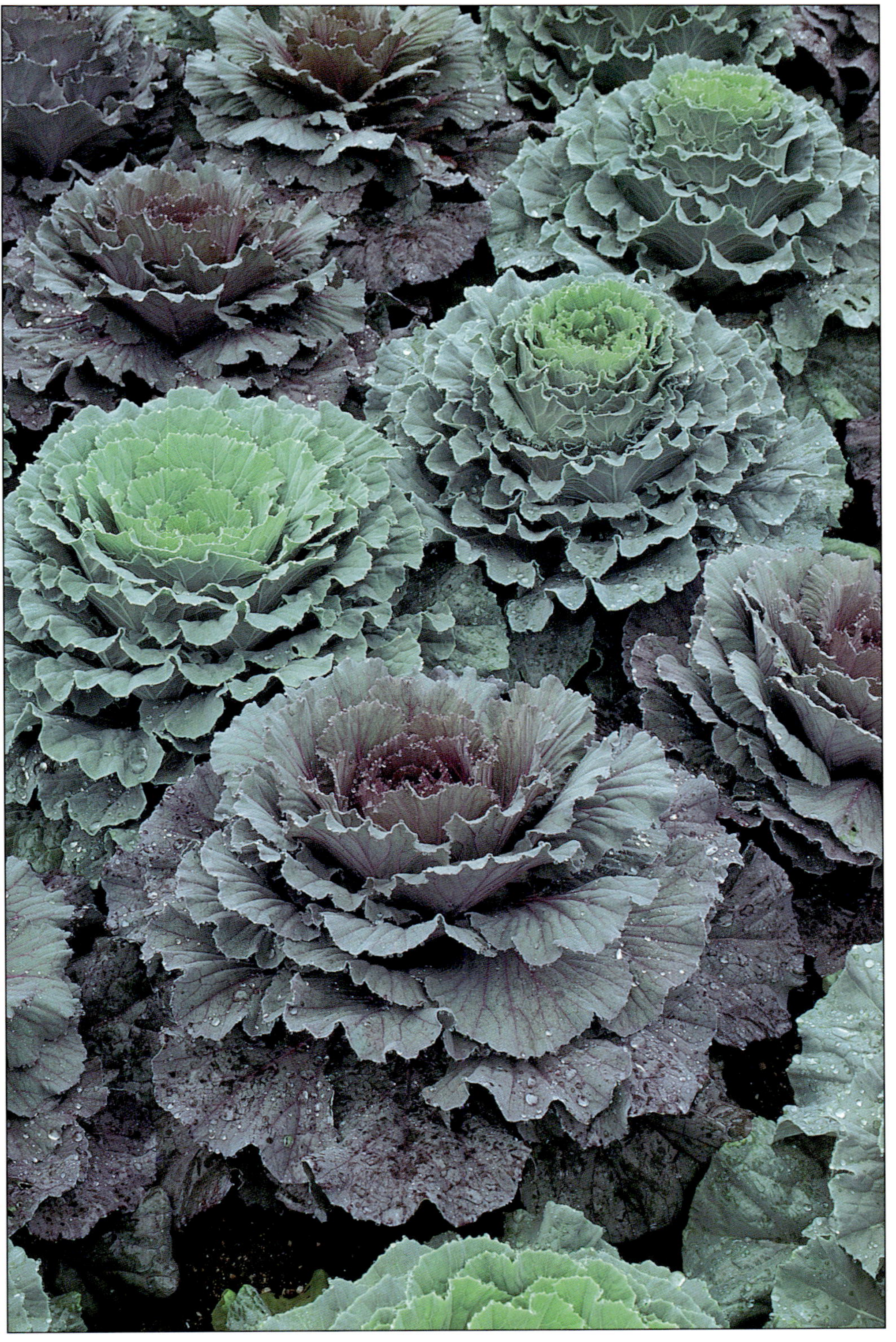

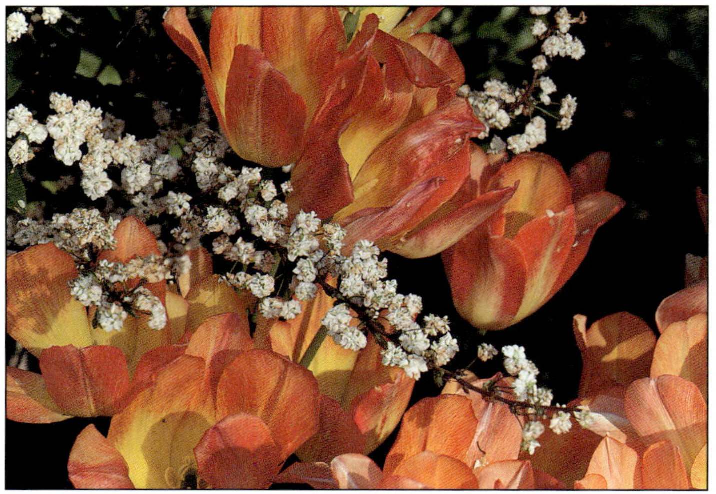

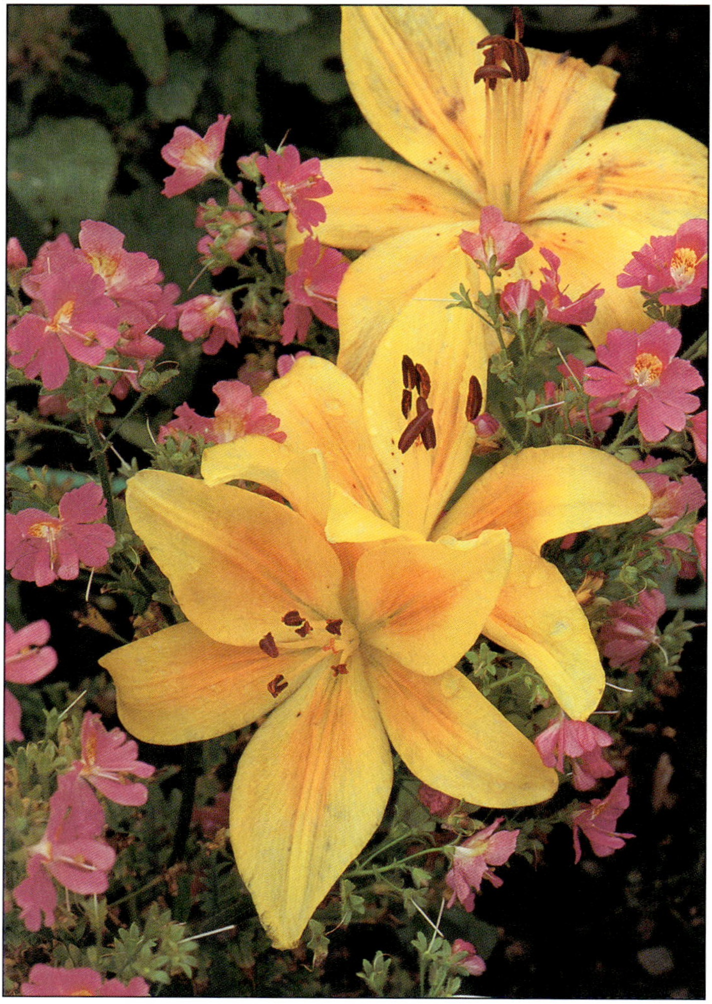

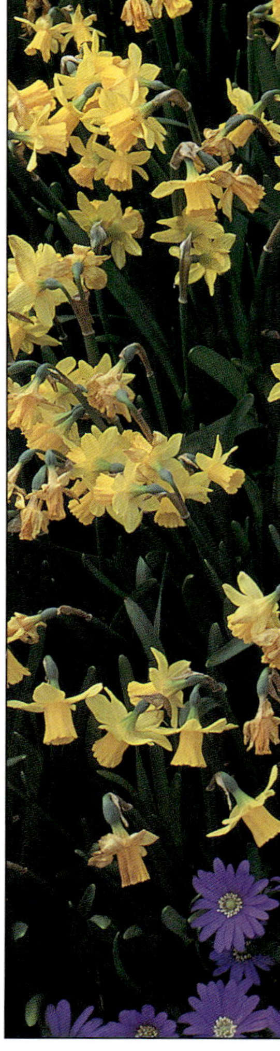

This detail shot taken at New York's Wave Hill was made with warm, low light and an odd framing of tulips and baby's breath against a backdrop of deep shadow. Shooting with a Zuiko 90mm macro lens, I exposed for 1/30 sec. at *f*/22 on Kodachrome 25.

Three lilies surrounded by miniature purple flowers in a private garden in Alaska fill the frame with rich colors and contrasting forms. With a Zuiko 35-70mm zoom lens set at 35mm, I exposed for 1/30 sec. at *f*/8 on Ektachrome LPZ.

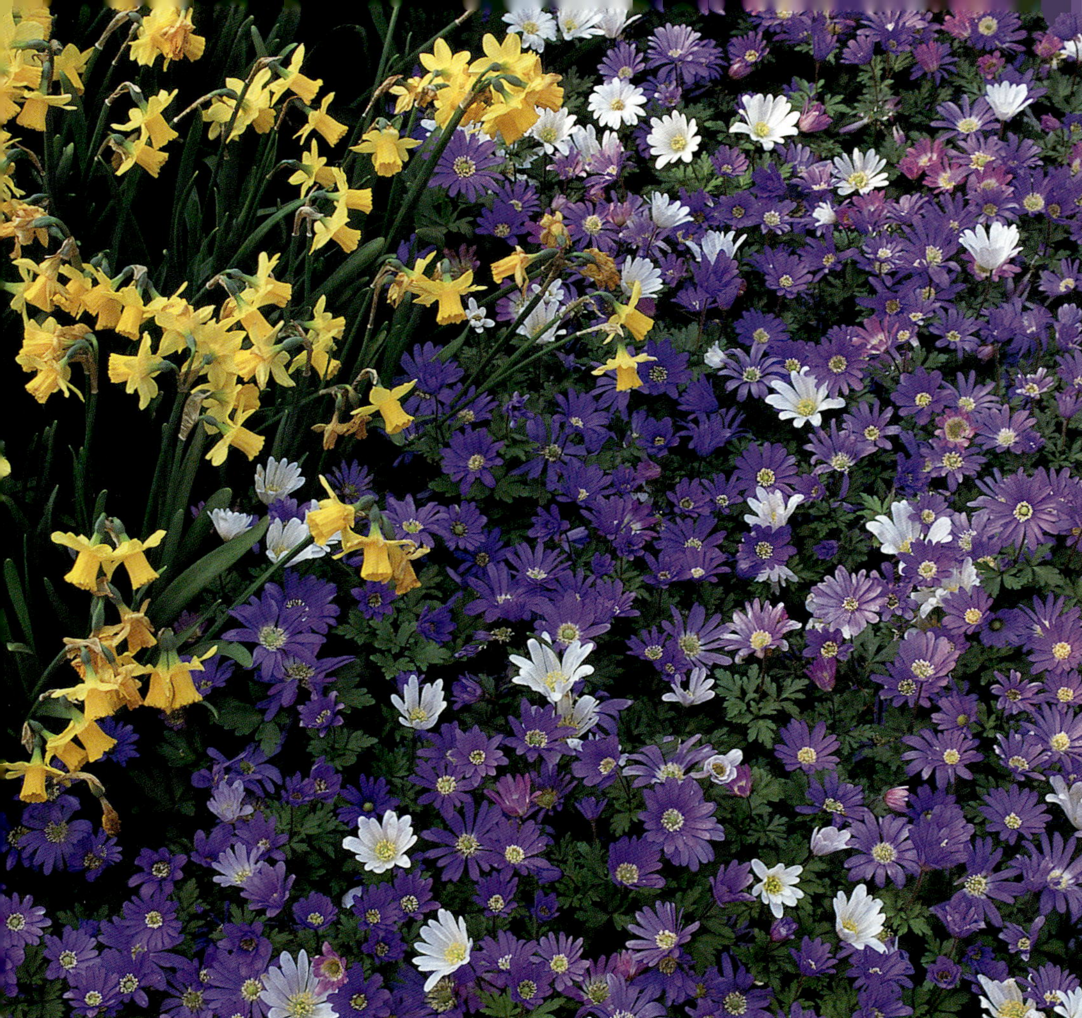

A downward perspective turns these bedding plants in a private Georgia garden into swaths of pure color and texture for a surprisingly abstract detail. I achieved this effect with a Zuiko 90mm macro lens and Fujichrome Provia, exposing for 1/15 sec. at f/16.

areas with blurs. And be sure to vary your perspective so you aren't always shooting from the front.

Most of all, simplify. If you want a true detail, be sure you keep the image spare and focused. Come in close to frame a tight composition, and don't include any more than is essential to your purpose. Turn the backdrop dark or make it a smooth blur of color, so that your primary subject really stands out. (For a far more comprehensive discussion about photographing flowers in detail, see *The Field Guide to Photographing Flowers*, a companion volume in this series.)

DEVELOPING AN AESTHETIC PERSPECTIVE

Besides expanding your photographic repertoire by shooting a mix of overviews, vignettes, and details, you should begin to think of your garden images not so much as documents of particular plantings and arrangements but as expressions of your personal aesthetic sensibility. Of course, the garden is what it is, which is why being able to appreciate what the designer has done will help you convey the ideas and intentions behind it. However, to truly evoke the essence of any garden, your photographs must also have your personality and style. You must bring your own vision, reveal your own awareness, and explore your own aesthetic philosophy in each photograph.

To create a romantic aura reminiscent of Monet's Impressionist paintings, I diffused the bright summer light on the waterlily pond at the artist's garden in Giverny, France, with a soft-focus filter on a Zuiko 180mm lens. The exposure was 1/4 sec. at *f*/8 on Ektachrome LPZ.

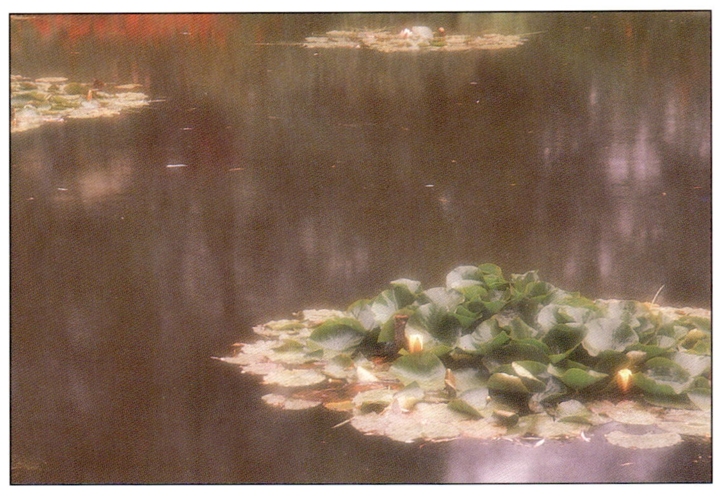

The ordinary, ragged gravel path winding into the undergrowth conveys the coolness, quiet, and naturalness so typical of Japanese gardens like this one in Kyoto. With a Zuiko 35-70mm zoom lens set at 40mm, I exposed for 1/30 sec. at *f*/11 on Fujichrome 100.

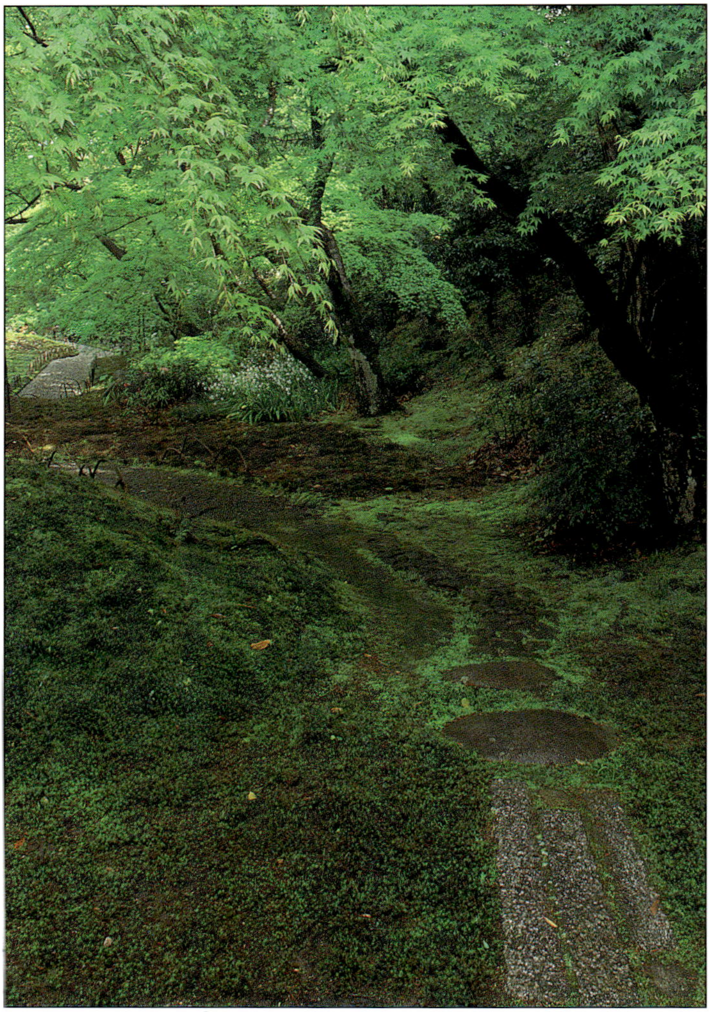

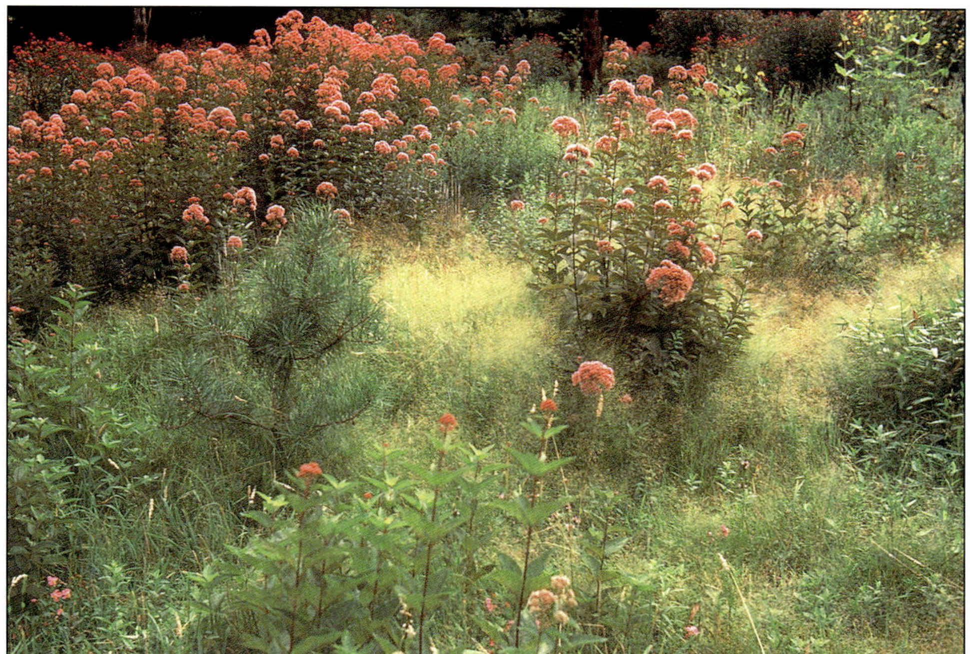

As late afternoon sunlight bathed this natural meadow at the New York Botanical Garden in the Bronx, New York, a gauzy partial blur emerged when some light flared into the lens. After setting a Zuiko 50-250mm lens at 180mm, I exposed for 1/60 sec. at *f*/8 on Ektachrome LPZ.

Begin to hone your perspective by thinking about what appeals to you in each garden. What mood or feeling does it generate? If you close your eyes, what is the image that stays in your imagination? Think about how you would portray the garden if you could paint it, with just the right light or with certain distractions removed. Such imaginative exercises will help you focus on exactly how you want to depict the garden.

Capturing the sense of place in an individual, creative way is actually much more challenging than straightforward documentation. But these are the kinds of photographs that will truly make you proud. And there is no end of possibilities once you get your creative juices flowing.

The next step is to determine how to translate that inner vision into an actual image on film. This requires a knowledge of the photographic tools you'll need, as well as a clear understanding of how to use them to get the results you want. This isn't particularly hard; but it does have to be conscious. Unfortunately, advertisers give the impression that all a photographer has to do is point and press a button to take a fabulous shot. In fact, great photographs take caring: caring to get the results you want. And caring takes a bit of time. So if you care enough to produce the very best images you can, you can learn how you can get them.

EXPANDING THE POSSIBILITIES

There is no end to the creative process, so continue to experiment with new ideas and approaches. These might not always be successful; in fact, most experiments aren't. But don't let that discourage you. Keep making attempts at techniques you haven't tried before, and you'll produce enough exciting results to make those efforts worthwhile.

Play with Blur. For example, try your hand at portraying motion in impressionistic ways. Instead of always going for maximum sharpness, develop an appreciation for the unexpected effects of letting the movement of plants register on film as a blur by using a slow shutter speed.

Experimenting with motion using a fast shutter speed, a telephoto lens, and a shallow depth of field resulted in this unexpected image of salvia growing in a private New Jersey garden. Here, I used a Zuiko 90mm macro lens and exposed Ektachrome SW for 1/250 sec. at *f*/4.

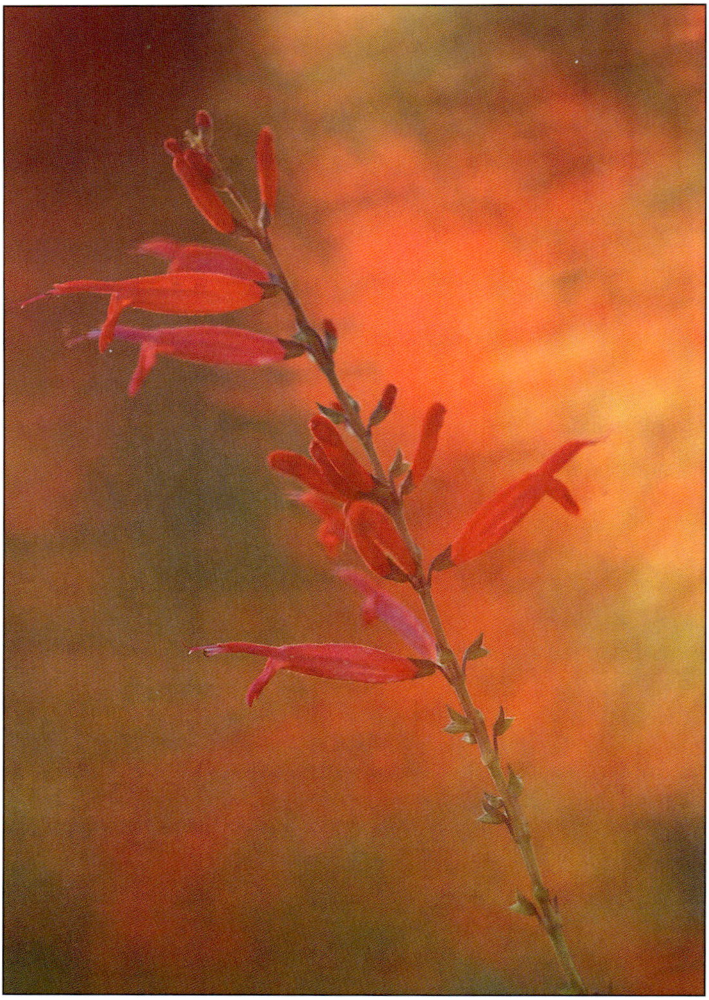

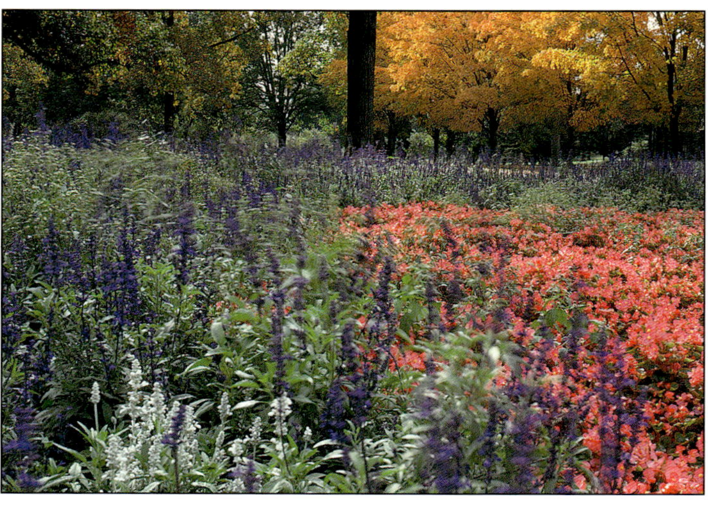

A slow shutter speed, 1/8 sec., conveys the movement of the foreground flowers and camouflages the fact that they were past their prime in this otherwise sharp image of the New York Botanical Garden in the Bronx, New York. Here, I set a Zuiko 28mm lens at *f*/16 and shot Kodachrome 64.

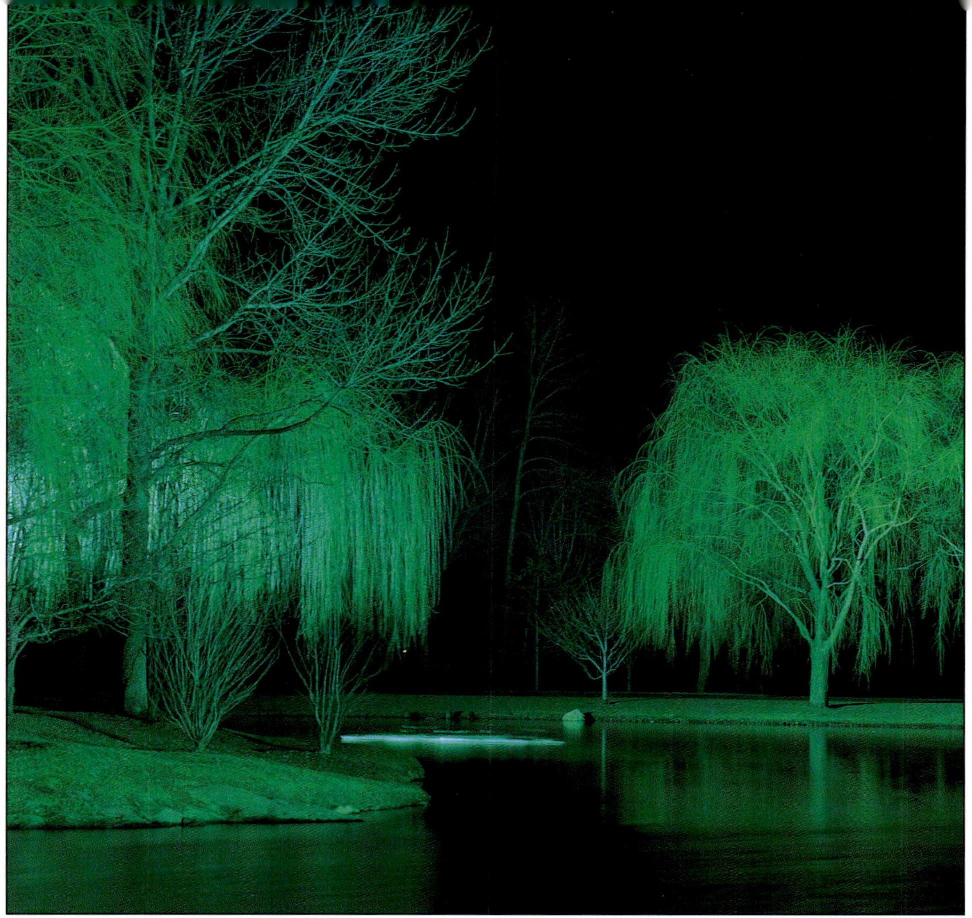

The eerie green of these trees at the Donald M. Kendall Sculpture Garden at PepsiCo World Headquarters in Purchase, New York, comes from combining daylight film with mercury vapor lights at night. Shooting with a Sonnar 150mm lens, I exposed at f/8 for 3 seconds on Ektachrome EPN.

How slow? This is where your experiment comes in. Try a variety of speeds, starting with 1/30 sec. or 1/15 sec., depending on how quickly the breeze is blowing. Then shoot a series of exposures at progressively slower speeds, remembering to place your camera on a tripod and to adjust the aperture setting to maintain a constant exposure (see Chapter 2 for information on equipment). Keep a record of the speeds you used, and match them with the results when they come in. Then decide which effect you like best, and try it with different subjects.

A variation of such deliberate blurring is called "rear-curtain flash" or "slow shutter synchronization." This technique entails putting your camera on a tripod, and using a slow shutter speed with your flash. The short burst of light from the flash unit freezes the motion of the foreground subject while the background appears to be in motion because of the longer exposure time. This effect works especially well with masses of flowers on a windy day.

Cross-Processing. Another interesting possibility is cross-processing. For example, try shooting slide film and processing it as if it were negative film, or vice versa. The chemical mismatch makes for some strange colors, which you might find pleasing. Again, try the effect with a number of different subjects, varying their colors and your compositions. What works with some colors might not work as well with others. Once you find the effect you like, you can turn to it whenever you think it will get you where you want to go. By keeping an open mind as well as an open eye, you'll discover all sorts of possibilities for photographing gardens.

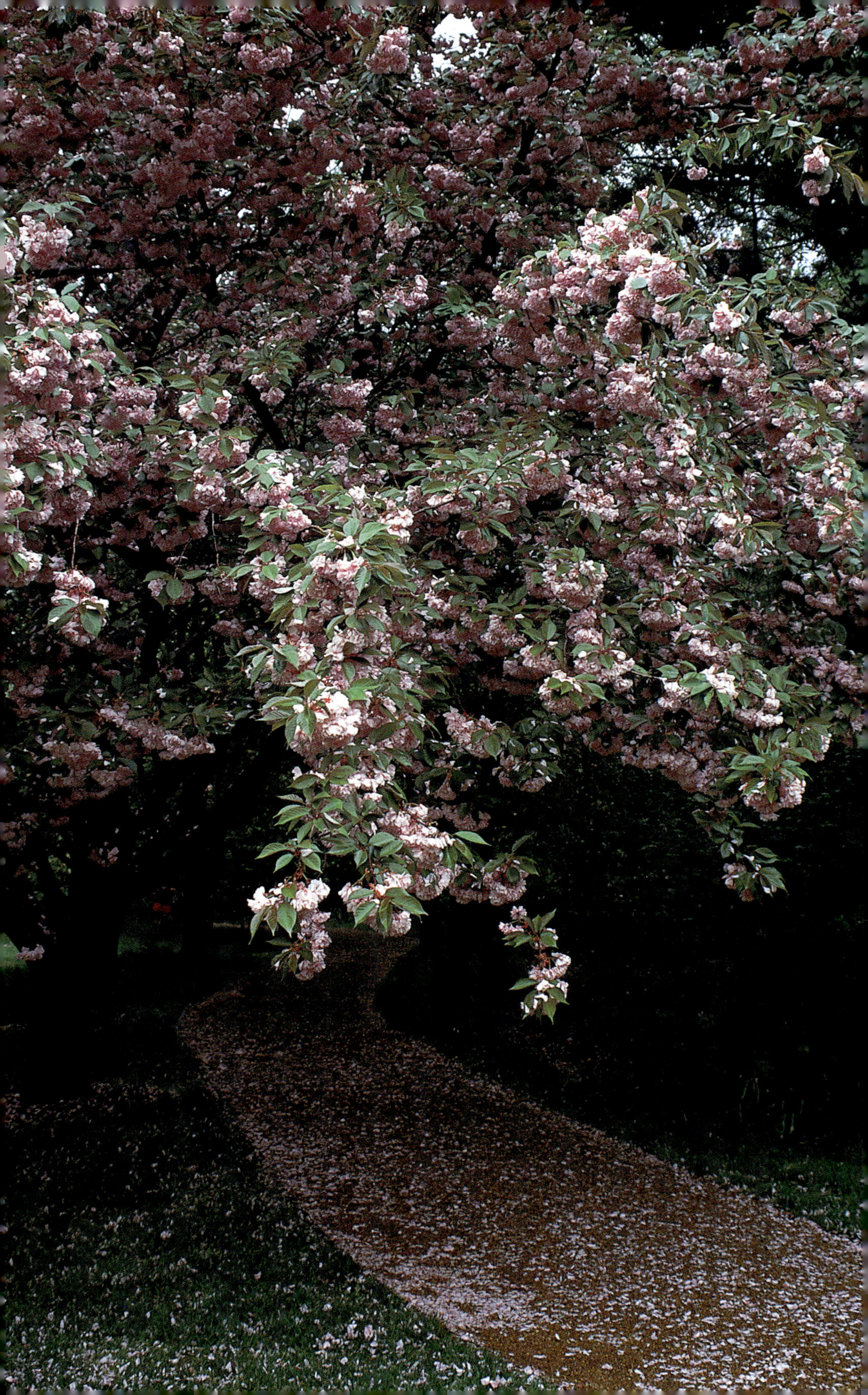

CHAPTER 2

Tools for Garden Photography

Not all lenses focus as close to the subject as the Zuiko 35-70mm zoom lens. Set at 35mm, this lens let me focus on the hanging branches of the flowering cherry tree at the Donald M. Kendall Sculpture Garden at PepsiCo World Headquarters in Purchase, New York. The 35mm setting kept both the foreground flowers and the vanishing path sharp. I exposed at *f*/8 for 1/30 sec. on Fujichrome 100.

When it is important to work quickly, use a zoom lens: it saves time and reduces hassle. A Zuiko 50-250mm lens set at 150mm enabled me to compose this shot at the Donald M. Kendall Sculpture Garden in Purchase, New York, as soon as the sun dropped to create the soft backlight on this perennial border. The exposure on Kodachrome 25 was *f*/8 for 1/60 sec.

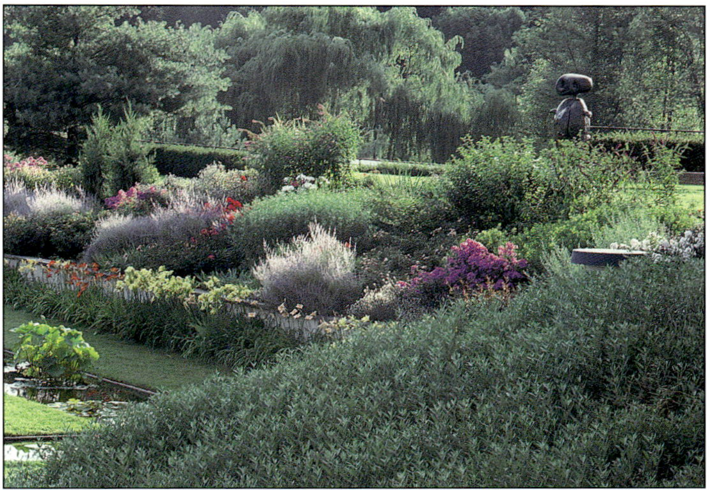

Garden photography depends, to some degree, on the effectiveness of the garden designers, who work without regard to the needs of photographers. Of course, knowledgeable photographers will find ways to portray any garden at its best, even if it has obstacles or flaws. Often, when clients hire professional garden photographers, they expect—and get—images that make the garden appear more beautiful than it is because the pros know how to camouflage the flaws.

When you don't have time to set up a tripod, you'll find that a light camera is easier to handhold than a heavy one. Shooting cherry trees in this Kyoto, Japan, shrine on the run, I was able to hold my lightweight 35mm SLR camera steady during a 1/60 sec. exposure. Here, I used a Zuiko 35-70mm lens set at 40mm, an *f*/5.6 aperture, and Fujichrome 100.

Since you can't control a garden designer's vision, at the very least you must be as clear as possible about your own. The clearer your photographic vision, the stronger your compositions, the more sensitive you are to light and color, and the better you have mastered fundamental camera techniques, the closer you'll be to creating great garden images.

To some degree, of course, your results depend on the photographic tools you use. Undoubtedly, you'll need some basic items of equipment just to get started. And you'll probably want to turn to specialized gear as your interests develop in particular directions. What you shouldn't do—and too many photographers make this mistake—is to run out and buy a trunkful of expensive equipment in the hope and expectation that your images will improve just because you've spent a bundle. Not so. You are much better off starting small with a few key items of the highest quality you can afford. Another option is to start using equipment you already own, beginning with basic items and adding new ones as you feel ready to stretch in new directions.

If you already own camera equipment, take stock of what you have and consider whether you've been using all its potential. If not, devote time to expanding your skills and technical repertoire. Then add to your photographic toolbox as you outgrow your current gear, knowing exactly which pieces you need to produce new kinds of images. Again, be sure to emphasize quality rather than quantity.

As photographers learn the limits of the equipment they have, they come to understand what they can and can't do with it. For example, if they don't have any closeup equipment but want to shoot closeups, they know that they have to purchase something that will enable them to do so. To decide exactly what to buy, they might talk to other photographers, consult books and magazines, visit a reputable camera shop, and discuss their needs with a salesperson.

The following pieces of essential photographic gear will help you get top-notch garden images right from the start. You'll learn how each item can help you achieve your photographic goals.

CAMERAS

First on your list of essentials, of course, is a camera. Today's sophisticated electronic cameras offer a wide range of options, and new models come out often in every price range. To keep up with the latest products, check a reputable magazine, such as *Popular Photography*, which regularly tests new cameras and other equipment and explains the results, usually with visual backup. You can use any of the following types of cameras to photograph gardens, but give priority to a model with interchangeable lenses or a built-in zoom lens, so you'll have the flexibility you'll want for composing.

Single-Lens-Reflex Cameras. The 35mm single-lens-reflex (SLR) camera is the one many professional and most serious amateur photographers prefer. The main advantage of an SLR is the degree of control it gives the photographer. It lets you fully command the technical and aesthetic aspects of your photograph to get the precise exposure and depth of field you want—provided you know what you're doing (by the time you finish this book, you'll have that understanding). And its through-the-lens viewing feature gives you the best mastery of your composition.

SLR cameras also let you choose from a wide range of lenses for the greatest latitude in composing and make it easy to add filters. If you plan to use electronic flash, these cameras provide an added advantage because their electronic linkage through the lens (TTL) to the flash is so

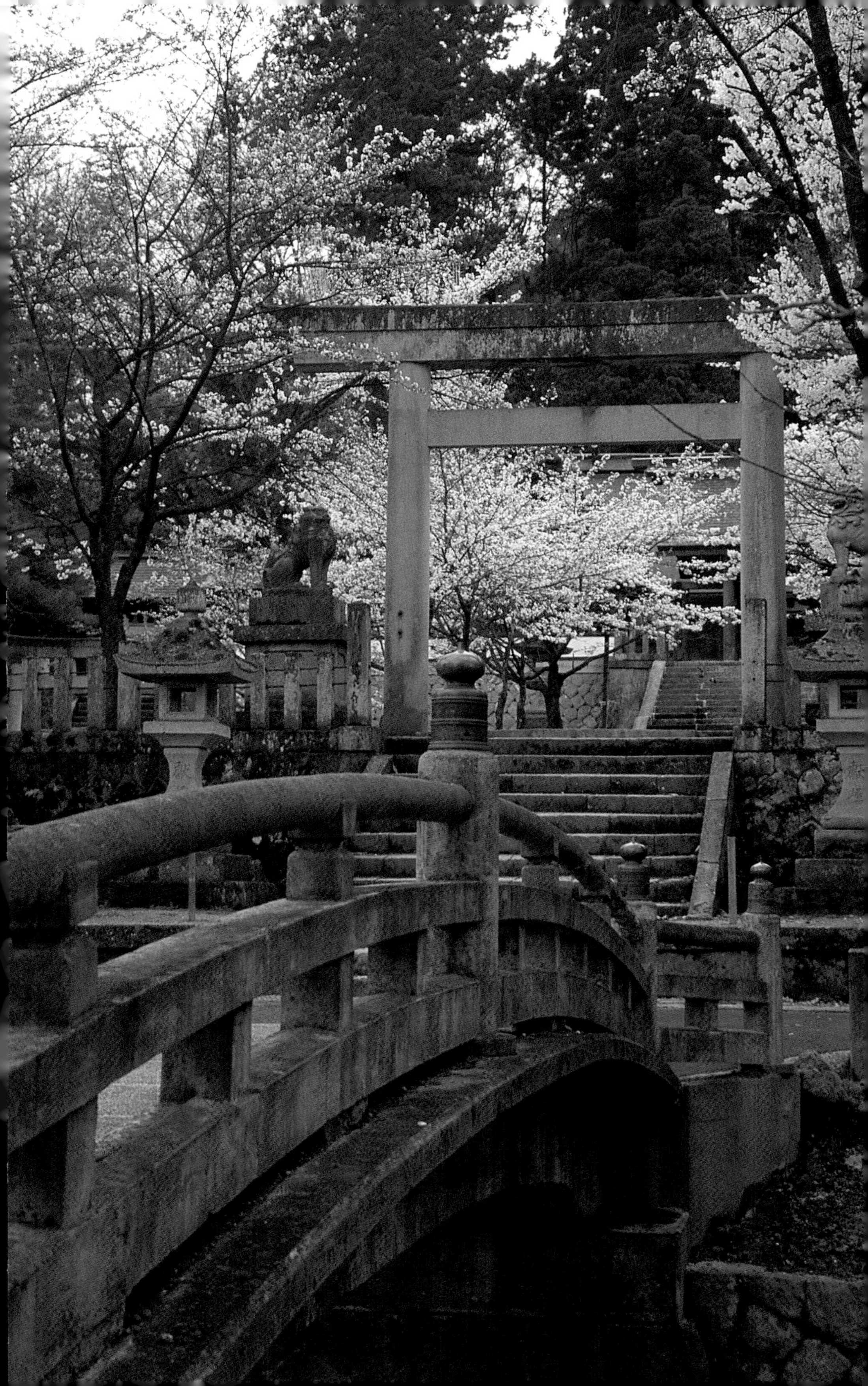

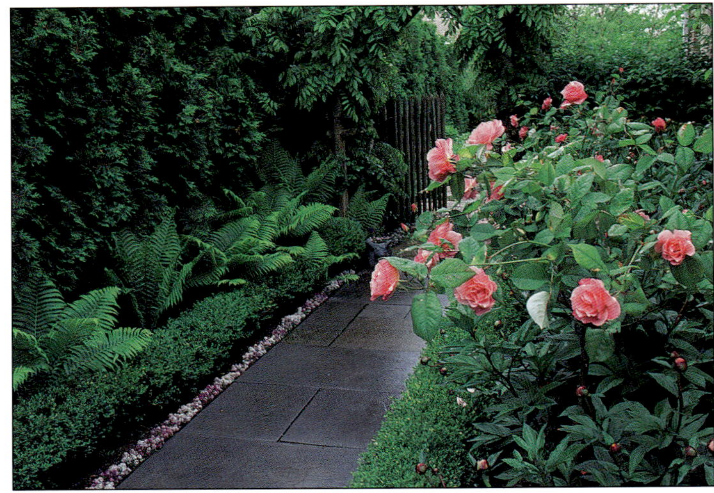

The sophisticated automatic aperture-priority metering system built into my Olympus OM-4T helped me accurately expose a rose bush during a quick shoot in this private garden in Illinois. A tripod was essential since the camera set the shutter speed, a slow 1/15 sec. I made this image with a Zuiko 35-70mm lens set at 35mm, exposing Fujichrome Velvia at *f*/16.

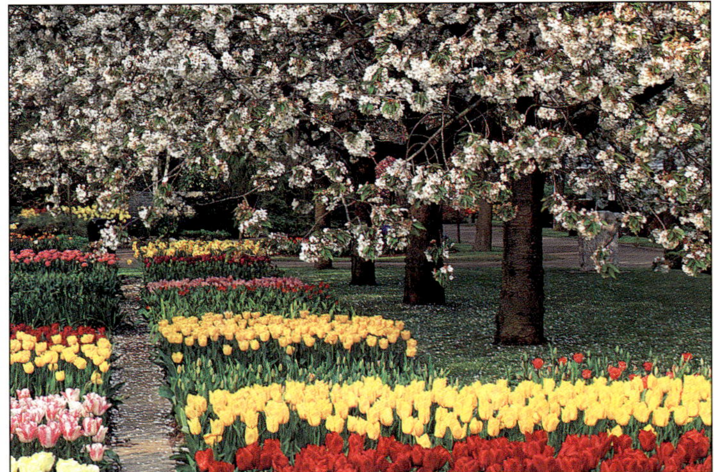

The camera's capacity to accept a variety of lenses provides photographers with creative control. Here, I mounted a Zuiko 50-250mm zoom lens set at 200mm on my Olympus OM-4T to create the telescoping effect that masses the bulbs at Holland's Keukenhof Garden. The exposure on Fujichrome Velvia was 1/30 sec. at *f*/11.

reliable it is almost foolproof. In addition, 35mm SLRs accept the greatest variety of films, and they are light, compact, and easy to use.

If you're looking at new cameras, keep in mind that models with the latest in automatic and electronic wizardry aren't necessary for photographing gardens. In fact, you'll probably find yourself overriding the autofocus feature more often than not. So unless you want those features for other photography you plan to do, you don't need to pay a premium for them.

However, some newer models, like the Olympus IS-3 and the Nikon N-90S, offer a feature useful for garden photography: a program mode with a landscape setting, which automatically produces the greatest depth of field from foreground to background. And some models, like the Olympus IS series, have attachments to extend the range of the built-in zoom lens to 300mm, in case you want to shoot more distant subjects.

Point-and-Shoot Cameras. With their built-in and automatic features, point-and-shoot (P&S) cameras have a place in garden photography, though a limited one. They are easy to use, and are smaller and lighter than SLRs. This makes them ideal for situations where you want the lightest gear possible, such as when you travel to places where you don't expect to see many interesting gardens. However, the range of lens options in P&S cameras is much narrower than those for SLRs; they offer little or no control over *f*-stops, shutter speeds, or focusing.

To make the most of these limitations for garden photography, check the program menus of the various P&S cameras on the market. Choose one that has landscape, backlight, and closeup modes. Using these modes will give you a modicum of control over depth of field and exposure.

Medium-Format Cameras. If extreme sharpness in your photography is an absolute must for you, you might prefer a camera with a larger format than 35mm. Medium-format SLR camera models produce a larger negative or transparency in three sizes: 2¼ x 2¼ inches, 4.5 x 6cm, or 6 x 7 cm. A bigger transparency might give you a somewhat sharper, clearer image than a 35mm transparency would afford, provided you already exercise extreme care in focusing and other techniques for achieving maximum sharpness.

This symmetrical composition of an allee of birches at the Stan Hyett Garden in Akron, Ohio, was enhanced with a square image framed with a medium-format Hasselblad CM and a Planar 80mm lens. I exposed at *f*/22 for 1/15 sec. on Fujichrome Velvia.

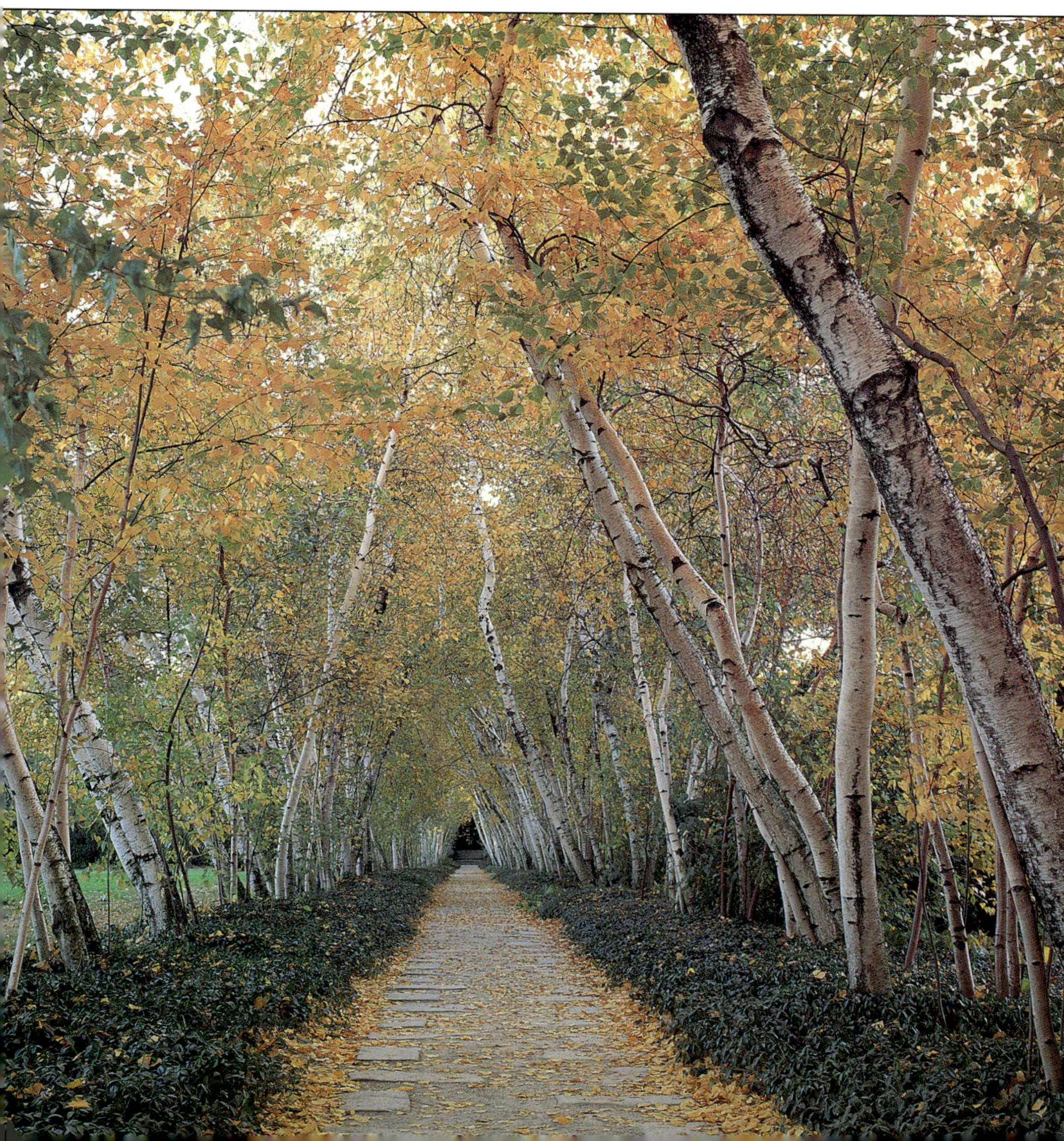

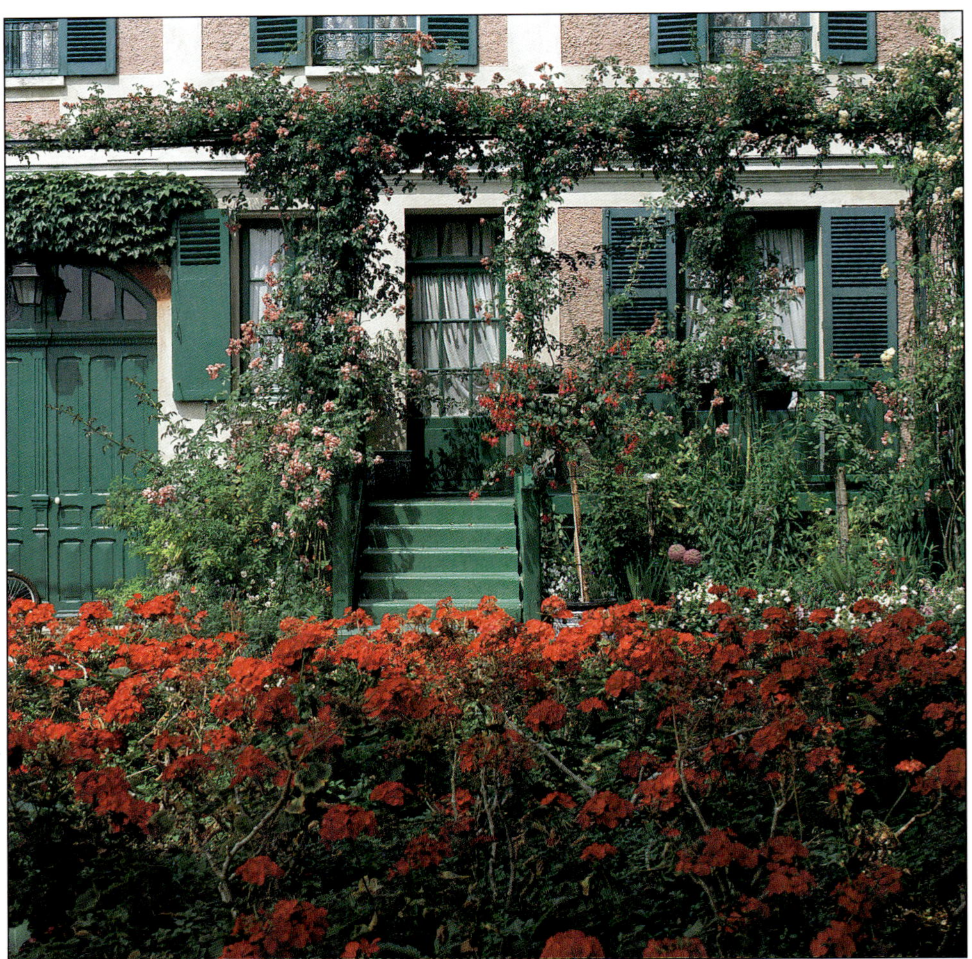

A square format offers a visual change of pace that makes viewers take notice. I made this image of Monet's house and garden at Giverny, France, with a medium-format Hasselblad CM and a Planar 80mm lens. Shooting Fujichrome RFP, I exposed at *f*/22 for 1/15 sec.

Medium-format cameras are available from Fuji, Mamiya, Pentax, Rolleiflex, and Hasselblad in square, rectangular, and panoramic formats. The cameras permit you to change lenses, from ultrawide-angle to telephoto. In addition, many of these cameras have removable film backs, so you can easily switch from one kind of film to another when you're photographing. This feature is a definite advantage if you use print and slide films interchangeably, or if you're working with variable light and you want access to different film speeds.

Keep in mind, however, that medium-format cameras are considerably bulkier, heavier, and slower to use than the compact 35mm SLRs. Another drawback is that not as many film types are made for medium-format cameras. Finally, these cameras, as well as the lenses and accessories made for them are more generally expensive than 35mm cameras and their accouterments.

Large-Format Cameras. Like some of the greatest landscape photographers of the past—Carlton Watkins, Timothy O'Sullivan, Ansel Adams, Edward Weston, and Eliot Porter—quite a few of the best landscape photographers today work with large-format cameras. Because the negative or transparency these cameras produce is very large, images can be espe-

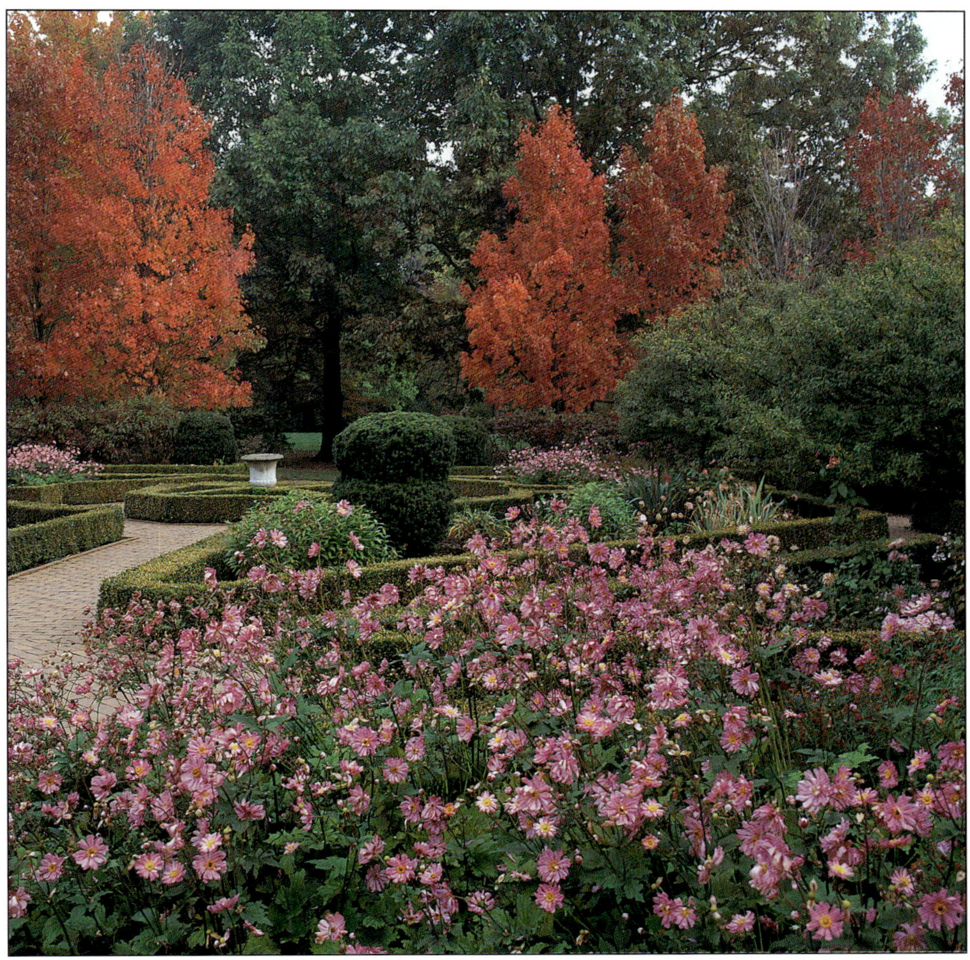

I chose a 2 1/4-inch square format to make this image of an autumn garden at the Kingwood Center in Mansfield, Ohio, extra sharp. Working with a Distagon 60mm lens, I exposed Fujichrome Velvia for 1/15 sec. at *f*/16.

cially sharp and rich in detail. The most common large-format view cameras come in 4 x 5-inch and 8 x 10-inch sizes and are made by Sinar, Linhof, and Arca.

However, large-format cameras are almost never used for garden photography because they are bulky and slow, and take some getting used to since you view the image upside down and backwards. The chief exception is when integrating the architecture is important since these cameras enable you to swing, twist, and tilt the lens and film planes. This gives you great control over focus, depth of field, and perspective.

Panoramic Cameras. The growing interest in panoramic images has spurred the development of a variety of equipment for this purpose. Top-of-the-line, sophisticated, electronic panoramic cameras can cost up to $15,000 and come in rotation and nonrotation models designed to record from 90 degrees to as much as 360 degrees. But unless you plan to do lots of panoramic shooting, you can get similar effects with special adapters for 35mm SLRs and P&S cameras or with disposable panoramic cameras made by Kodak and Fuji. For the most part, though, panoramic shots of gardens are gimmicks: they are fine for an occasional flourish, but far from essential.

I wanted to compress the cascading flowers around these benches at the Chicago Botanic Garden in Glencoe, Illinois, so I chose a moderate telephoto setting, 70mm, on a Zuiko 35-70mm lens. The exposure on Fujichrome Velvia was 1/15 sec. at *f*/16.

LENSES

If you're working with an SLR camera, you can expand your visual options with an array of interchangeable lenses. Newcomers to photography usually react with amazement when they first glimpse a scene through some new lens because the transformation is so unexpected and exciting. Try to retain that feeling of wonder even as you become familiar with the effect of each kind of lens. (If you're using a P&S camera with a built-in zoom lens, the lens descriptions below will help you understand what you can do by setting your zoom lens to a particular focal length.)

Begin with the lenses you already own, using this chapter to alert you to new ways to make the most of them. As you begin to outgrow what you have, use this chapter to help you make decisions about which new lenses to buy. You have dozens of fine lenses to choose from. In fact, almost all name brand lenses on the market today have excellent resolution and sharpness.

But don't make the mistake of buying more than you really need. Always base your choice of lens on the kind of image you want to create. Buy the best quality you can afford in the lens type you want. And keep in mind that for photographing gardens, you don't need to pay a premium for very fast lenses. This is because you're working with a stationary subject and you are likely to be shooting with your camera on a tripod and with your lens closed down to a small aperture. Whether you're buying new lenses or using those you already own, keep the following factors in mind.

Standard Lenses. A 50mm standard lens is often bought with the camera body, is inexpensive, and approximates the perspective of the unaided eye. It is fine for most overview shots and for intimate garden landscapes or vignettes. If you plan to shoot closeups in the garden, though, you might be better off forgoing the 50mm lens and substituting a macro lens in the 50mm to 60mm range. Such a macro lens can do everything a

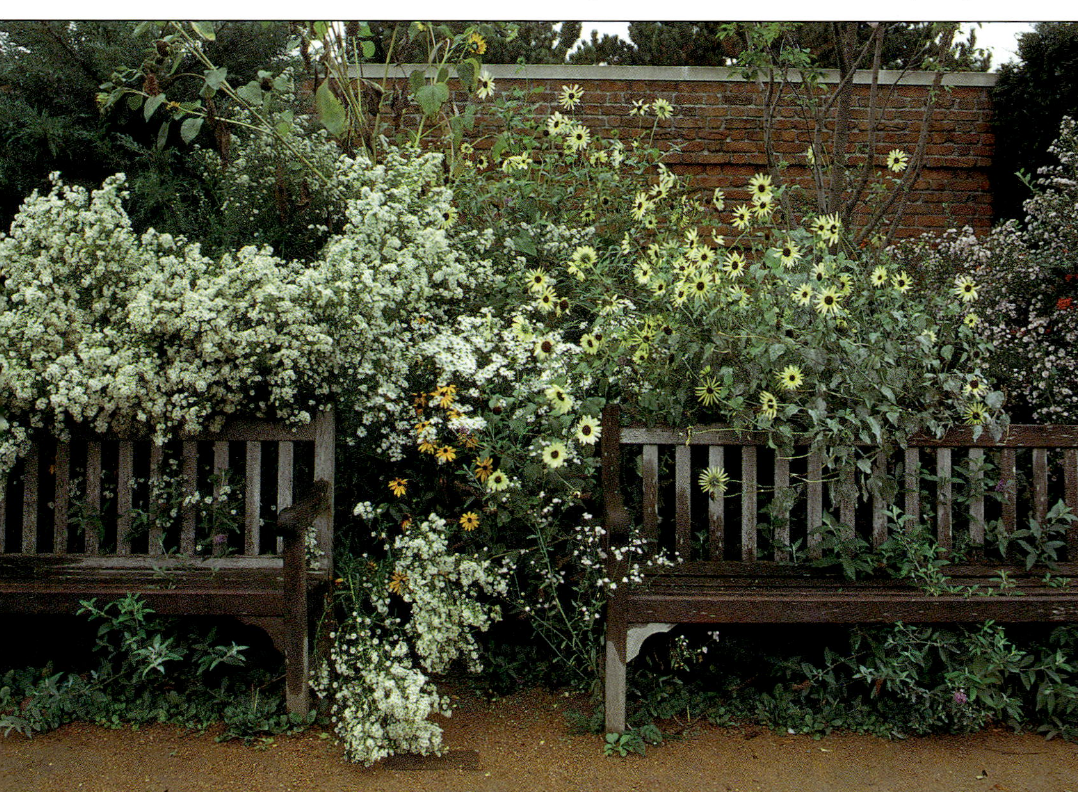

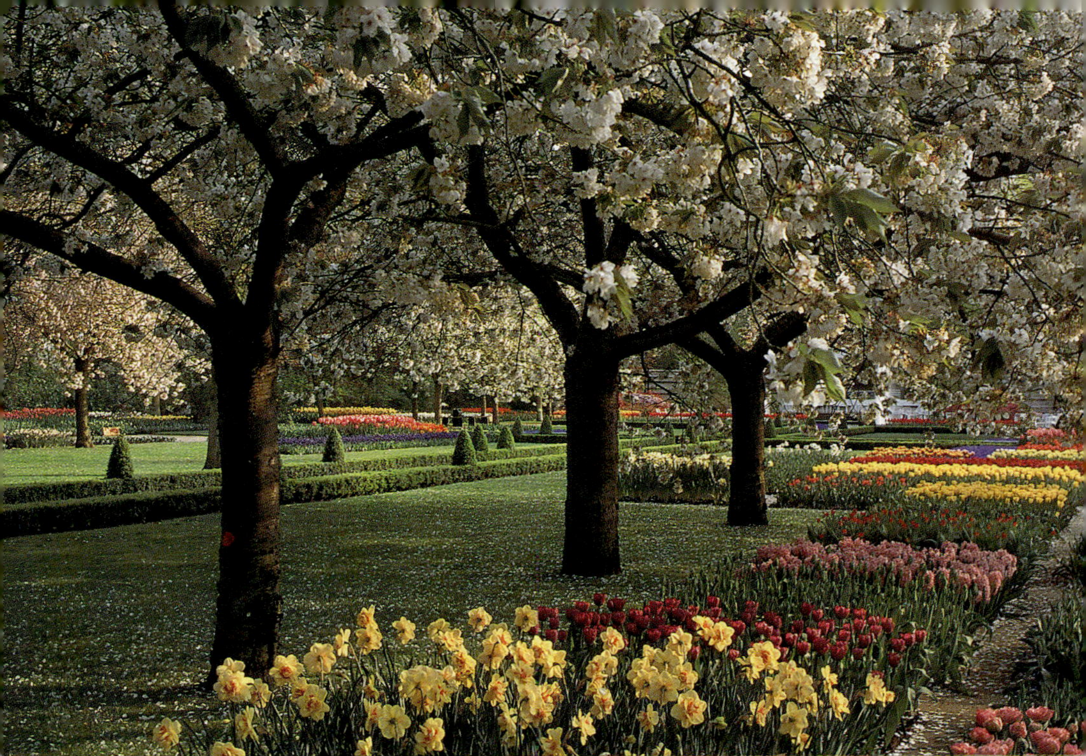

A telephoto setting of 150mm on a Zuiko 50-250mm lens enabled me to compose this image from a distance of about 80 feet and concentrate on the cherry blossoms in Holland's Keukenhof Garden. Here, I exposed at *f*/11 for 1/30 sec. on Fujichrome Velvia.

standard lens can do, as well as enables you to work at distances of only a few inches. This feature is an advantage most garden photographers want for shooting closeups.

Wide-Angle Lenses. Any lens with a perspective wider than 50mm is considered a wide-angle lens. The wider the angle of the lens, the more exaggerated the perspective will appear. For gardens, most photographers prefer lenses between 24mm and 38mm. But some experiment with more extreme wide-angle lenses—18mm or wider—that can produce interesting "fisheye" effects.

Since wide-angle lenses can achieve great depth of field, they are particularly handy for portraying an entire garden overview in sharp focus. They are also invaluable for integrating foreground and background areas in a garden. This feature lets you combine a nearby subject with the broad expanse of its setting with little or no loss of sharpness in either.

Wide-angle lenses are also excellent for photographing in narrow or confined spaces, such as when you're working inside a conservatory, shooting in a small cottage garden, or not allowed to stray off a path. They also can create offbeat perspectives in a garden, especially from close to the ground.

Telephoto Lenses. Telephoto lenses are the orphans of garden photography. They're underutilized because many amateur photographers think of telephoto lenses for long distances, not the relatively shorter distances you find in gardens. Many photographers also don't appreciate what a telephoto lens can do beyond enlarging distant subjects, such as blurring backgrounds and compressing space. Telephoto lenses open up many creative possibilities:

- Turn to your telephoto lenses to magnify a subject. For example, enlarge flowers that you can't get close enough to photograph with a standard lens, such as waterlilies in a pond.

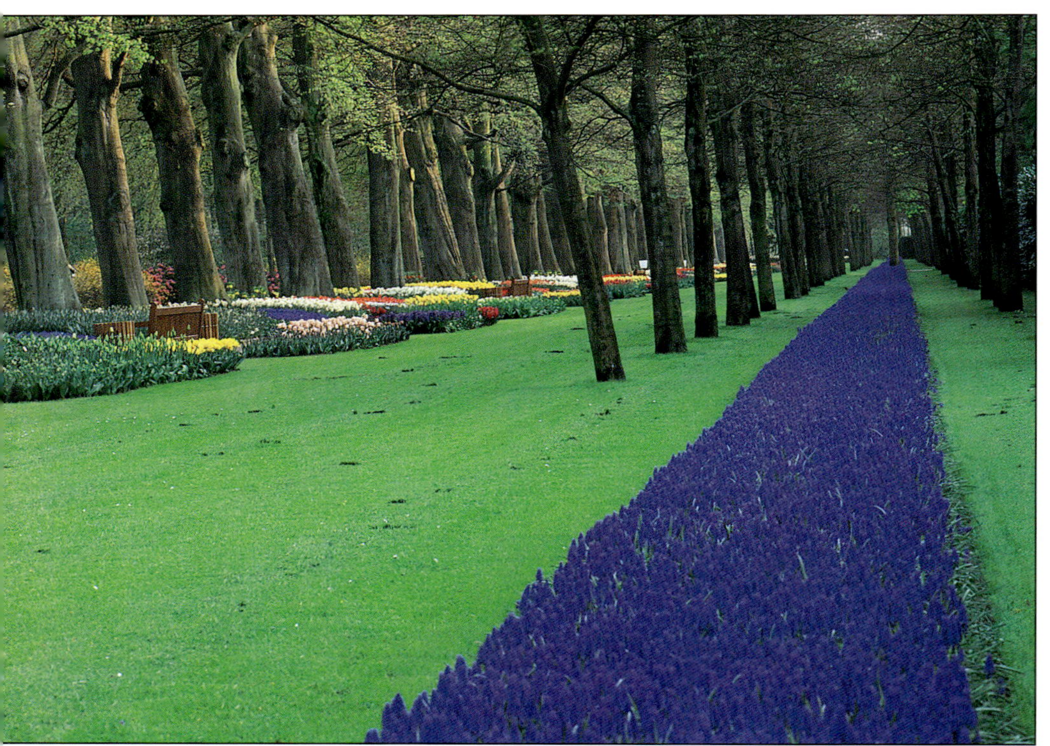

The slight wide-angle distortion of a Zuiko 35-70mm lens set at 35mm exaggerated the converging lines of this bed of grape hyacinths. This creates a great sense of depth while maintaining good proportions in the surroundings. The exposure on Fujichrome Velvia was 1/8 sec. at *f*/16.

- Use these lenses to separate a portion of a garden scene from its surroundings. Telephoto lenses are the perfect tools for isolating small visual gems in the huge mine of the garden.
- The lenses' narrow depth of field enables you to blur unwanted foreground or background foliage in order to focus on the main subjects in a vignette or detail.
- Telephoto lenses let you telescope the field of view, flattening and compressing space to visually juxtapose areas that are some distance apart. This interesting effect works best when the subjects have simple shapes, lines, and colors. The compression intensifies color, which is something to keep in mind if you're shooting a sparsely planted flower bed, for example. This effect also highlights textures and brings out the abstract design of your composition.

Lenses between 80mm and 200mm are best for garden photography. But be aware that the more a lens magnifies, the heavier and bulkier it is likely to be and the harder it will be to handle. When using a telephoto lens, always mount your camera on a tripod to eliminate camera shake and the resultant unwanted, blurred images.

As mentioned earlier, most amateur garden photographers don't turn to their telephoto lenses enough. Start experimenting with these long lenses as soon as possible. You'll quickly discover their impressive results.

Zoom Lenses. Zoom lenses give you many of the compositional advantages of changing lenses without the extra gear. A single zoom lens ranging in focal length from 28mm to 200mm or from 35mm to 350mm can take the place of several single-focal-length lenses, at less weight and without appreciable loss of sharpness. But for garden photography, you'll find that several less grandiose zoom lenses tend to do a better job.

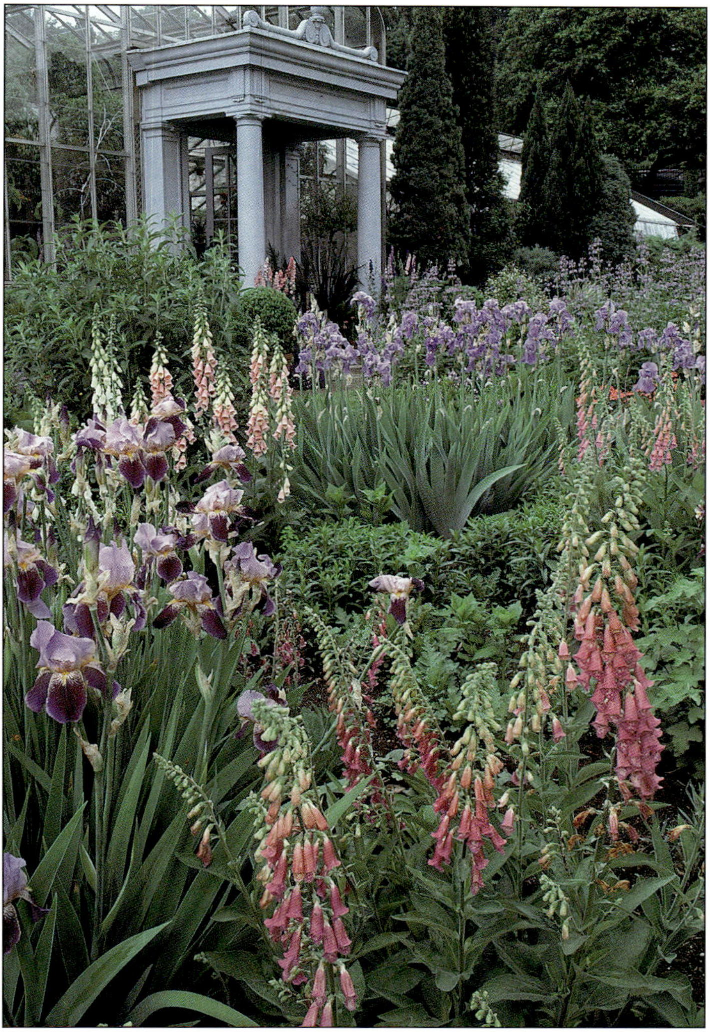

The wide perspective and extensive depth of field of a Zuiko 24mm lens integrate the foreground foxgloves with a sharply rendered architectural setting at Wave Hill in New York. I exposed for 1/30 sec. at *f*/11 on Kodachrome 25.

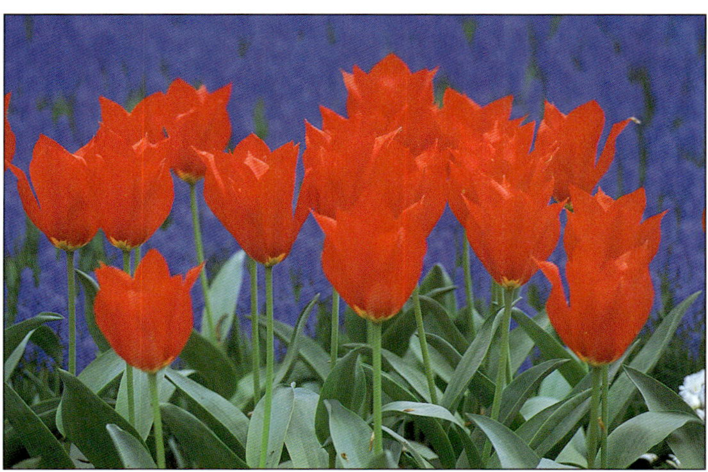

Under conditions that didn't permit me to enlarge the flowers with a macro lens, the magnifying power and narrow depth of field of a Zuiko 300mm lens plus a 25mm extension tube produced this moderate closeup of tulips set against a deliberately blurred backdrop of grape hyacinths at Holland's Keukenhof Garden. The exposure was *f*/5.6 for 1/15 sec. on Fujichrome Velvia.

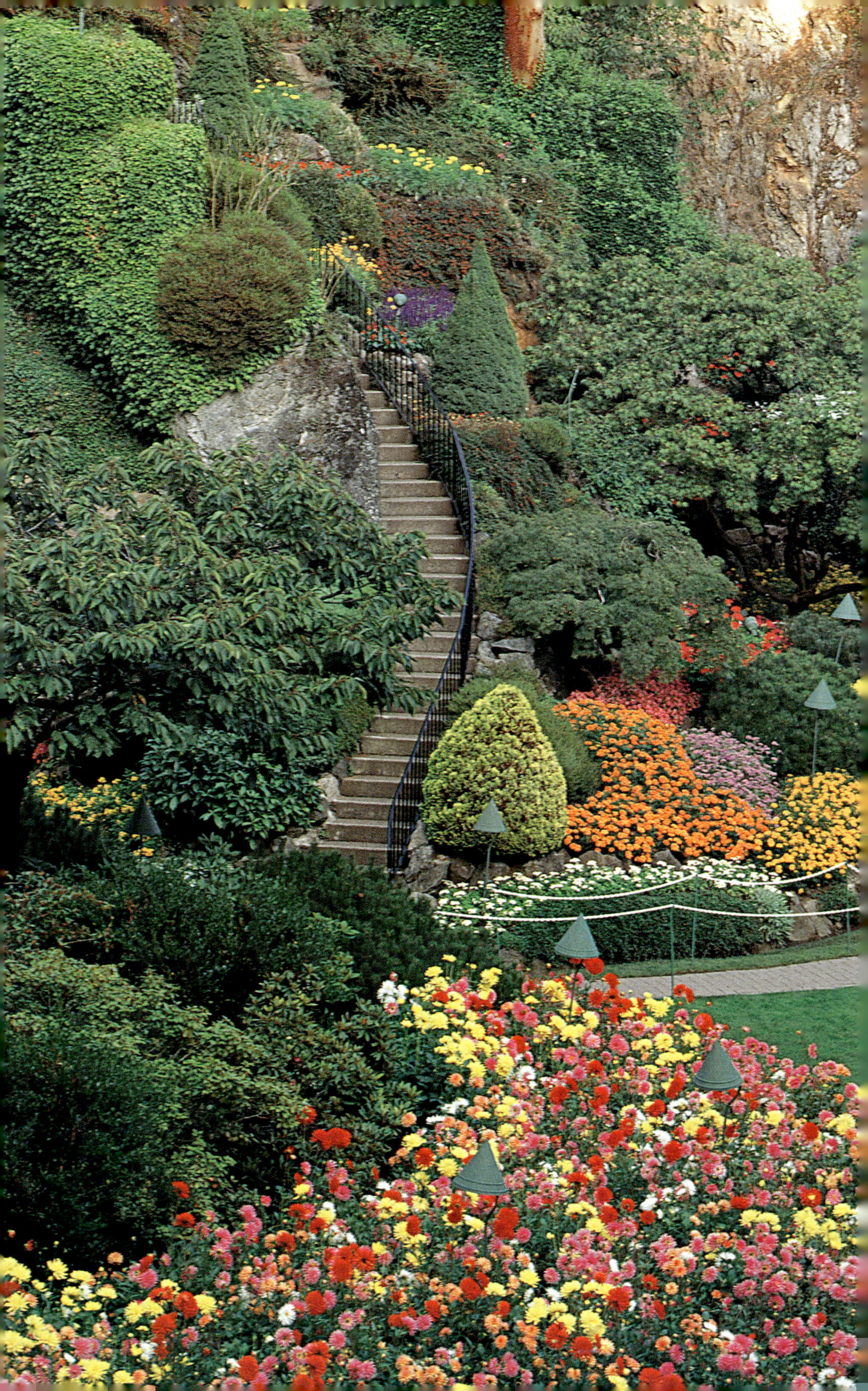

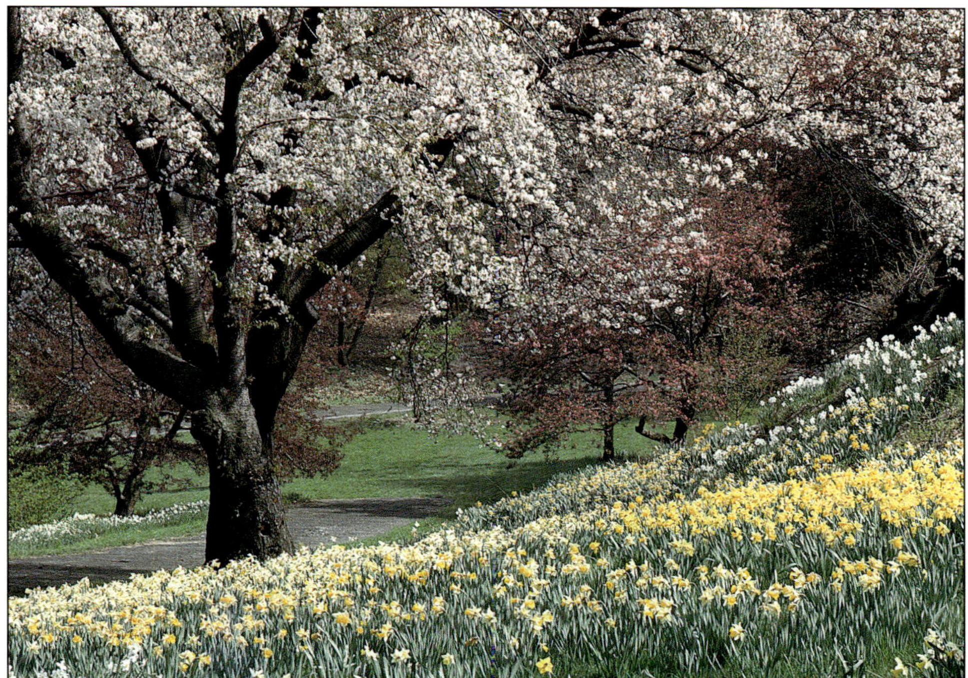

Here, a Zuiko 35mm lens harmoniously combined the flowering crabapple tree and the daffodils beneath it for an image that truly conveys the spring bloom at the New York Botanical Garden in the Bronx, New York. Shooting Kodachrome 64, I exposed for 1/60 sec. at f/8.

Set at 70mm, a Zuiko 35-70mm lens was ideal for isolating this portion of the Buchart Gardens in Victoria, British Columbia, from a distance of 150 feet, compressing the foreground plantings in the process. The exposure on Fujichrome Provia was f/16 for 1/30 sec.

The most consistently useful and effective lenses are the 35-70mm zoom, the 80-200mm zoom, and the 50-250mm zoom. These lenses offer convenience, portability, versatility, and speed.

While the ability to shoot quickly isn't a priority for most garden photography, all outdoor photographers want to be able to react quickly to shifts in light. When a sudden and possibly short-lived change in the quality of light takes place, a zoom lens will help you react quickly to capture a sight that can make the difference between an ordinary and a spectacular image.

FILMS

A growing number of films on the market can serve the needs of garden photographers. Recent years have seen a veritable revolution in films, with dozens of new ones released in the last few years alone. But while serious amateur photographers often devote lots of attention to the latest gear, they don't often give the same importance to choosing the best film for a particular shot. In fact, the type of film you choose could play a significant role in the way your final image looks.

In the broadest sense, you can choose among three categories of film: black-and-white print film, color print film, and color transparency film. Although each group offers many good options, films still vary in their strengths and their differences can be quite visible. For example, films differ in terms of color rendition, contrast, grain, and responsiveness to light (indicated by film speed), as well as in how they're processed.

Your own sense of aesthetics and how you plan to use the images will help you make the choice you like best. You can develop a clearer sense of how each film renders color and responds to light several ways:

- Do what the pros do. Load two or more cameras with different films, and shoot the same garden subjects. Comparing the results could be a real eye-opener.

Fujichrome 100 film helped create the vibrant greens in this detail of a perennial garden shot at the New York Botanical Garden in the Bronx, New York. Working with a Zuiko 50-250mm lens set at 120mm, I exposed for 1/60 sec. at *f*/11.

In the diffused backlight of a summer afternoon at the New York Botanical Garden in the Bronx, New York, Ektachrome LPZ film, with its low contrast, helped to unify and soften the greens throughout, to keep shadows from losing detail, and to produce clear whites. I made this shot with a Zuiko 35-70mm lens set at 40mm and exposed at *f*/8 for 1/125 sec.

When some rays of sun filtered through this cloud cover, I switched to Fujichrome 100 to increase contrast. This gave the same scene a sunnier look and snappier greens. I made this shot with a Zuiko 35-70mm lens set at 40mm, exposing at *f*/8 for 1/125 sec.

- Test before you invest. Shoot at least one roll of any film you aren't familiar with before you buy it by the caseload. Put it through the gamut of situations you expect to encounter, keeping careful records about lighting conditions and your camera settings for each shot. Then study the results carefully.
- Consult a reputable photography magazine, such as *Popular Photography*, in order to learn about and compare the new films that hit the market.
- Read the captions throughout the book, and note the type of film used in each shot. Then decide which you prefer.

Color Transparencies. If richness of color and fine grain for sharpness are important to you, shoot color transparencies. Professionals use this type of film to produce slides for most editorial photography, including the kind you see in garden and nature magazines. Slide film is less expensive to process per roll than color print film, and you can easily produce an enlarged print to frame from a transparency.

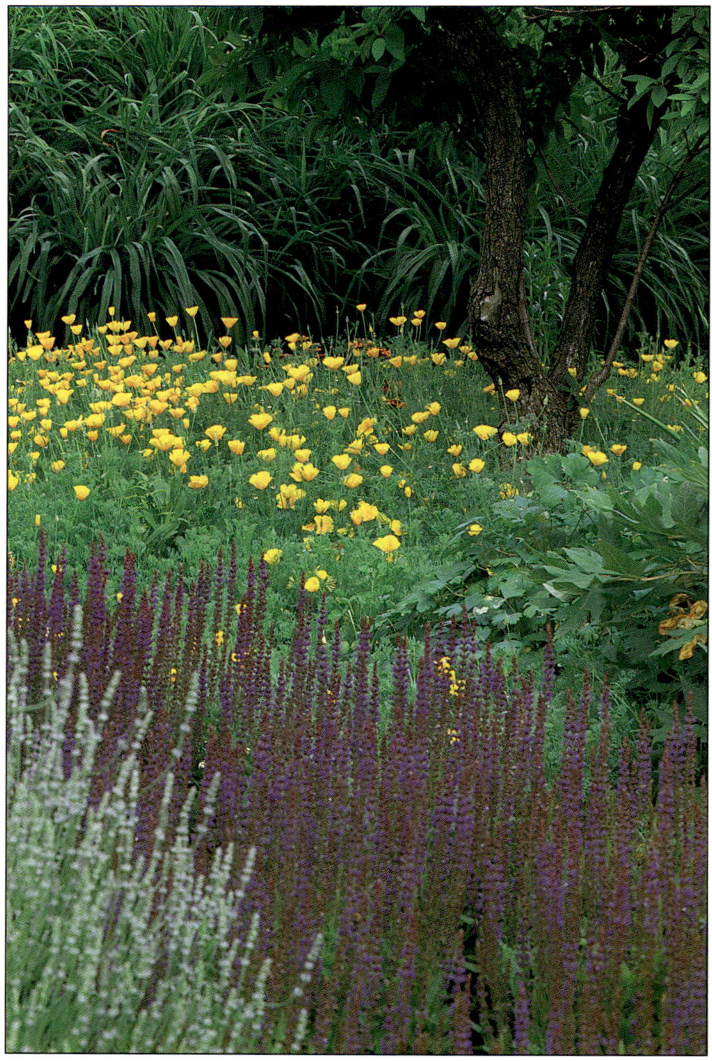

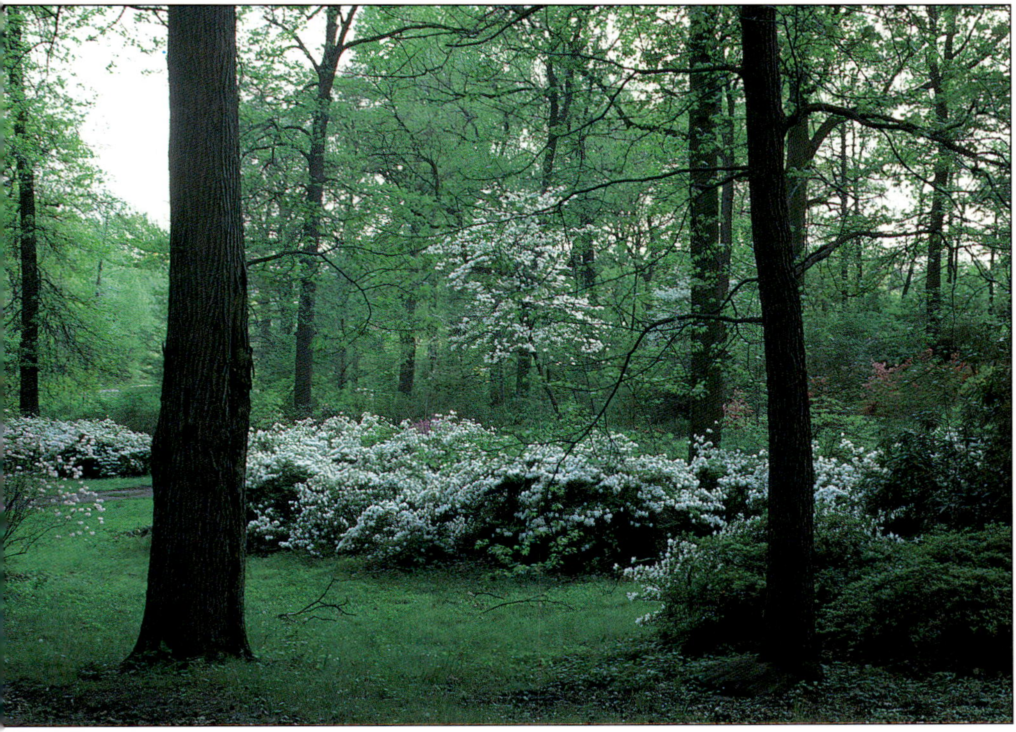

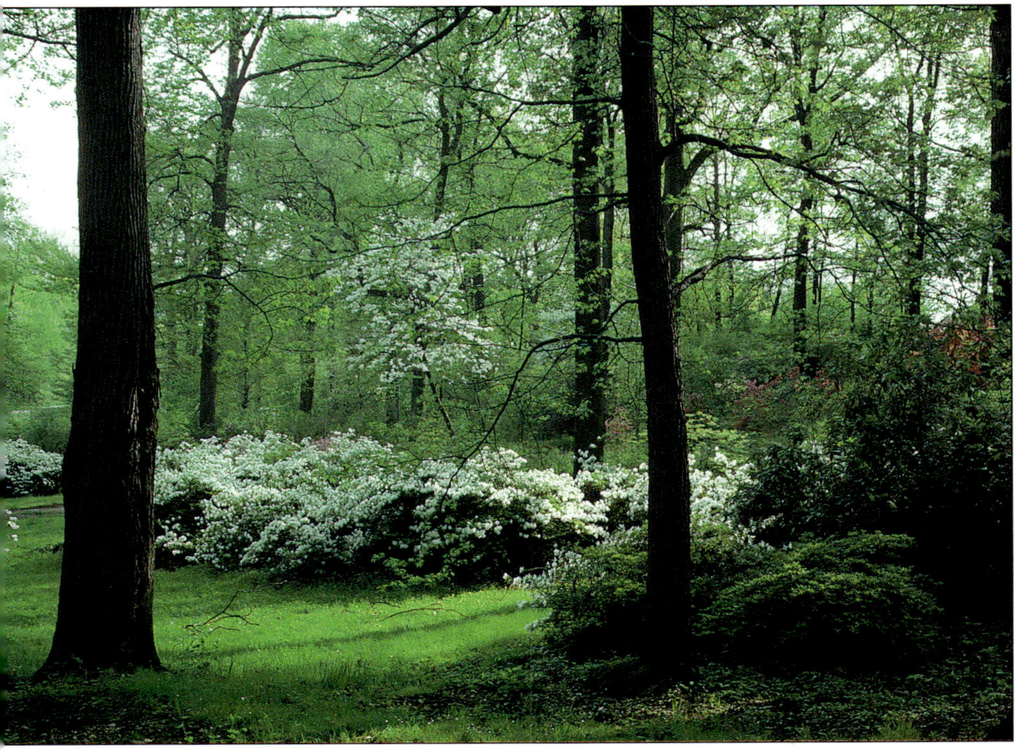

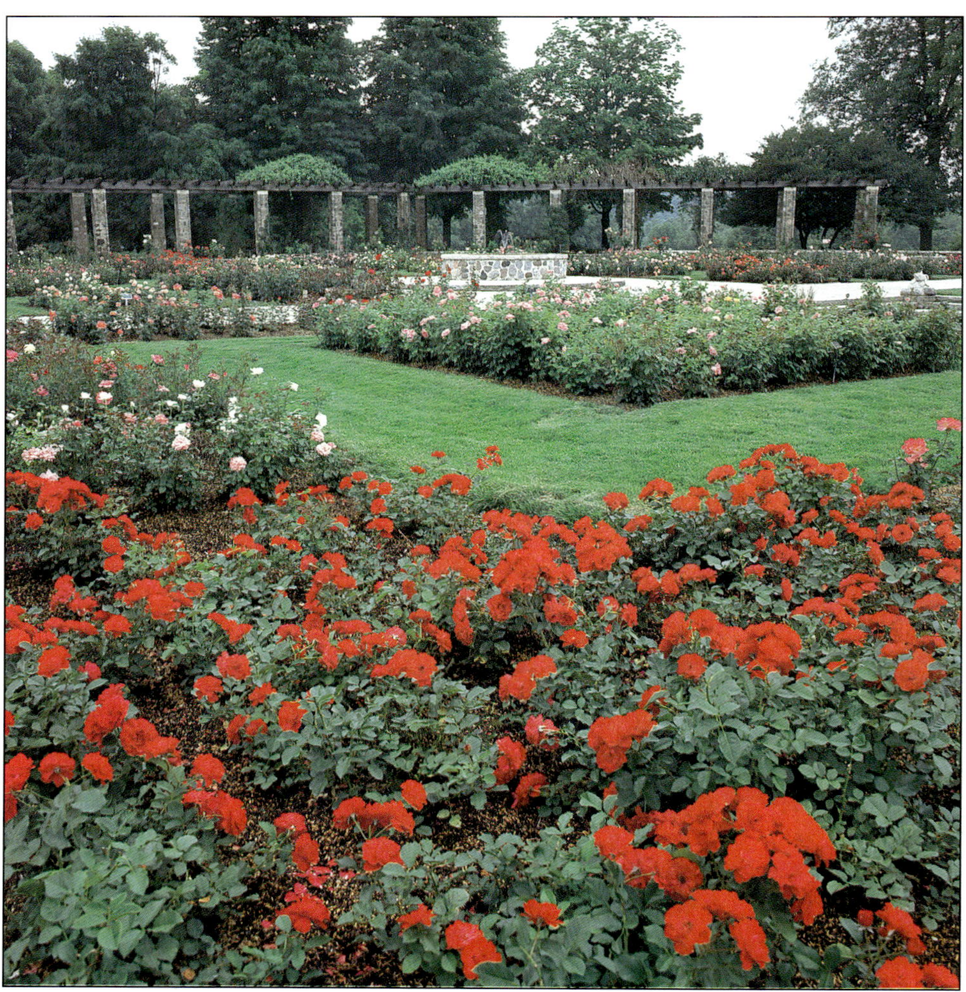

In low-contrast light, Fujichrome Velvia is ideal for keeping both reds and greens sharp and pungent. That is why I chose it for this shot of a rose garden at Mansfield, Ohio's Kingwood Center. Working with a Distagon 50mm lens, I exposed for 1/8 sec. at *f*/16.

The following films are all excellent choices, although they differ considerably from one another:

- **Fujichrome Provia 100** offers vibrant greens and blues and is also excellent for pastels in the cool hues. It has fine grain for sharpness, pushes well to ISO 200, and uses standard E-6 processing, which can be done in a few hours.

(When you "push" film, you make the film act as though it were a faster film than it is rated. Simply override your camera's automatic ISO setting—check your camera's instructions—and use a higher setting. In other words, shoot ISO 100 film at ISO 200, for example. Then tell the processing-lab staff member how much you pushed the film: one *f*-stop or +1 if you doubled the ISO, as above; two *f*-stops or +2 if you increased it even more, such as shooting ISO 100 film at ISO 400, for example, etc.)

- **Fujichrome Velvia** is favored by professional photographers for its brilliant colors, fine grain structure, and ability to handle low-light and low-contrast conditions well. However, it is slow; it is rated ISO 50, although it pushes well to ISO 100. Velvia is a contrasty film and tends to overexpose, making it a poor choice for P&S cameras.

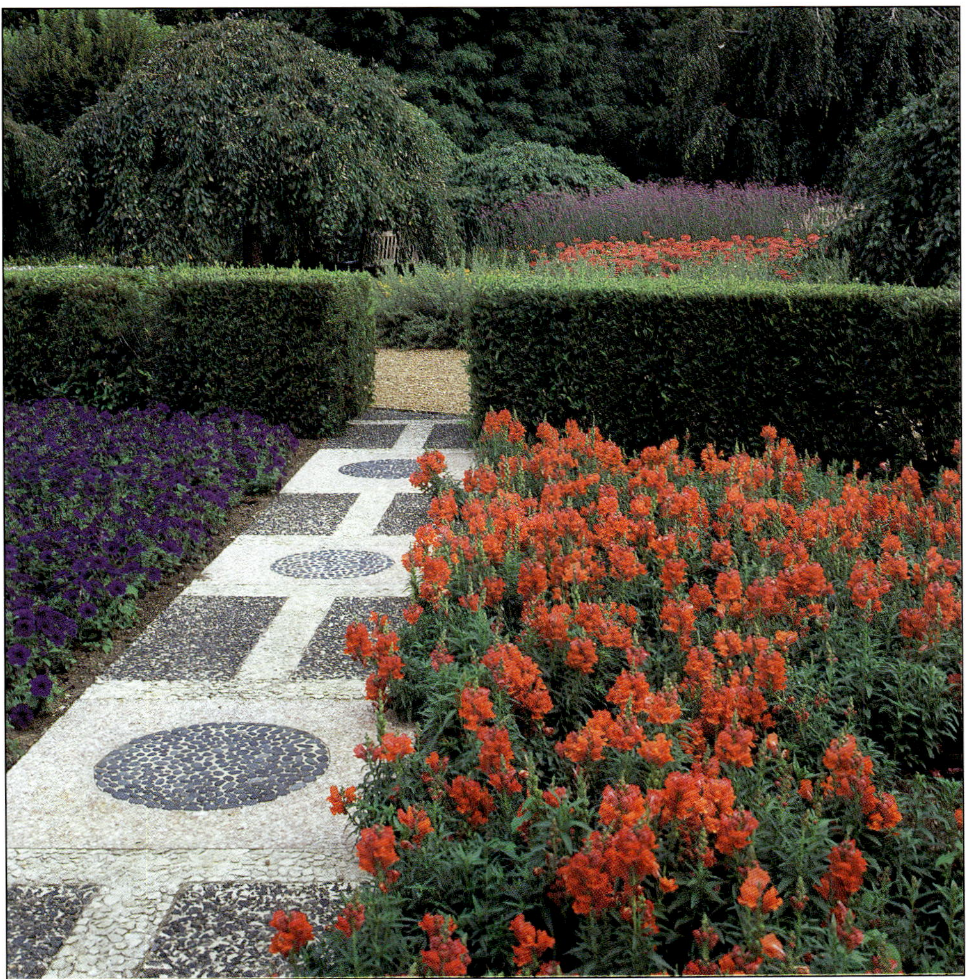

Fujichrome Velvia increases contrast in bright light, a feature that helped delineate the shapes and textures in this annual garden at Cantigny Garden in Wheaton, Illinois. Working with a Distagon 60mm lens, I exposed for 1/15 sec. at *f*/22.

(Slow film reacts more slowly to light than faster films. So when you shoot slow-speed films, you need longer exposure time or less depth of field. For garden photography, you generally want to use a reasonably fast shutter speed—at least 1/60 sec., except for special effects—and reasonable depth of field—at least *f*/8. So unless the day is bright, the wind isn't blowing, or you have extraordinary patience, you are better off using somewhat faster film.)

Kodak's Ektachrome 100 S and **100 SW**, both rated ISO 100, are excellent new Kodak films that many garden photographers now favor over the Fujichrome films. These films, especially the SW film, are less contrasty than Provia 100 but are as fine-grained as Velvia. Like both Provia and Velvia, these new films use E-6 processing.

Kodak's Ektachrome EPX and the slightly faster EPZ 100 are fine-grained films that render warm colors beautifully and produce a cool blue tone in sky, water, and mist. They are excellent films that enhance sunsets and fall foliage because they do wonders with yellows and earth tones, and because they render greens in a more muted—some say more natural—way than Fujichrome films do. EPX and EPZ do tend to underexpose easily, though, so take careful meter readings (see page 88) and

Under diffused light conditions, Fujichrome Velvia's latitude effectively accommodates the range of bright to dim areas, as in this image shot at Cantigny Garden in Wheaton, Illinois. Here, I used a Planar 80mm lens and exposed for 1/60 sec. at *f*/11.

By shooting Kodachrome 200, a fast film, I was able to increase the shutter speed to help handle breezy conditions on a cloudy day at the New York Botanical Garden in the Bronx, New York. With a Sonnar 150mm lens, I exposed for 1/60 sec. at *f*/5.6.

To maintain the soft, muted pastels of this private garden in Atlanta, Georgia, while shooting under diffused light and windy conditions, I selected Fujichrome Provia for its low contrast and extra speed. I used a Zuiko 28mm lens and exposed at *f*/16 for 1/30 sec.

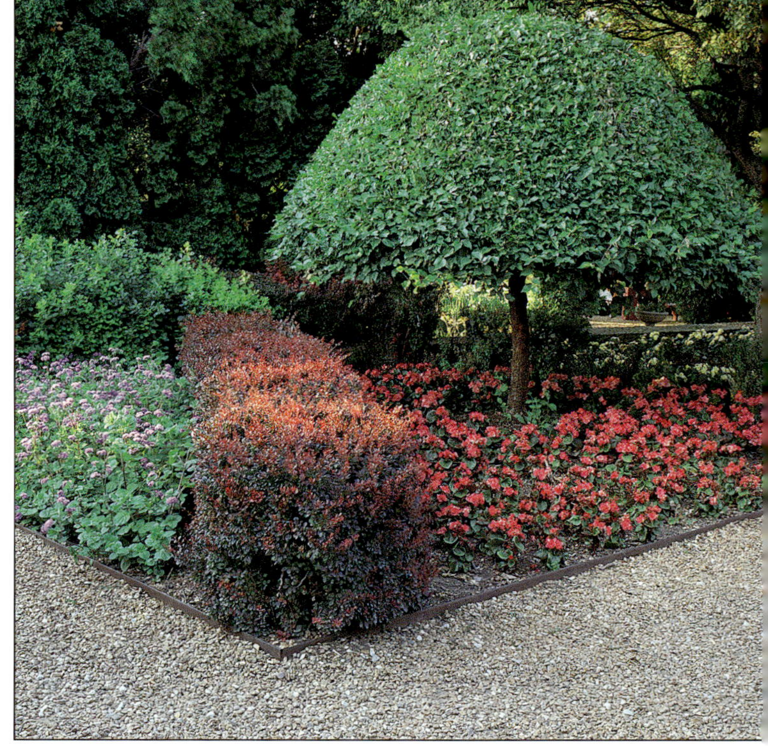

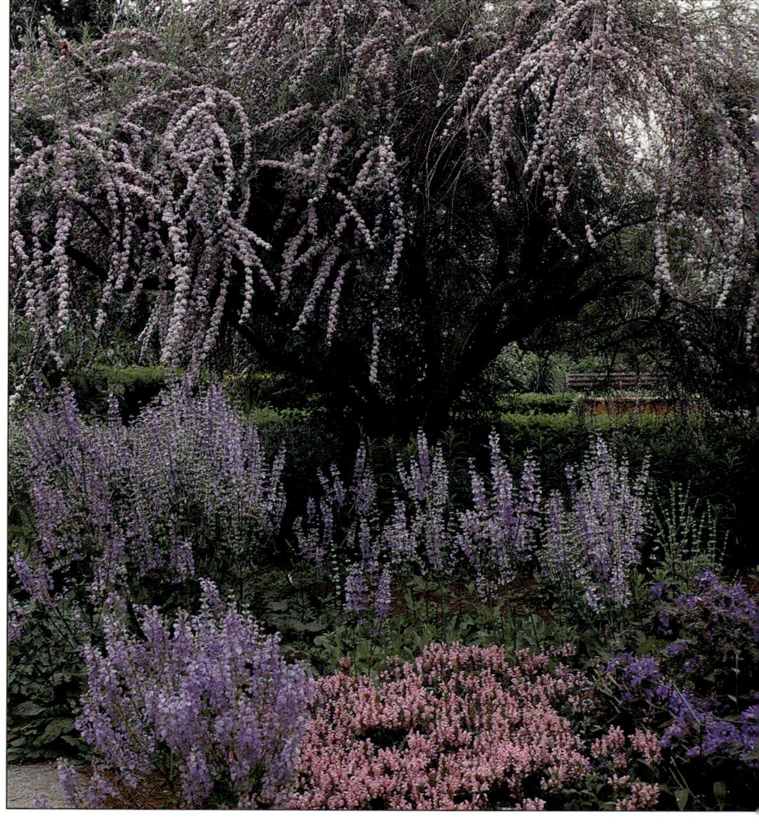

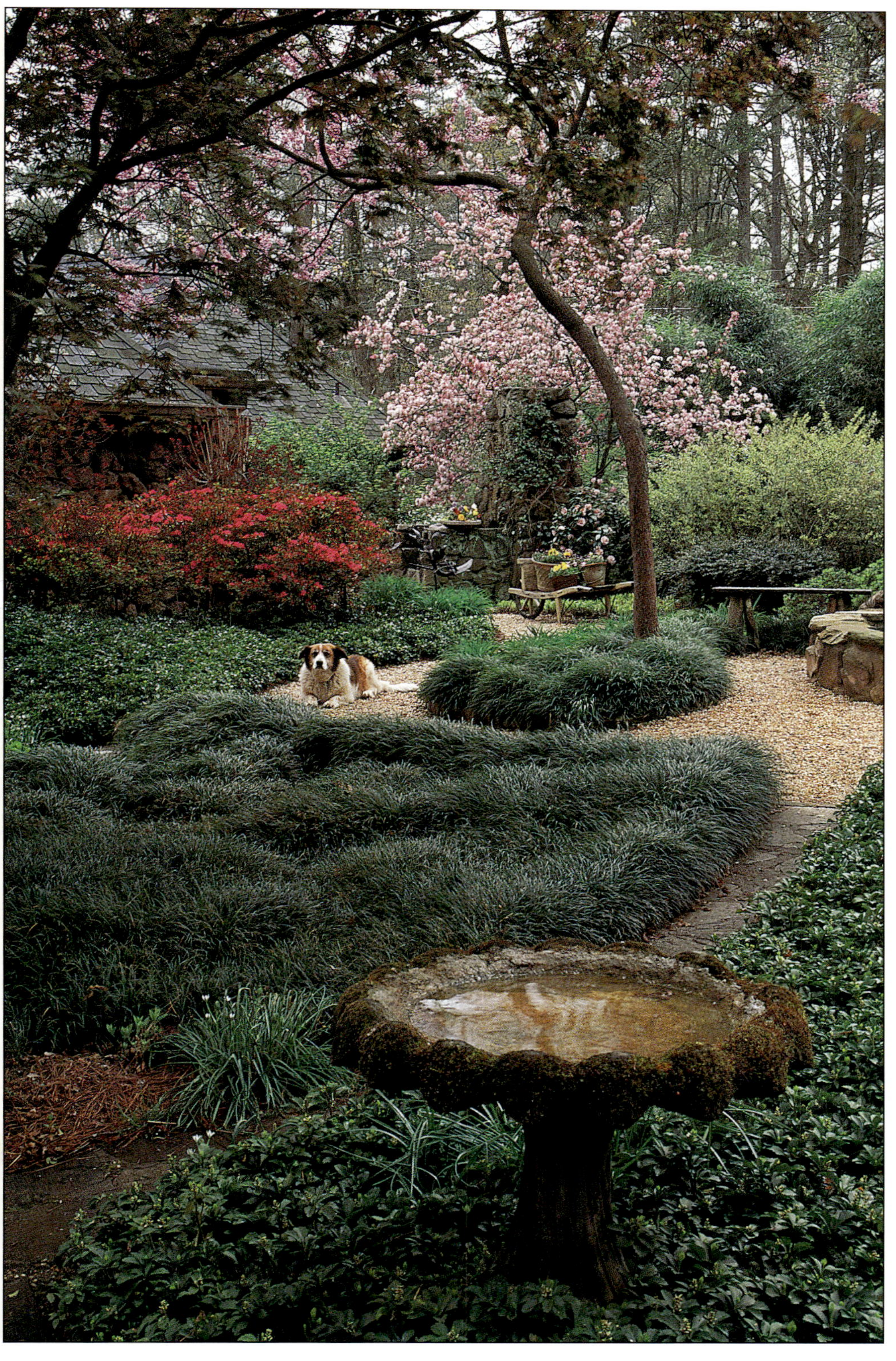

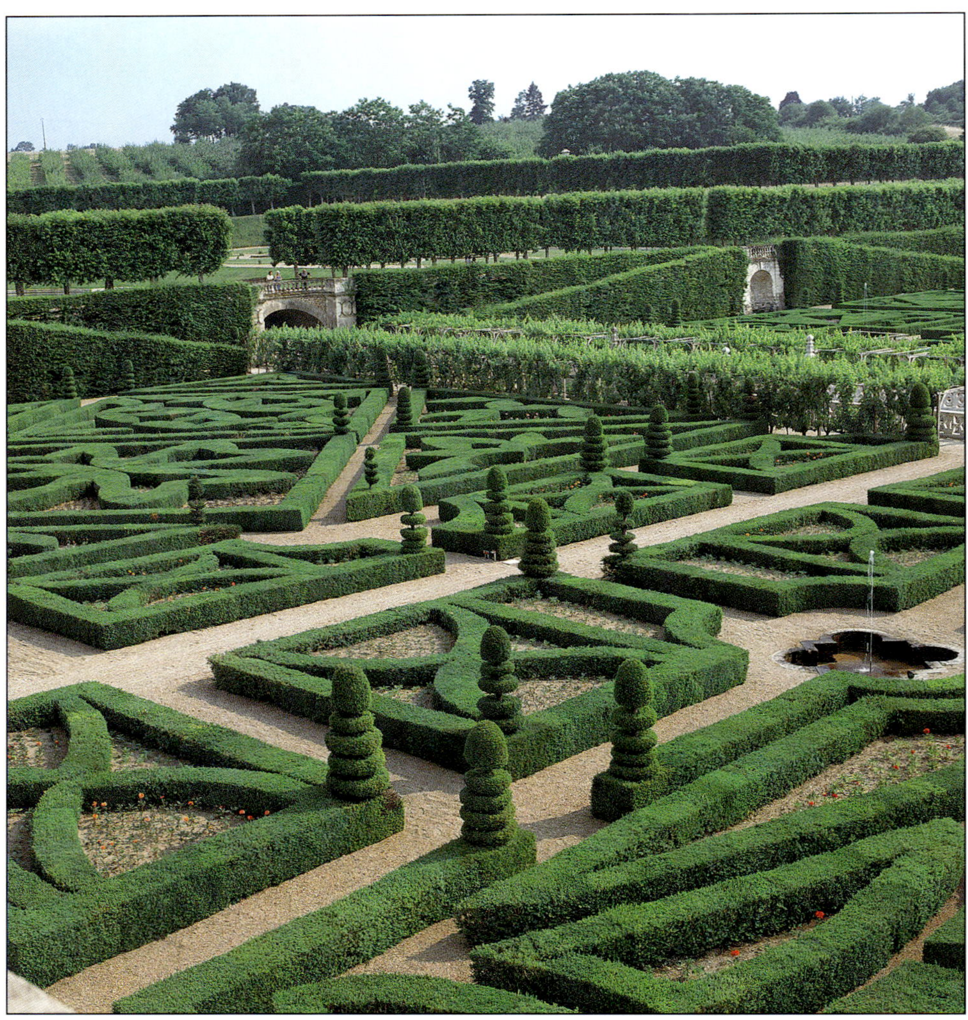

Fujichrome Velvia brightened the dull greens in the formal hedge and topiary garden in Villandry, France. With a Planar 80mm lens, I exposed at *f*/16 for 1/30 sec.

bracket liberally. To do this, shoot at higher and lower exposures than the meter reading to allow for possible inaccuracies in the reading or to ensure a good exposure in complex lighting conditions.

Kodachrome 25 is the slowest, most fine-grained film in this category. Many photographers favor it for its rich color saturation, especially its vibrant, warm reds and warm-tone pastels. This film requires special processing and, therefore, isn't recommended for P&S photographers.

Color Print Films. This film, which is also called color negative film, is for those photographers who prefer to display their work in albums. But it is also suitable for shooting fine prints to hang on the wall and is now commonly used for newspaper reproduction. Keep in mind, though, that it isn't the film of choice for reproduction in books or magazines.

Color negative film is easier to expose than slide film because it responds with greater tolerance to high-contrast lighting situations. If you're bracketing, bracket toward overexposure because an overexposed negative is easier to correct in printing than one that is underexposed. The best options, Kodacolor Gold and Fujichrome Reala 100, are both

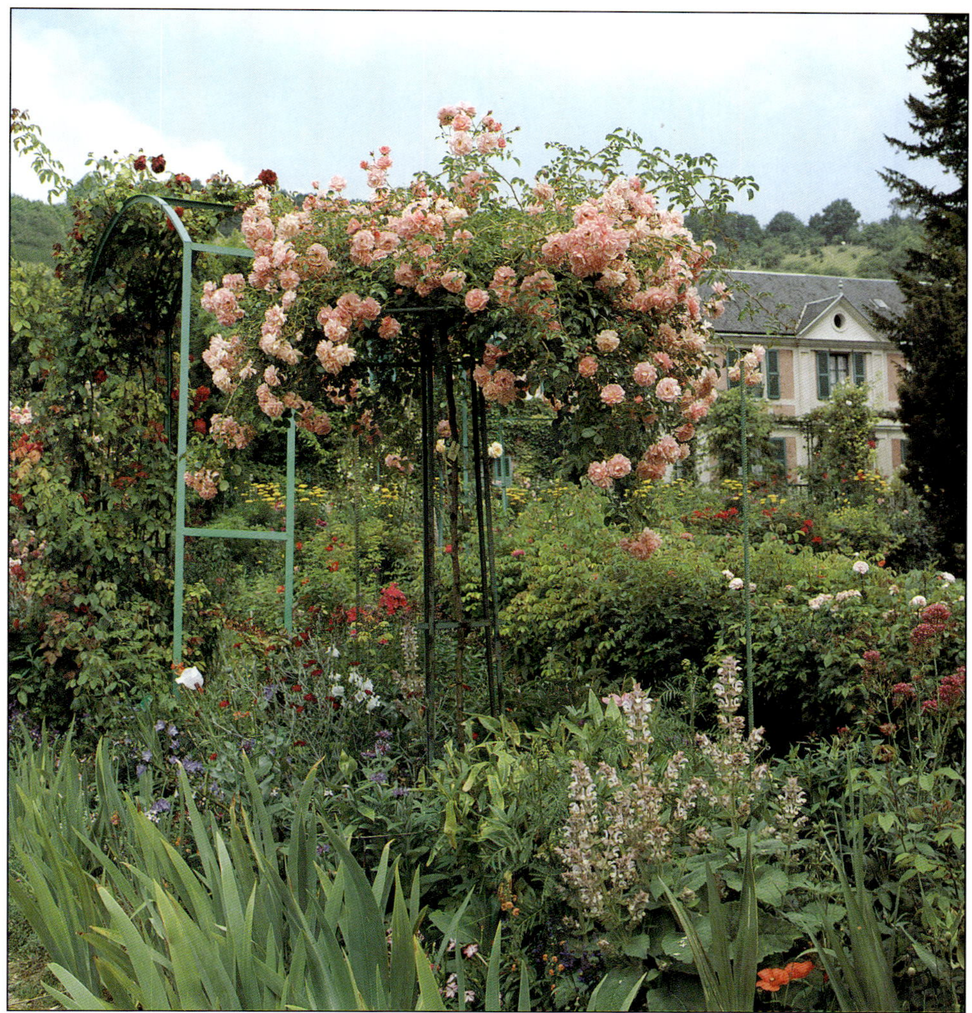

Here, I opted for Ektachrome EPN, a low-contrast film, to keep the colors of the delicate pink roses soft despite the harsh light at Monet's home in Giverny, France. Shooting with a Planar 80mm lens, I exposed for 1/30 sec. at f/16.

very fine-grained films that produce rich, vivid colors. Reala has snappy cool greens and blues, while Kodacolor favors warm reds, yellows, oranges, and browns.

Black-and-White Print Films. Very few photographers use black-and-white print, or negative, film to shoot gardens unless they are in the fine-art field. Kodak's T-Max 100 film has very fine grain and good contrast, qualities that produce extremely sharp, snappy prints; as such, it is ideally suited for purely graphic portrayals of trees. Kodak Plus-X film, rated ISO 125, is slightly less contrasty but is almost as sharp. Its great range of tonalities makes it an excellent choice whenever middle gray tones are important to the image.

Kodak's Tri-X film, rated ISO 400, is a faster version of Plus-X and is a bit grainier, less sharp, and more contrasty. Its fast speed makes it a good choice if you must handhold your camera while it is set for a small aperture. To achieve an interesting grainy look, you can push Tri-X to ISO 1600 or 3200.

FILTERS

Filters can give you the creative edge you want, and quite a few are almost indispensable to garden photography. Glass filters, which are made to screw onto most camera lenses, are preferable to plastic filters. Glass filters have better optics, can be cleaned more readily—just breathe on them and wipe with lens tissue—and don't scratch as easily. Since they are small and light, you should bring them with you at all times; carry them in specially designed filter packs, such as those Tiffen makes. Experiment with the effects the filters produce. They can enhance your image in a variety of ways. You can get started with the following assortment of filters.

Neutral-Density Filters. A plain gray neutral-density (ND) filter lets you use a slower shutter speed than you otherwise could. This is especially handy if you want a milky effect for moving water on a very bright day. A graduated ND filter, which is part clear and part gray, helps balance bright and shaded areas in a scene. Just be sure to position the dark side of the filter over the bright area in the frame, such as the sky.

Polarizing Filters. On bright, sunny days, polarizing filters, or polarizers, can restore the true natural colors in a garden scene, deepen the blue of the sky, and whiten clouds. Polarizers accomplish all this by reducing or eliminating glare and reflectivity from foliage, water, and other shiny garden surfaces. As you rotate these filters, you can control exactly how much glare and reflectivity you want to remove. Simply watch the effect through your lens.

Each lens might need its own polarizer to fit properly and prevent vignetting. When this occurs, you'll see dark corners where the polarizer cuts into the frame. Be especially careful with wide-angle lenses. Polarizers aren't available for most P&S cameras, and some of the new

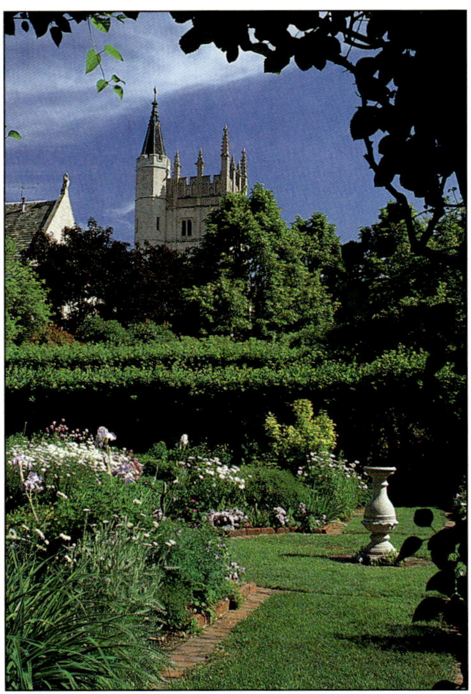

This shot was taken at the Shakespeare Garden at Northwestern University in Evanston, Illinois, without a filter. Working with a Zuiko 35-70mm lens set at 35mm, I exposed Fujichrome 100 for 1/60 sec. at *f*/11.

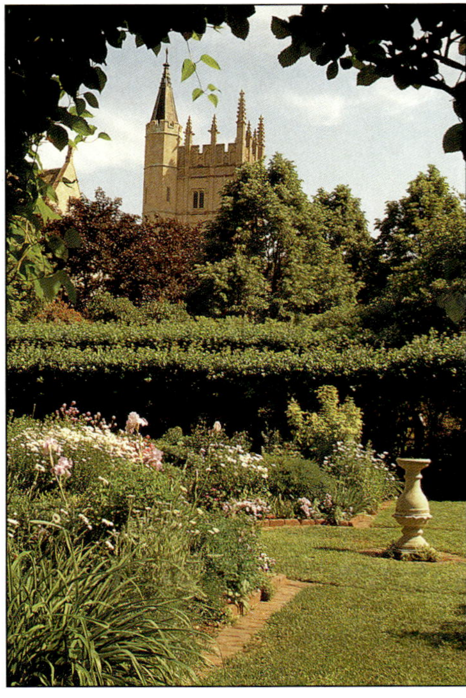

This shot illustrates the effect of an 85 deep warming filter. In this case, the filter dulled the garden scene and muddied its colors. You should use a filter only when it will actually enhance an image, and be sure to check through the viewfinder to see if the effect works. Once again, I used a Zuiko 35-70mm lens set at 35mm and exposed Fujichrome 100 at *f*/11 for 1/60 sec.

autofocus SLRs require a special polarizer that works in a circular rather than linear pattern. Check before you buy.

Skylight Filters. A 1A or 1B skylight filter or an 81A warming filter can protect your lens from dust, scratches, and abrasions. These filters also give a slightly pink cast to your image, warming a scene and counteracting atmospheric blue tones. If you like the warming effect, try the KR red 1.5 filter, which truly intensifies green foliage in a garden.

Soft-Focus Filters. Soft-focus filters, which are also called fog filters, diffuse and soften your garden images. The misty, romantic, or mysterious aura they produce can be particularly appealing for shooting spring's flowering trees or fall's warm colors and works best in diffused backlight. You can simulate the effect of a soft-focus filter by slipping a nylon stocking over your lens or, in a pinch, breathe on your lens and work quickly to retain the foggy effect.

The exact amount of diffusion depends on the specific filter. Some manufacturers calibrate by using +1, +2, and +3 designations for increasing degrees of diffusion. Other manufacturers use such descriptive terms as "haze," "mist," and "fog." These labels aren't consistent, so you should look at a filter's effect before you buy it.

Ultraviolet Filters. To cut through atmospheric haze, use an ultraviolet (UV) filter. This haze is most noticeable at high elevations; on hot, humid days; and in places with a great deal of air pollution.

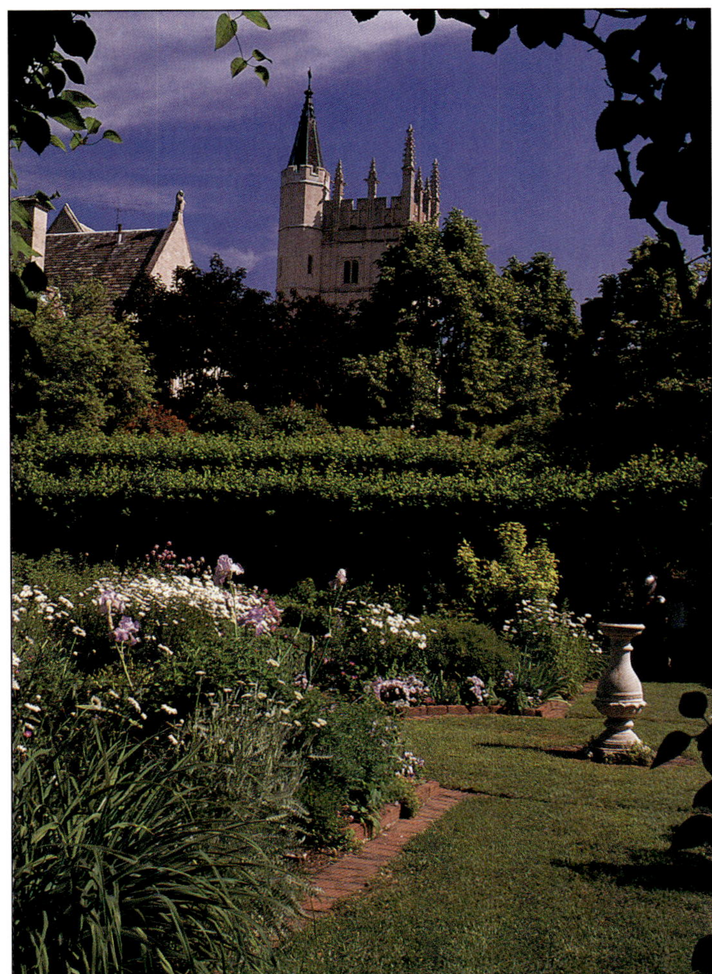

In this shot of the Shakespeare garden scene, a warm-toned polarizing filter helped remove reflections, turned the sky a deep blue, and made the green a bit more natural. With a Zuiko 35-70mm lens set at 35mm, I exposed for 1/60 sec. at *f*/11 on Fujichrome 100.

A mist filter softened the harsh reflections and added atmosphere in this otherwise simple shot of a canal at the garden of Courrances in France. Working with a Zuiko 50-250mm lens set at 180mm, I exposed Fujichrome 100 for 1/60 sec. at *f*/8.

A polarizing filter removed glare from the surface of the pond at the Chicago Botanic Garden in Glencoe, Illinois, thereby turning the water into an effective dark backdrop for the waterlily. I made this shot with a Zuiko 50-250mm lens set at 250mm and exposed at *f*/5.6 for 1/250 sec. on Ektachrome 100 EPP.

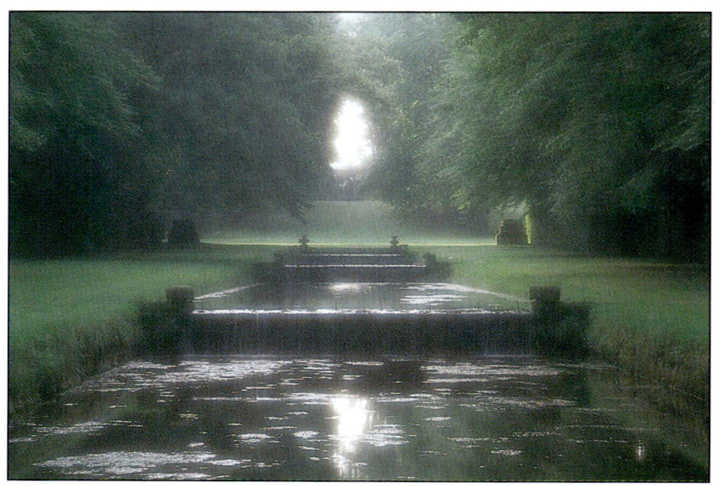

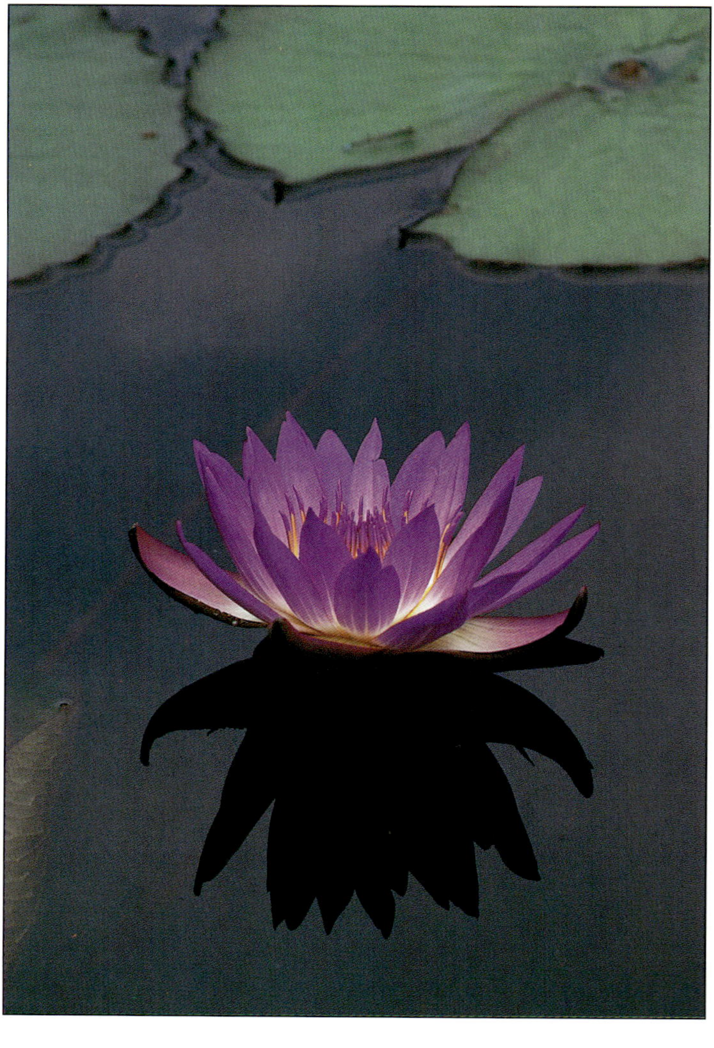

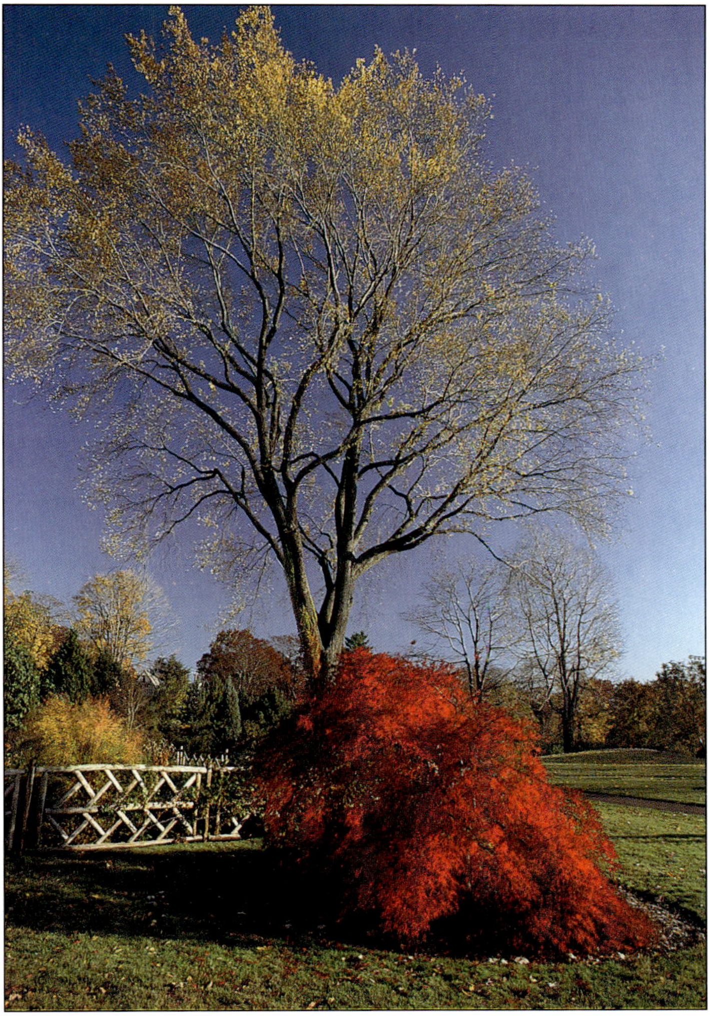

An 81B warming filter intensified the red of the split leaf maple, and a polarizing filter strengthened the blue of the sky in this shot taken at Wave Hill in New York. Here, I used a Zuiko 35mm lens, exposing Kodachrome 25 for 1/125 sec. at *f*/8.

You can successfully combine filters. Here, an 81A warming filter slightly enhanced the orange color on the roses at Giverny, France, while a polarizing filter removed reflections and deepened the blue of the sky. Shooting with a Zuiko 90mm macro lens, I exposed Fujichrome 100 at *f*/5.6 for 1/500 sec.

(Overleaf) A graduated sepia filter warmed an otherwise blandly illuminated scene of a temple lake garden in Bali. With a Zuiko 50-250mm lens set at 80mm, I exposed at *f*/11 for 1/125 sec. on Fujichrome 100.

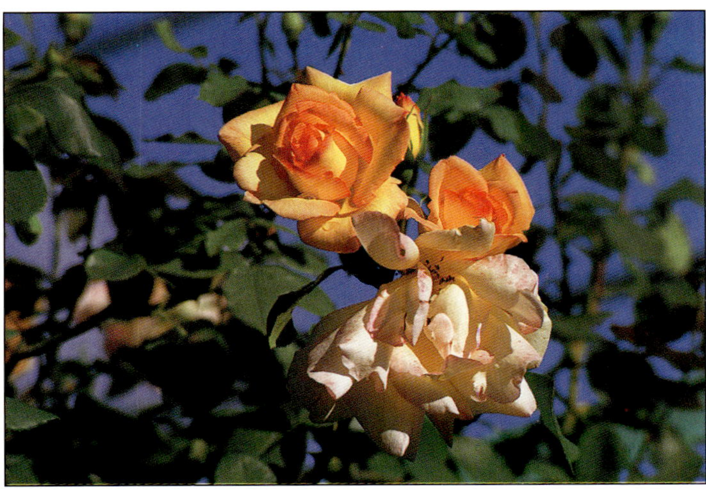

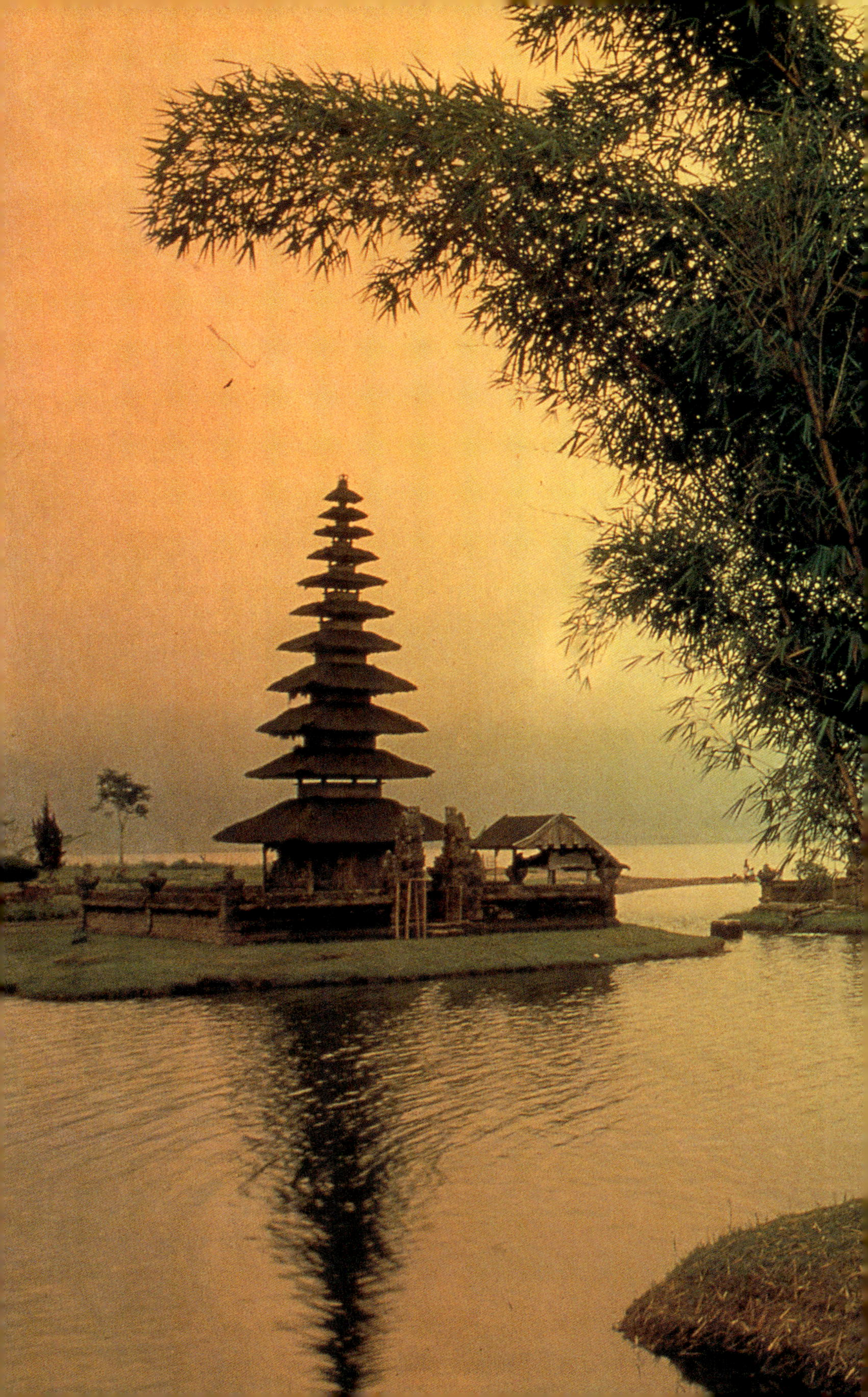

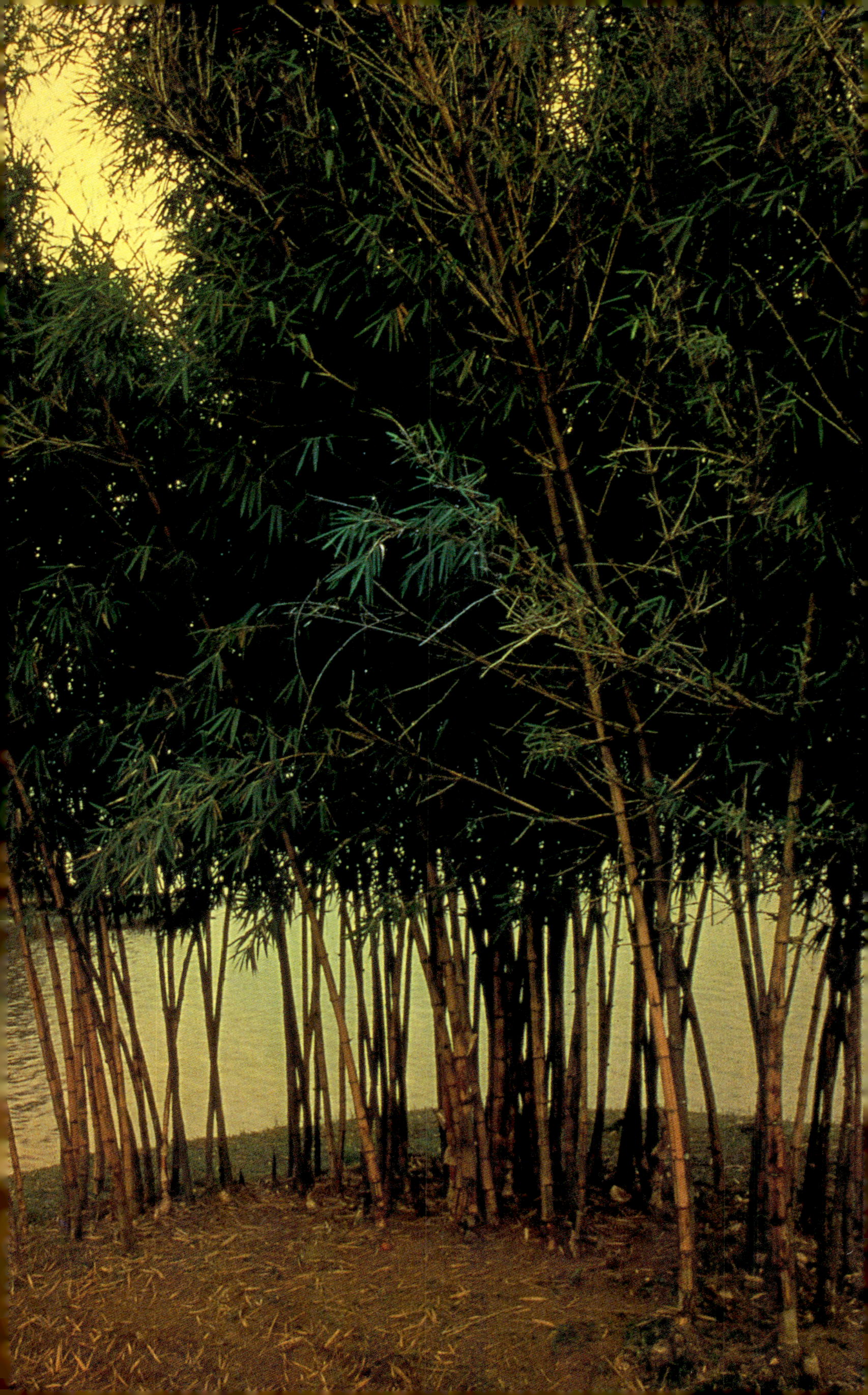

A tripod was essential for framing this detail of a border at Inniswood Garden in Columbus, Ohio. The tripod allowed for careful focusing, as well as permitted me to keep the camera steady for extra sharpness with a 1/30 sec. exposure. Shooting with a Zuiko 35mm lens, I exposed Ektachrome 100 SW at *f*/11.

Shooting these hydrangea in the shady part of a private garden in Natchez, Mississippi, at 1/30 sec. required the steadiness a tripod provides. With a Zuiko 35-70mm lens set at 35mm, I exposed for 1/30 sec. at *f*/16 on Ektachrome 100 SW.

Warming Filters. These sepia-tone filters can boost the golds, oranges, and yellows of fall foliage; enhance the colors of sunrise and sunset; and warm the cool blue light found near bodies of water or in wooded garden settings. They come in two series of varying intensities: 81A, 81B, and 81C, and 85A, 85B, and 85C. The 85 lens series is more of an orange-toned sepia than the 81 lens series; the filters increase in intensity from A to B to C.

Color-Correction Filters. Although color-correction (CC) filters are designed to increase or decrease contrast in black-and-white photography, they have their place in color photography as well. Some photographers use them to enhance a specific color in the image. For example, a yellow filter intensifies fall foliage, while a green filter boosts spring and summer leaves. However, unless you're aiming for a surreal special effect, you should use these filters judiciously: avoid an unnatural look by working with the least intense filter in a particular color and checking that it doesn't dominate or distort other hues in your image. CC filters range from 10CC to 40CC; for color photography, work with the 10CC intensity.

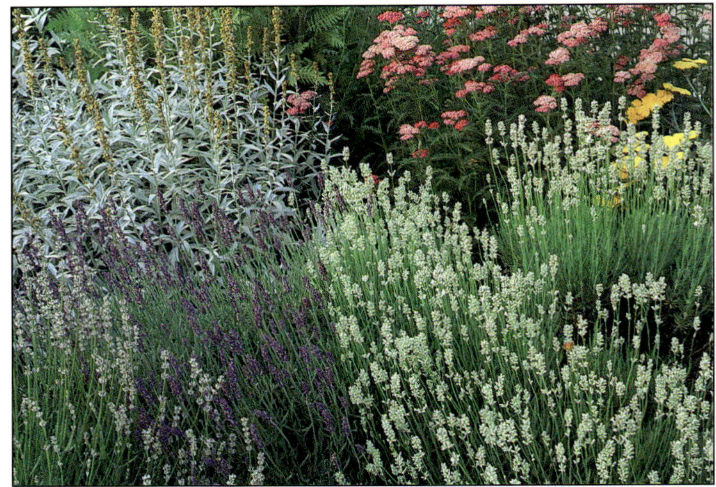

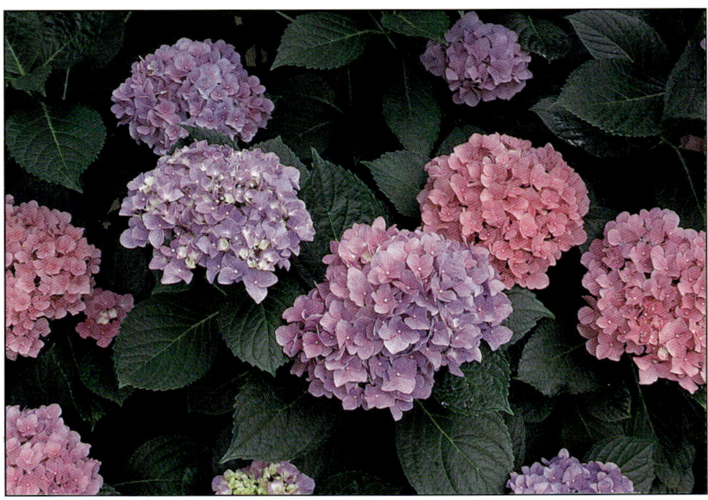

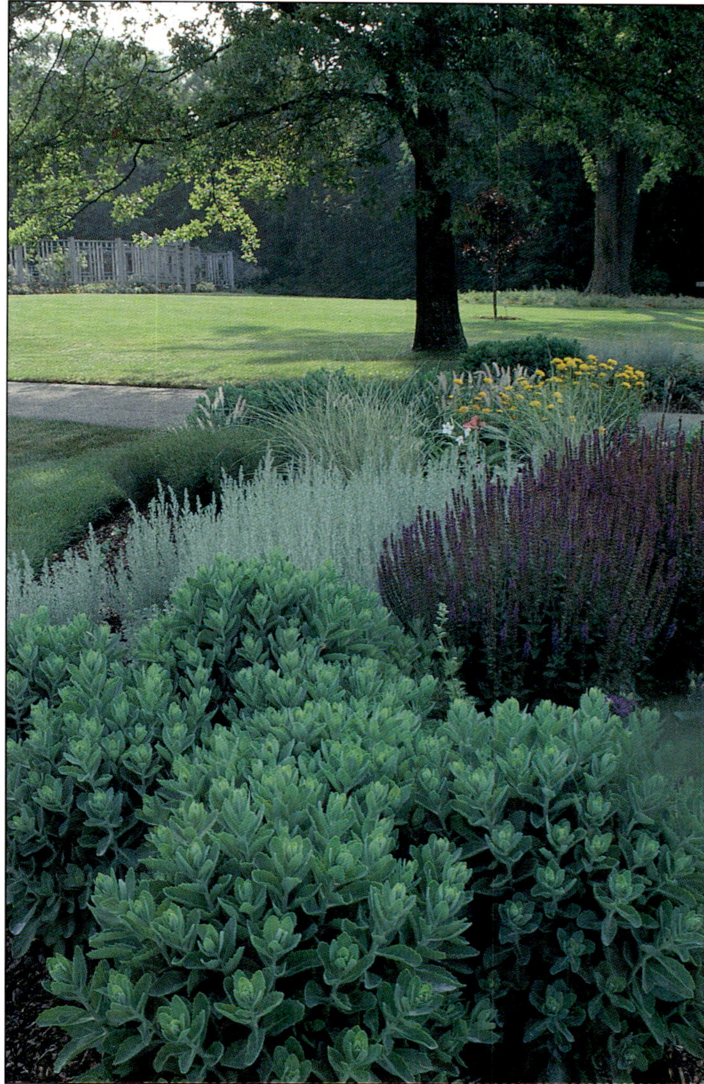

A spot-meter reading on the foreground green plantings properly exposed the important shaded area in this shot of Inniswood Garden in Columbus, Ohio; at the same time, it caused a slight overexposure of the background lawn. Shooting with a Zuiko 35-70mm lens set at 35mm, I exposed Ektachrome LPZ for 1/15 sec. at *f*/16.

TRIPODS

A strong, stable tripod is the most essential accessory for garden photography. It lets you compose carefully and precisely, as well as permits you to maintain any position, no matter how awkward, through any number of exposures. And, unlike a monopod, a tripod enables you to leave your camera unattended. Without having to worry about a steady hand, you can use slow shutter speeds and small aperture settings for greater depth of field and maximum sharpness. Since a fine tripod can last a lifetime, buy the best you can afford. You might, for example, consider the Bogen #3221 with its lever tightening system or the Gitzo with its screw tightening system. Both tripods are reliable, sturdy, and user-friendly.

With your tripod, you'll need a solid ball-joint head. A ball-joint head that allows you to maneuver your camera to any angle with ease and locks with a single turn makes using a tripod a breeze. Take a look at the Linhof Profi II, Bogen 3036, and the Foba Superball.

OTHER ESSENTIAL GEAR

There is no end to the accessories you can accumulate, from those you "can't do without" to those that are just good to have. The following items are the most important for garden photography.

Camera Bag. A suitable camera bag is a must. It should be stable, strong, and light, with enough space to comfortably and firmly hold your gear in separate compartments. A bag that is too large might let your equipment to bounce around. Conversely, a bag that is too small risks having items fall out. Snap-together closure devices are more reliable than zippers and snaps. Bags that Tamrac and LowePro AW make are good options.

Photo Vest/Belly Pack. In addition to a camera bag, some photographers like the convenience of a photo vest or a belly pack, such as those that LowePro offers. These items come in handy when you don't expect to carry much gear with you or you have some items you like to have at hand. But they are no substitutes for a good camera bag.

Cable Release. This device screws into the shutter-release button on your camera and lets you release the shutter without touching the camera in order to reduce camera shake, especially during long exposures. A cable release that is at least 12 inches long completes the "tripod package."

Spot Meter. A handheld spot meter permits you to meter specific details in the garden, even at a distance, with pinpoint accuracy. This is a real boon in high-contrast or variable-light conditions. This type of meter also serves as a check or a backup to your camera's built-in meter. The Minolta Spotmeter F and the Gossen Luna Star F are both excellent models.

Don't confuse a spot meter with a handheld incident light meter, which is also useful but optional. An incident light meter discounts extraneous light from bright reflections in high-contrast light, giving you a less accurate gauge.

Lens Shade. A lens shade prevents extraneous rays of the sun from entering the camera and causing flare or glare. Buy the deepest lens shade available for each lens, and be sure it is the right size for that lens. The wrong size lens shade may cause vignetting. Look for possible vignetting whenever you use a wide-angle lens or zoom lens, or if the lens shade is mounted on a filter. A thick, collapsible rubber shade also helps protect your lens from rain, snow, and fingerprints, as well as against accidental damage that a bump or fall might cause.

Camera Strap. Since you should have your camera on a tripod whenever possible, a comfortable camera strap is only a must if you plan to wear your camera over your neck for any length of time. The strap should be wide enough to rest easily around your neck without cutting or chafing. Also, be sure that the strap is made of a high-grade material that won't unravel after a few uses.

Cleaning Kit. Check your gear, and clean it thoroughly right after each shoot. That way, surface dirt won't have a chance to settle in and cause serious or expensive damage. A small cleaning kit should include a soft cloth, lens tissue, and a bulb-type blower with a brush. Use the appropriate item to gently remove the moisture and surface grime on your camera and lenses. (For stubborn smudges, breathe on your lens before wiping it with lens tissue.) Don't try to clean the inside of your camera; let a professional do this every two years for ordinary use. However, if your camera has been exposed to harsh conditions, such as sand, salt-water spray, or dust, take it for a professional cleaning immediately afterward.

Closeup Equipment. For taking closeups in the garden, you'll want to have some special equipment on hand. You have three options.

- **Macro Lenses.** Specially designed for closeups, these self-contained lenses are easy to use and don't reduce light intake. They are, however, the most expensive option. If you plan to do closeup work regularly, you should invest in a 50-60mm or a 90-105mm macro lens.
- **Extension Tubes.** This option is cheaper than macro lenses, but you must mount extension tubes between the camera body and lens. The main disadvantage associated with extension tubes is that they restrict the working distance from the subject, forcing you to work within certain limits.
- **Closeup Screw-On Lenses.** These lenses comprise the most economical choice. You can combine these lenses for more magnification. For example, you can combine +2 and +3 diopter screw-on lenses to achieve a +5 magnification. Always mount the highest diopter lens onto the lens itself, then add the next diopter. Be aware, though, that these lenses are the least sharp and must be used within a very limited working distance.

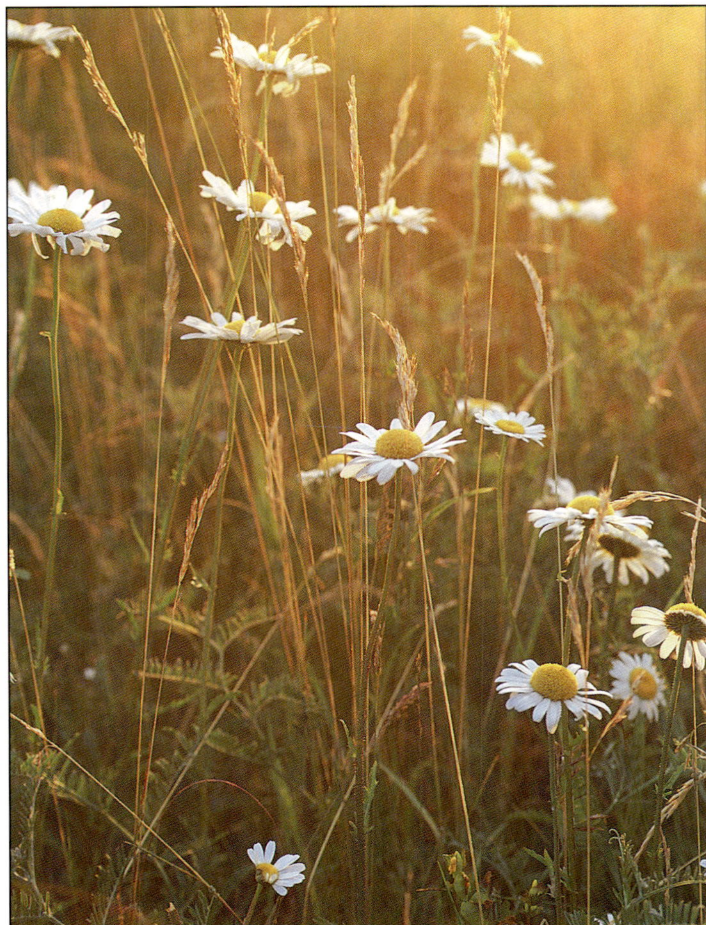

A lens shade helped minimize the flare from the bright backlight on these daisies in Maine, and a ball joint enabled me to compose quickly under changing light conditions. Here, I used a Zuiko 50-250mm lens set at 200mm. The exposure on Fujichrome 100 was 1/250 sec. at *f*/5.6.

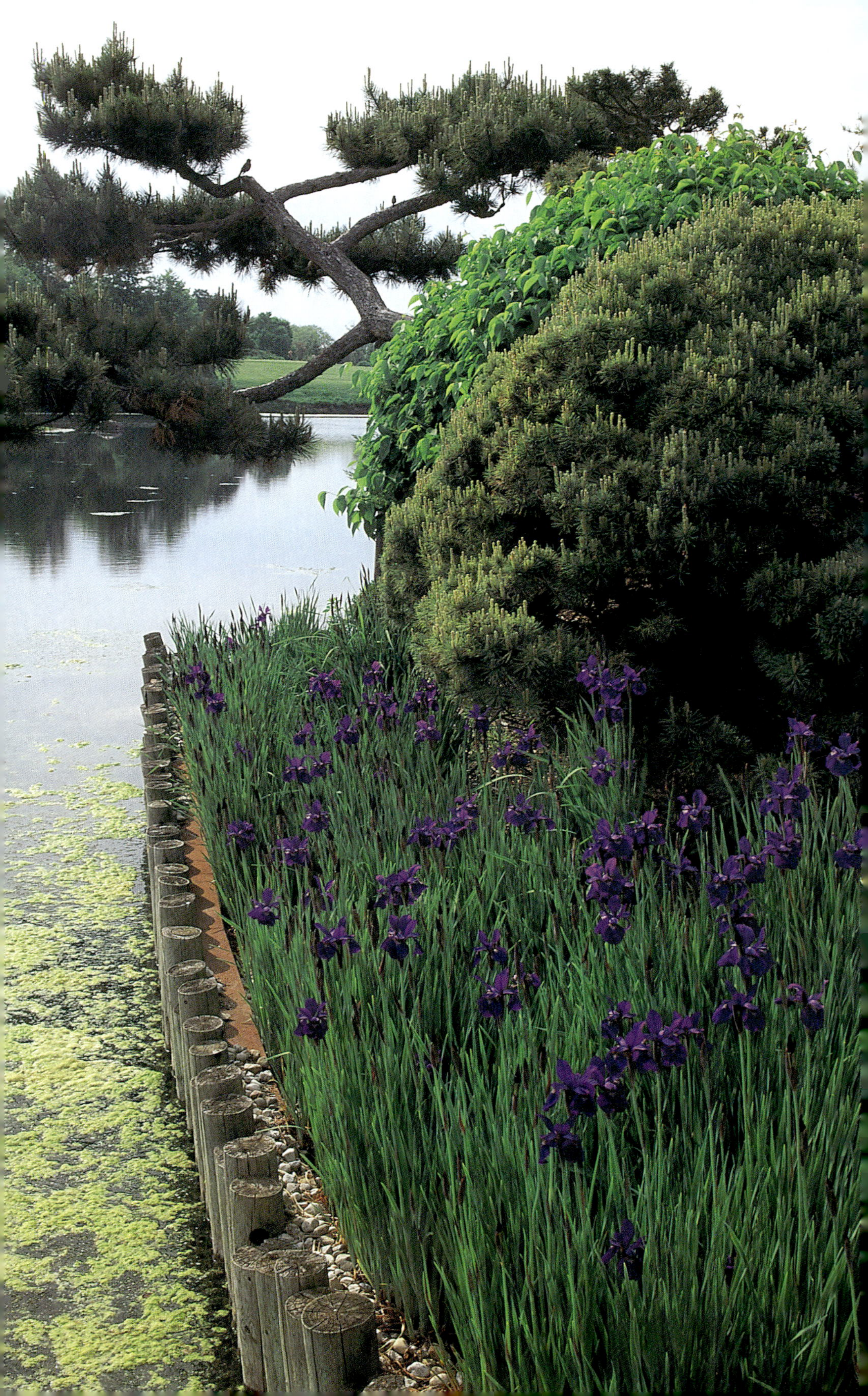

CHAPTER 3

Designing a Garden Photograph

Here, the log border separating the land and water gardens works as a strong directional line pointing toward the distant pine in this shot made at the Chicago Botanic Garden in Glencoe, Illinois. With a Zuiko 35-70mm lens set at 35mm, I exposed Fujichrome Provia for 1/60 sec. at *f*/11.

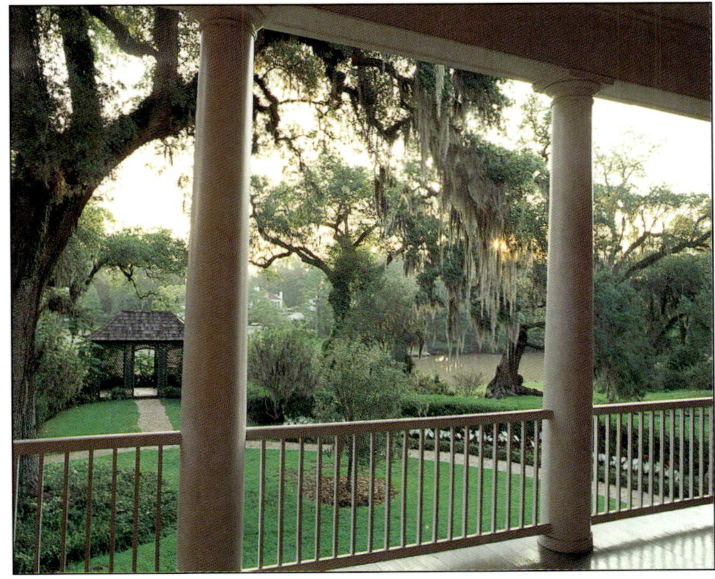

Framing the garden scene at Louisiana's Shadows on the Teche through the columns of a porch emphasized the relationship between the house and the garden. Here, I used a Mamiya 65mm lens and exposed Fujichrome Provia for 1/15 sec. at *f*/22.

Decisions! Decisions! Participants in our photographic workshops are always amazed by how many decisions they have to make. Isn't it enough to be in a stunning garden and work with the best camera equipment? Can't everything else just fall into place? Not only can't the rest just happen by itself, but you wouldn't want it to.

Filling the frame completely with this bed of colorful summer annuals at the Minnesota Landscape Arboretum gave this vertical shot great impact. Working with a Zuiko 28mm lens, I exposed for 1/60 sec. at *f*/16 on Ektachrome 100 SW.

The most fascinating and rewarding part of becoming an accomplished garden photographer is taking an active role in the design of each shot. Think of each image as a partnership between the garden designer and yourself. Like any artist, you take what is given—the garden design, the seasonal mix of plants, the light on a particular day—and you shape it according to your own vision.

While you certainly have decisions to make, they are far from overwhelming—not if you understand the basic photographic variables. In this chapter, you'll discover how to make informed decisions about those variables. But keep in mind that our advice is just that. There are no hard and fast rules. As you begin to photograph with greater awareness, keep a journal. Take notes on each shot to remind yourself about what your intentions were and the decisions you made. Then review the results and see if they met your expectations. If not, adjust your decisions the next time, repeating the review process until you're satisfied with your images.

VARYING THE FORMAT

Cameras are shaped to be held most comfortably in a horizontal format, and many photographers forget that they have another option. One of the simplest choices you have concerns how you'll hold the camera: to vary the design of your image, simply shift to a vertical format. In garden photography, you'll find that the difference between vertical and horizontal formats can be quite considerable. Make it a habit to shoot in both formats as you explore this design dimension, comparing the balance of

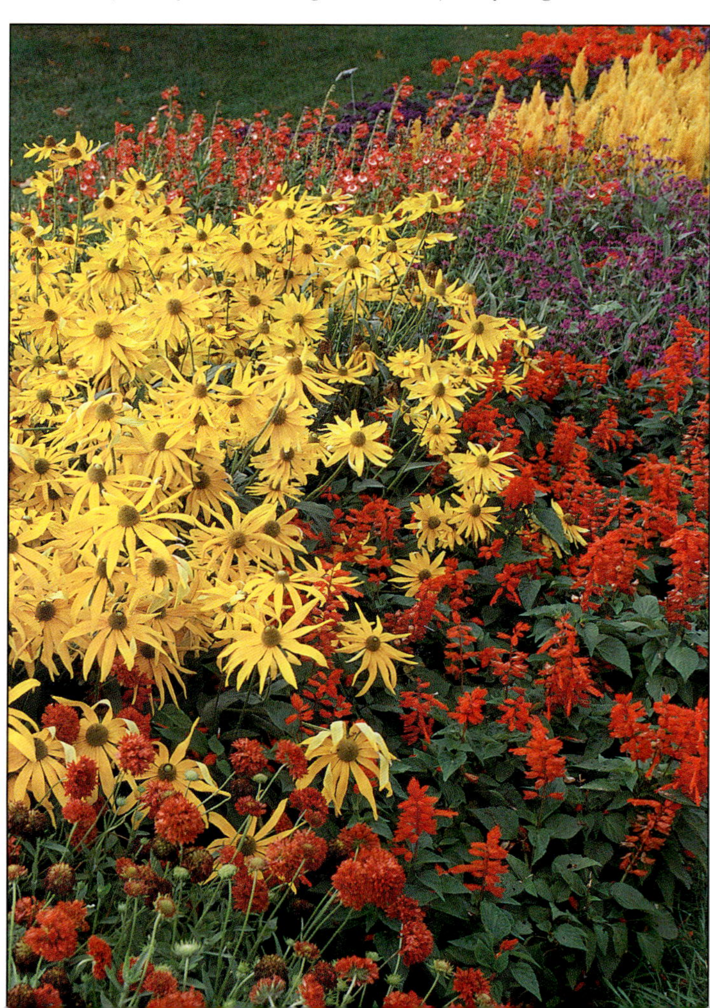

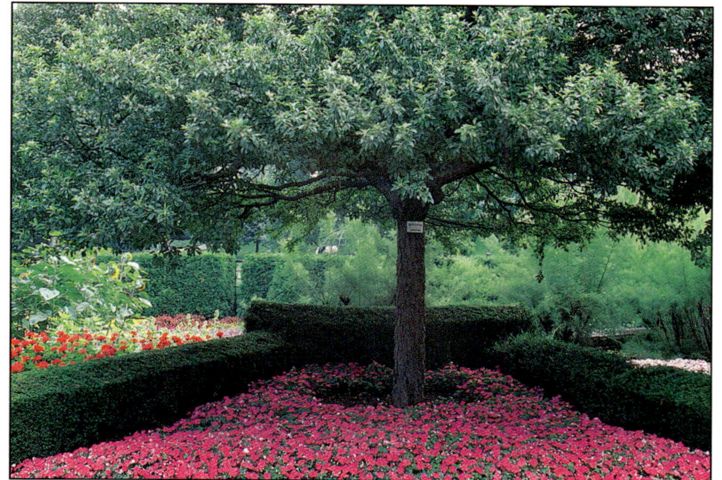

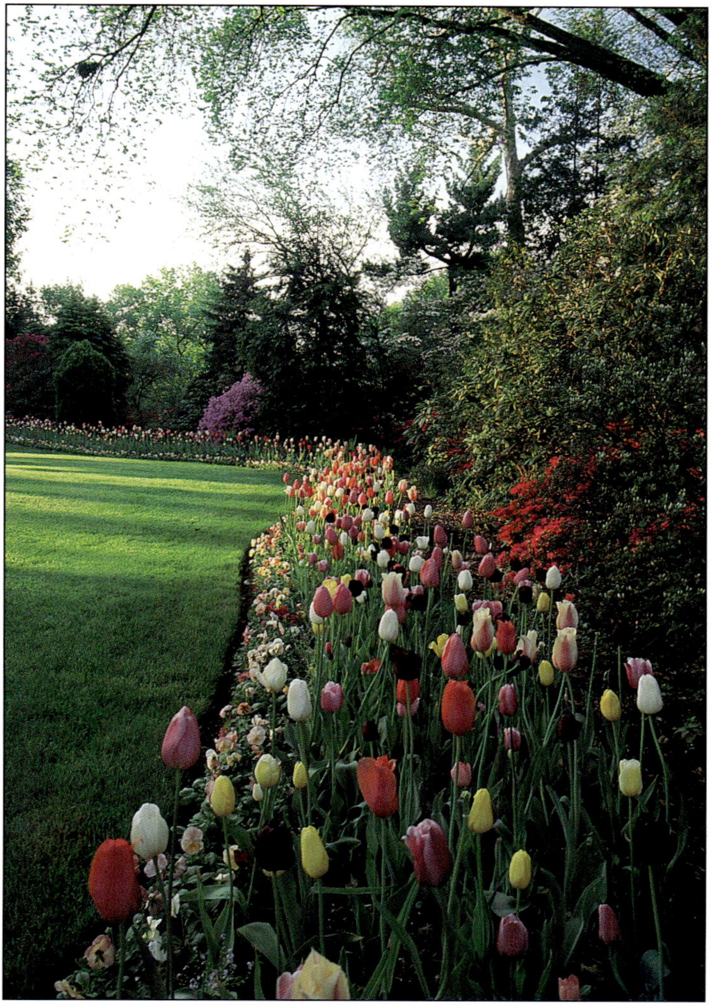

Although the tree at the center of this image is tall, I decided on a horizontal format to call more attention to the graphic lines and shapes in this vignette taken at Cantigny Garden in Wheaton, Illinois. Shooting with a Zuiko 35-70mm lens set at 50mm, I exposed for 1/30 sec. at *f*/8 on Fujichrome 100.

Here, the vertical format emphasized the converging lines that create a sense of depth and incorporated the fronds of a tree to hide part of the pale sky in this shot taken at a private Washington, DC, garden. I set a Zuiko 35-70mm lens at 35mm and exposed Fujichrome Velvia for 1/4 sec. at *f*/16.

A standard 50mm lens setting successfully documented this overview of a backyard garden in Illinois. With a Zuiko 35-70mm lens, I exposed for 1/30 sec. at *f*/8 on Fujichrome Velvia.

elements within the frame. Then as you become more confident, continue to at least consider both formats each time you frame an image, just in case your first inclination wasn't your best.

Try not to be too conventional in your approach. Just because a tree or tulip is taller than it is wide doesn't mean it is best shot in a vertical format. Go for the unexpected and original and your photographs will never be dull.

Most of all, be sure you utilize and fill the entire frame. There should be no wasted space in either format. If your primary subject is too small to fill the frame by itself, photograph its setting in a meaningful way so that it contributes to the impact of your image. Notice the sky in your composition, and minimize it unless it contributes to the effect you want. And always scan the edges and corners of your shot in order to eliminate any stray or distracting features by moving slightly or reframing before you release the shutter.

CHOOSING THE BEST LENS

Which lens to use goes hand in hand with your decision about format. But with many lens options, this is a tougher choice—and one that

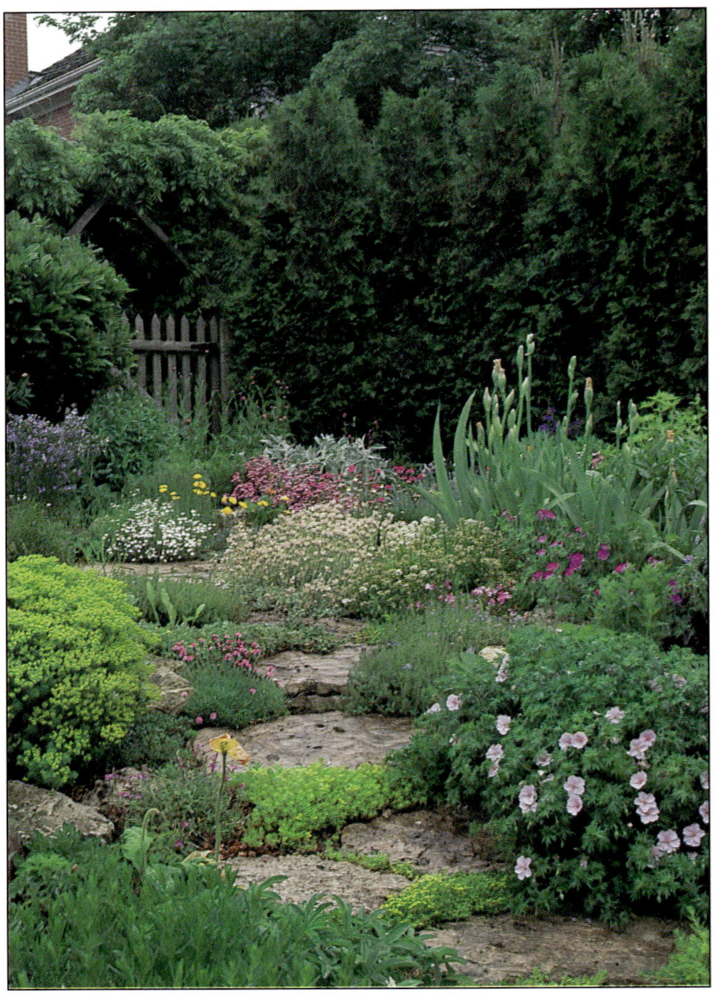

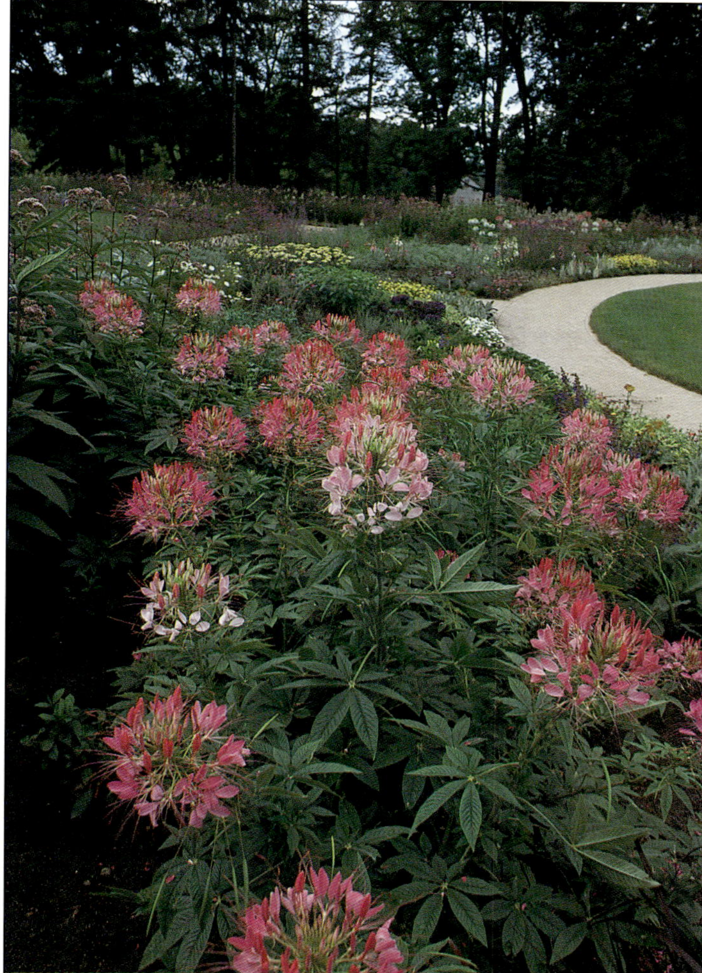

I needed a wide-angle lens in order to feature the spider flowers prominently in the foreground while integrating a fair amount of the surroundings in this broad overview of the Noerenberg Garden in Lake Minnetonka, Minnesota. I used a Zuiko 24mm lens and exposed for 1/8 sec. at *f*/16 on Fujichrome Provia.

affects many aspects of photographic design. Remember, each kind of lens has a specific purpose, but the true test takes place in the field. Beginners often need the actual experience of looking through each lens to see exactly how different their image will be from one to the next.

How do you know which lens to choose? Start by thinking back to the basic kinds of garden images: overviews, vignettes, and details. In general, the broader the view, the wider the lens should be; the tighter the view, the narrower the scope of the lens should be. For overviews, you'll probably turn to wide-angle to standard lenses, or to zoom lenses that span that range. For vignettes, you're most likely to choose standard to moderate telephoto lenses or a zoom lens in that range. And for details, your best bet would be standard to macro lenses if you can get close to your subject, or more powerful telephoto lenses if you have to keep your distance.

Another excellent learning strategy is to stick to just one lens during a particular outing. While this limits you in some ways, it also shifts your decision-making from "Which lens do I use?" to "How do I make the most of the one lens I have?" This is an excellent way to push your creativity and discover the capabilities of each lens.

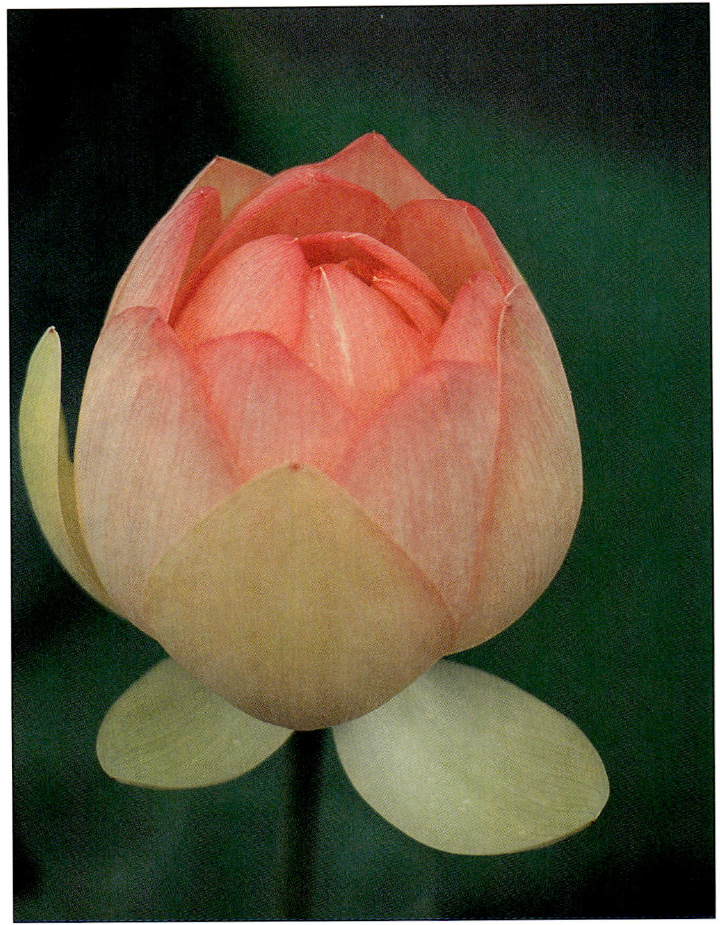

A telephoto macro lens enables you to capture detail images, such as this closeup of a single lotus flower at the Chicago Botanic Garden in Glencoe, Illinois. The lens lets you get close enough to keep the subject sharp while throwing the backdrop out of focus. Working with a Nikkor 200mm macro lens, I exposed at *f*/8 for 1/30 sec. on Ektachrome 100 SW.

With today's wide array of zoom lenses, some of this decision-making has been simplified. While one zoom lens can offer a range of compositional options, you'll still need a discerning eye to choose the best lens and lens length to encompass the garden scene to the scope and scale you envision. With more experience, you'll gain confidence about which lens to turn to for the garden image in your mind's eye. But even veteran photographers can find surprises when they change lenses, so keep experimenting even if you think you know just what you want and like. This will enable you to fine-tune your photograph in terms of composition, color, and texture.

ARRANGING LINES AND SHAPES

Framing a shot isn't the same as composing one. Before you release the shutter, take the time to create the best composition you can. This will make the difference between an acceptable garden image and a truly outstanding one.

The easiest, and the most difficult, way to conceptualize your composition is in the abstract. This is easy because once you distill your subject to its essential lines and shapes, the task of arranging them in a pleasing, balanced way becomes much simpler. The hard part is forgetting that you're looking at a garden—at flowers, shrubs, trees, and all the other elements. You might find it helpful to look at your subject as if you were a child trying to draw or paint it. A child is likely to apply gobs of color in simple shapes and to add bold lines at the edges or to represent a path or stream.

Why is abstracting the image so important? Because most people have a hard time detaching the visual from the actual or, in other words, what they see from what things are. People think they're capturing flowers, trees, and other garden features on film. But in fact, they're merely recording the light reflected from these objects. On film, they register as shapes with contours, as lines demarcating sections of a flat surface, and as colorful forms across a chemical canvas. That is why analyzing your subject according to its basic geometry will help you see the scene as a visual entity, regardless of the actual physical components. Then your task is to organize the shapes and lines into an effective, harmonious whole based on your personal aesthetic sensibilities.

Experiment with lines that converge to create a sense of depth or lines that divide the film frame into bold flat areas. For symmetrical,

Flower beds, trellises, and trees turned into abstract bands in a graphic design in this image, shot at Buchart Gardens in Victoria, British Columbia. With a Zuiko 35-70mm lens set at 35mm, I exposed for 1/30 sec. at *f*/8 on Ektachrome 100 SW.

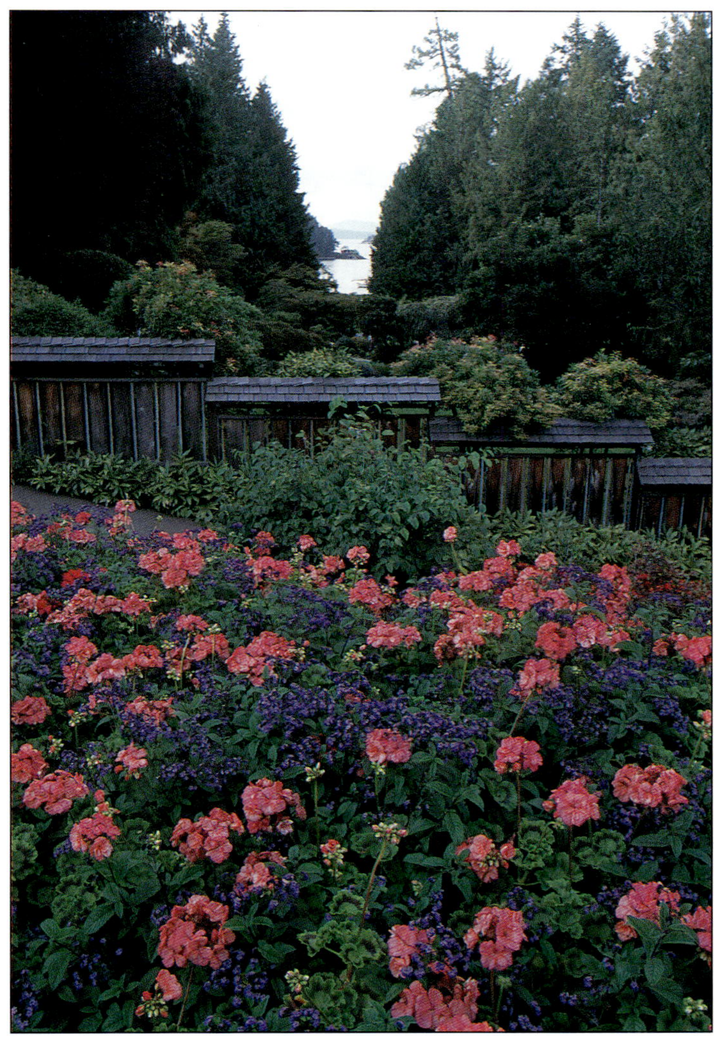

I composed this image so that the paths and borders separating the various beds in the vegetable garden at Villandry served as lines that draw the viewer's eye into the image. Shooting with a Zuiko 24mm lens, I exposed for 1/60 sec. at *f*/4 on Fujichrome 100.

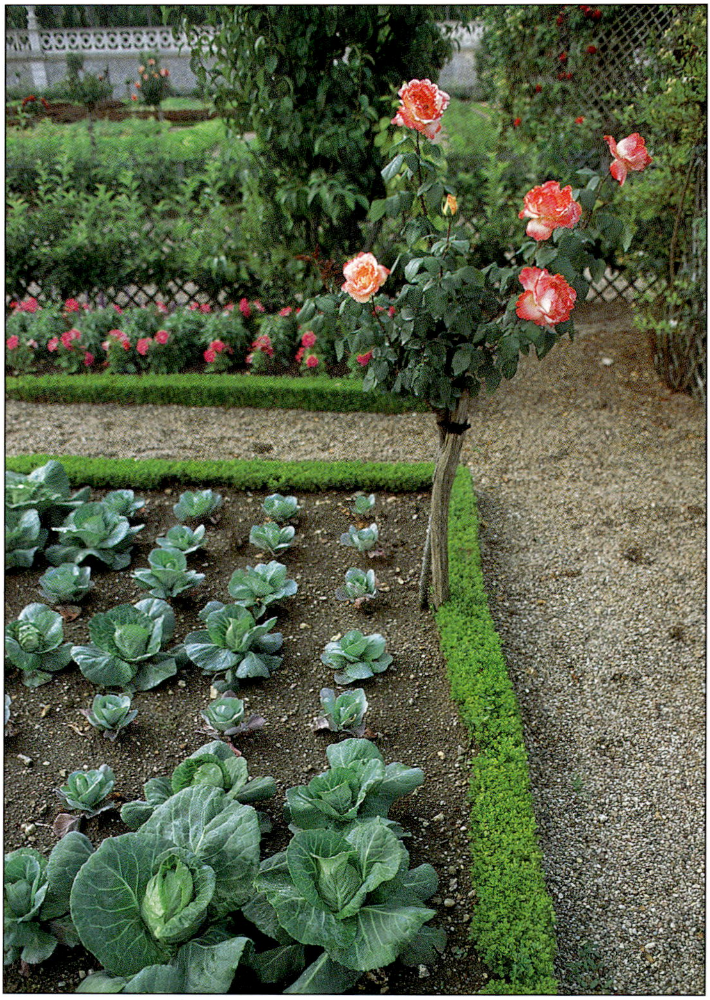

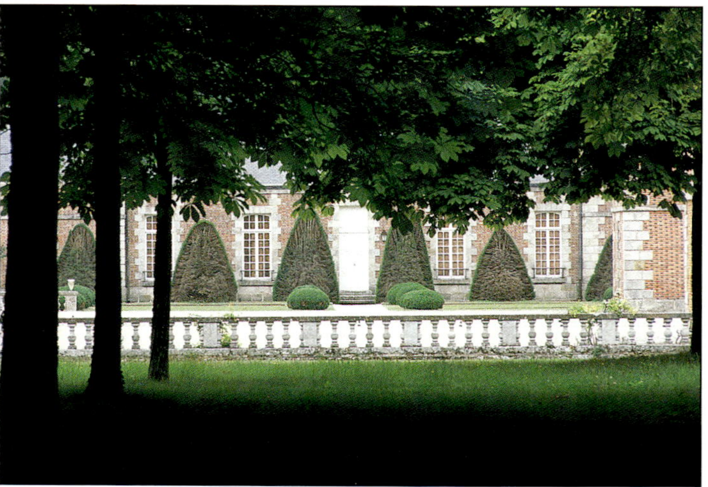

Bars of light and shadow, as well as the shapes of tree trunks and hedges, play against one another in this austere portrayal of the gardens at Courrances in France. Here, I used a Zuiko 50-250mm lens set at 180mm and exposed Fujichrome 100 for 1/125 sec. at *f*/8.

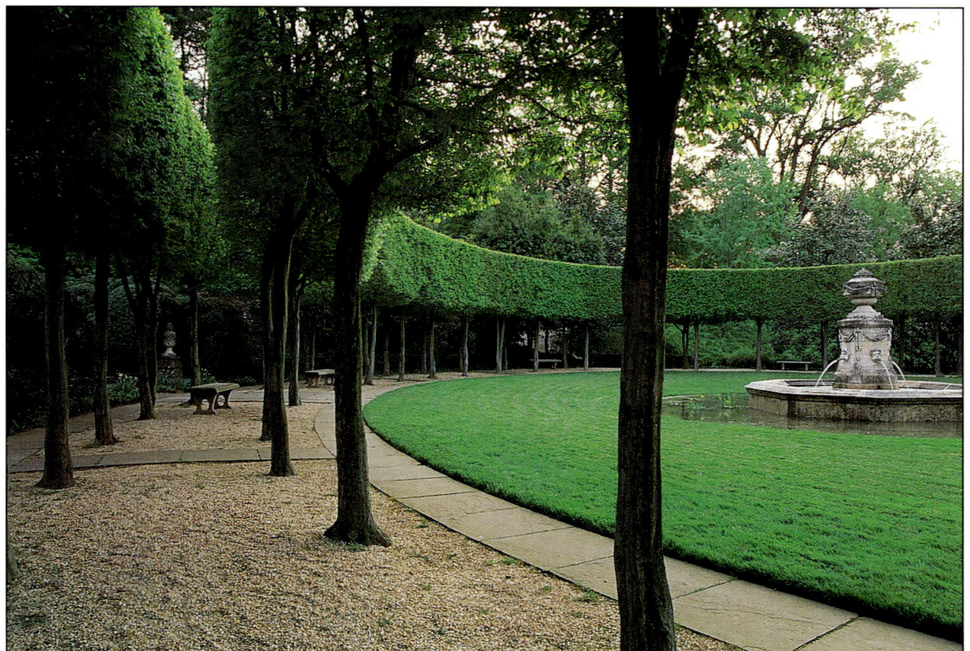

The sweeping curve of the path, echoed in the allee of trees, becomes the dominant line in this overview shot of Dumbarton Oaks in Washington, DC. I set a Zuiko 35-70mm lens at 35mm and exposed at *f*/16 for 1/4 sec. on Fujichrome Provia.

orderly images, think in terms of shapes that repeat across the film plane: flowers with the same shape in a bed, for example. For asymmetrical compositions, emphasize one dominant shape, such as a tree on the horizon. You can also try juxtaposing contrasting shapes and sizes or bringing out the irregular, undulating lines of grasses for more freeform, impressionistic effects. Soon you'll discover that your way of looking at gardens might be quite different from the way others see the same setting. And that is as it should be.

ENHANCING THE COLOR PALETTE

Color is an aspect of photographic design that combines aesthetics and technical know-how. Of course, the garden designers have already brought their own sense of color into the picture. Consider monochromatic gardens that highlight a subtle, soft color palette. Other gardens are gaudy and brightly colored and almost make your eyes pop. As a photographer, you'll want to use the colors you encounter in a way that respects the garden designer's intentions.

But you'll also want to put your own stamp on them, taking into account the quality of the light and your willingness to test the aesthetic potential of the scene. For example, on a misty day, you might choose to create a soft color effect by overexposing from the meter reading. On the other hand, you might prefer to underexpose a brightly illuminated scene to saturate the colors. (For now, the point to understand is that you have a good deal of control over how colors appear in your image. Chapter 4 more fully discusses the technical aspects of working with natural light and getting the best exposure.)

In garden photography, learning how to control color rendition is an essential skill. You can't change the colors of the plantings or the available light, but you have considerable control over your perspective on the light, your exposure settings, and your choice of film. Together, these factors will determine color rendition.

Diffused light and Fujichrome Velvia film enhance the subtle palette of this private natural garden in Atlanta, Georgia. With a Zuiko 35-70mm lens set at 50mm, I exposed for 1/30 sec. at *f*/16.

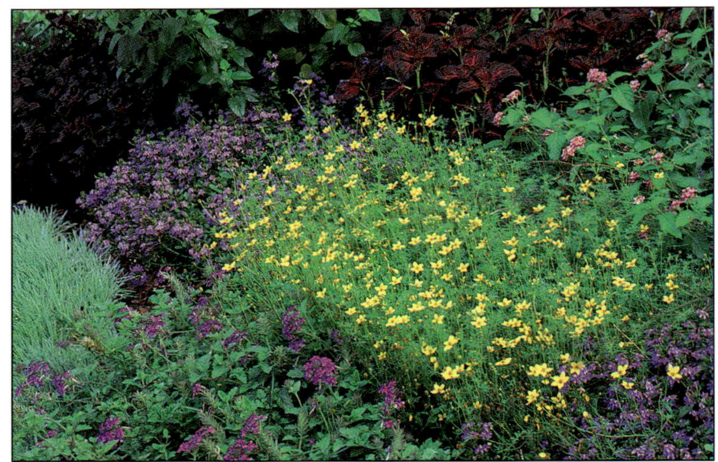

Slight overexposure helps maintain the soft, cool colors, both in the sunnier foreground area and the shadow-flecked background in this border at Florida's Epcot Center. Shooting with a Zuiko 35-70mm lens set at 50mm, I exposed Ektachrome 100 SW at *f*/11 for 1/60 sec.

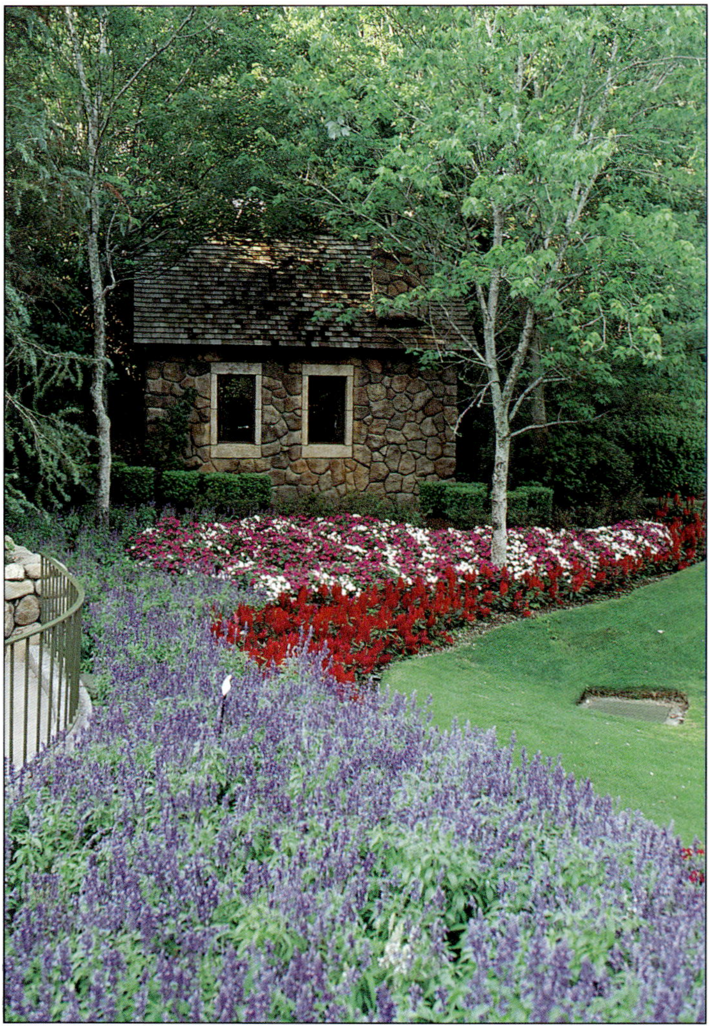

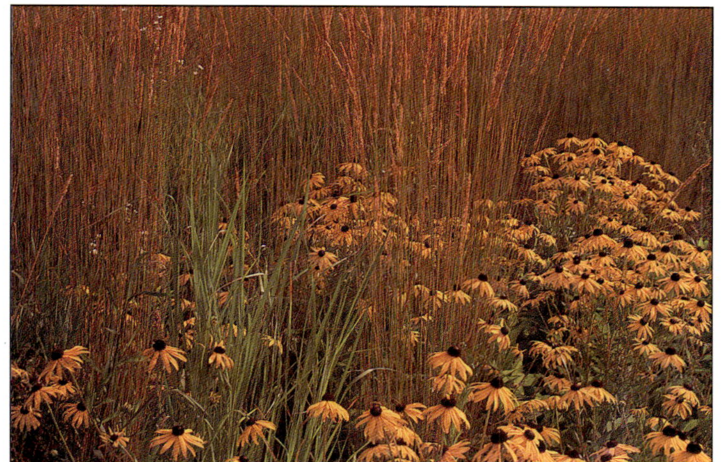

Ektachrome 100 film and late afternoon sunlight enrich the warm tones of this grass garden at the Minnesota Landscape Arboretum in Minneapolis. For this shot, I used a Zuiko 50-250mm lens set at 120mm and exposed for 1/30 sec. at *f*/16.

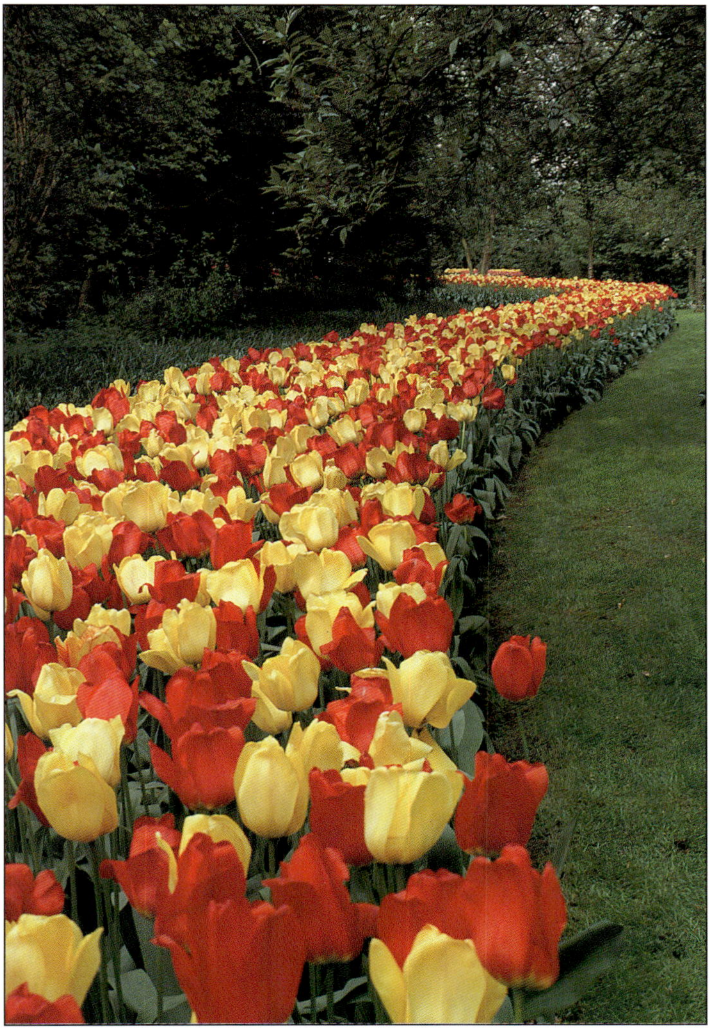

Exposing for the eye-popping colors of this tulip bed meant losing some brightness in the greens in this dramatic wide-angle shot at Holland's Keukenhof Garden. Working with a Zuiko 28mm lens, I exposed Ektachrome 100 SW at *f*/22 for 1/8 sec.

The contrasting textures in this vignette of a natural setting at Cantigny Garden in Wheaton, Illinois, depend on the sharpness of a small aperture and careful focusing. Here, I used a Zuiko 50-250mm lens set at 150mm and exposed for 1/15 sec. at *f*/16 on Ektachrome 100 SW.

High-contrast light brings out the spiny texture of this barrel cactus at Wisconsin's Mitchell Park Conservatory in a detail that also derives visual impact from its lines and shapes. Shooting with a Zuiko 90mm macro lens, I exposed Ektachrome LPZ at *f*/16 for 1/15 sec.

- Move your camera position to achieve frontlighting, sidelighting, or backlighting (see Chapter 4).
- Return to a garden on a day with a particular quality of light.
- Set or program your camera to overexpose or underexpose from the meter reading in order to lighten the color palette or to saturate colors.
- Select a film that will enhance the particular colors you're working with. Remember to choose a film that favors warm colors for fall foliage or film that sharpens greens if you're shooting in early spring.

DEFINING TEXTURES

Perhaps the most intriguing and frustrating aspect of garden photography has to do with trying to capture the tactile qualities of plantings. In life, you can simply reach out and touch most plants, luxuriating in the velvety feel of rose petals or marveling at the leathery surface of tree bark. How can you translate those physical sensations into a visual medium like photography? By portraying the textures of garden plantings. Since communicating the surface texture of plants depends on visual clarity, the main technical challenge is to achieve maximum sharpness (see Chapter 5 for explicit guidance on the techniques involved). Textures captured with absolute clarity can give any garden photograph a greater sense of reality.

Interesting textures work particularly well for vignettes and detail shots, which home in on the feel of the plantings. Be sure to look at ground covers, grasses, and other filler plantings for attractive possibilities. Then, study the contrasting textures in the garden. Garden designers often do the hard work for you by combining plants that complement one another. But even individual plants can be rich in textural contrasts. Think of flowering cacti, thorny roses, and magnolia trees, to name just a few. When you can work with all the elements—line, shape, color, and texture—you'll be well on your way to mastering the design of your garden photographs.

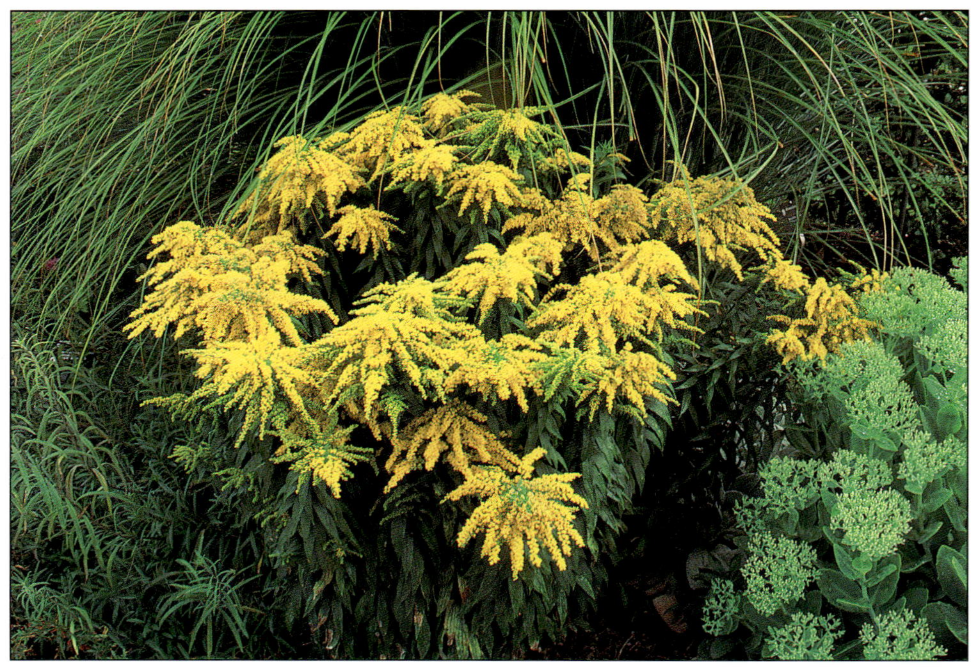

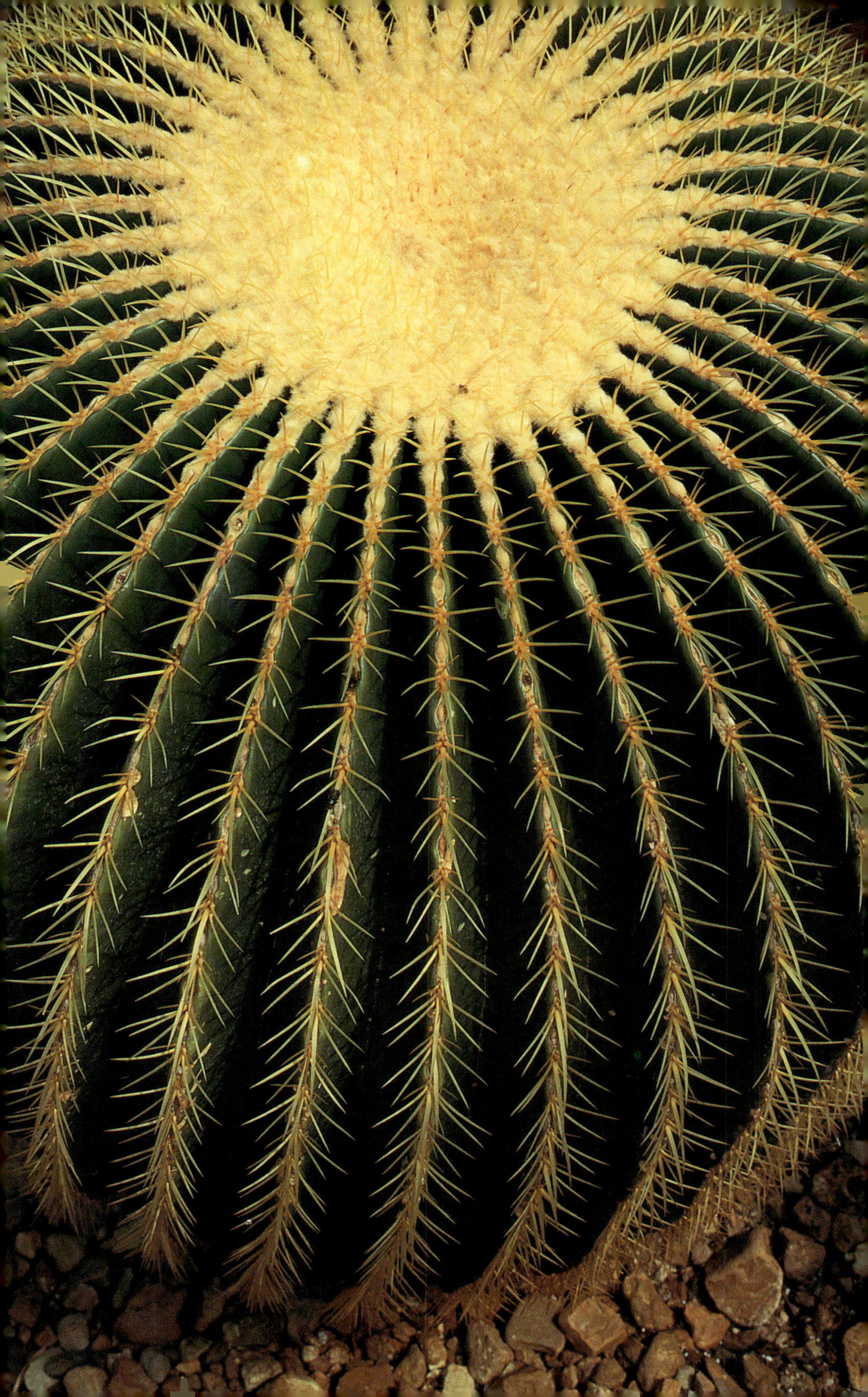

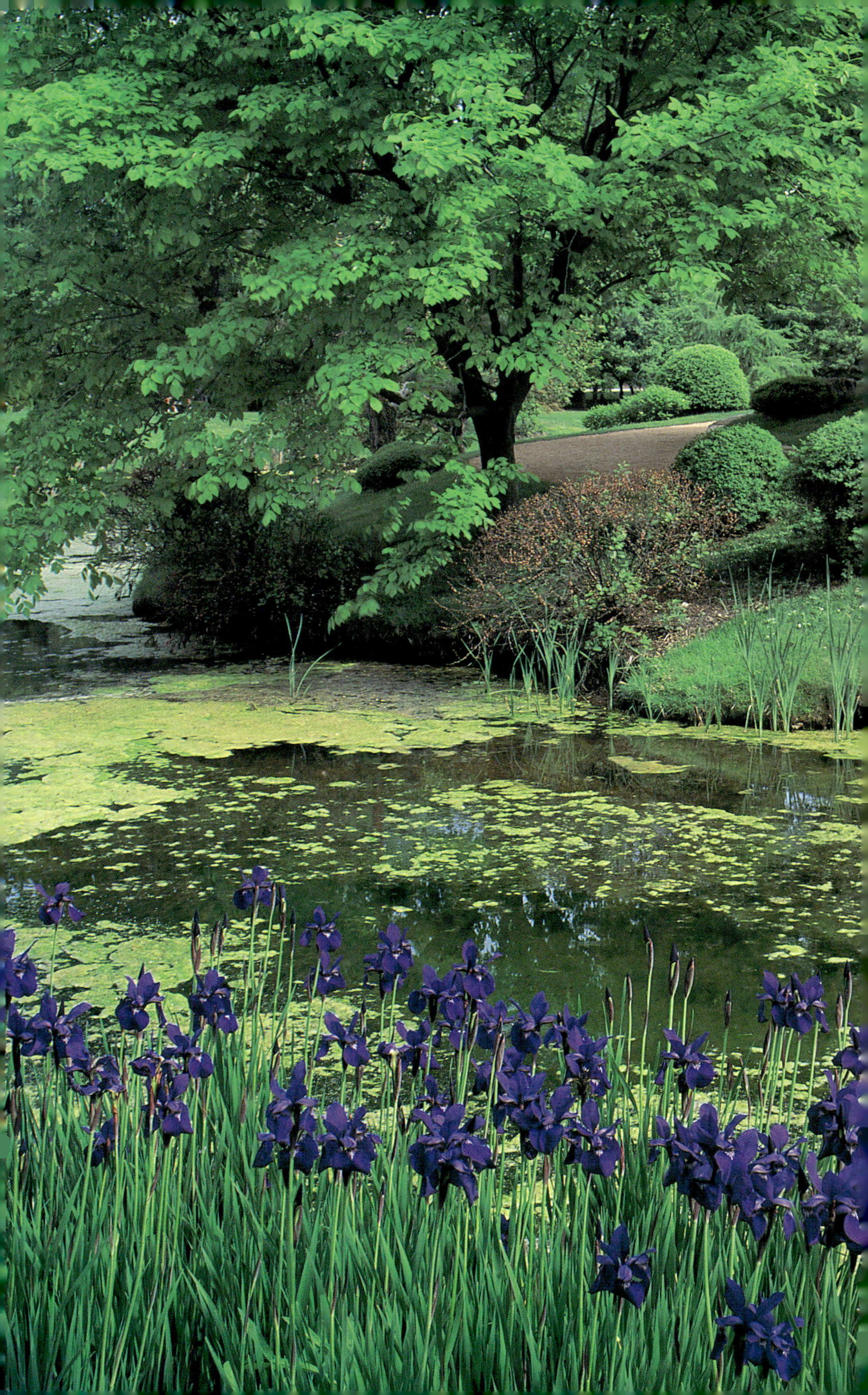

CHAPTER 4

Working with Natural Light

Diffused sunlight softens the contrast between bright and shadow areas and minimizes harsh reflections in this lakeside scene at the Chicago Botanic Garden in Glencoe, Illinois. Working with a Zuiko 35-70mm lens set at 40mm; I exposed for 1/60 sec. at *f*/16 on Fujichrome 100.

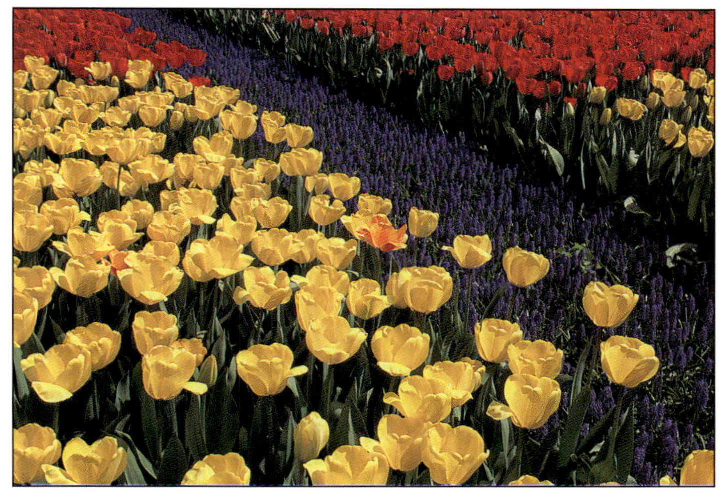

High, bright backlight and a telephoto lens intensified the radiant colors of these tulips in the Keukenhof Garden in Holland. Here, I used a Zuiko 50-250mm lens set at 200mm, exposing Fujichrome Velvia for 1/30 sec. at *f*/11.

Serious garden photographers understand that while good design and composition are basic to an image, they aren't enough. Outdoor photography depends on the interplay of natural light with the subjects that are portrayed. Light can make a garden subject glow, enrich its colors, set it off from its surroundings, and give it an aura worth noticing. In other words, light can make a subject photogenic.

Bright, high contrast side-light casts deep shadows that are integrated into the design of this overview of the Bahai Temple gardens in Illinois. Here, I used a Distagon 60mm lens and exposed at *f*/22 for 1/15 sec. on Fujichrome Provia.

As a garden photographer, you must pay special attention to the light at hand, analyze its evocative qualities, and develop the technical know-how to make it express your aesthetic values. To do all that, ask yourself the following questions:

- How intense is the light, and how will that intensity affect the scene?
- Where should I position myself to get the lighting direction I want?
- What is the color of the light, and how will that enhance or distort my image?
- How will I get the best exposure?

Through all this analysis, keep in mind that the photographic process will register the light somewhat differently from the way your eye ordinarily would. For example, film might exaggerate contrast in bright light, deepening shadows that your eye tends to overlook. If you can, seek out the kind of light that will help you create the impression and atmosphere you want: a bright sunset light or a soft, misty look. Otherwise, learn to define the assets and limitations of every lighting situation, so you proceed with a good sense about what you can and can't achieve. As with all learning, becoming familiar with this kind of analysis is slow and painstaking at first. But the more you make it part of your photographic routine, the more it will reward you with truly special images.

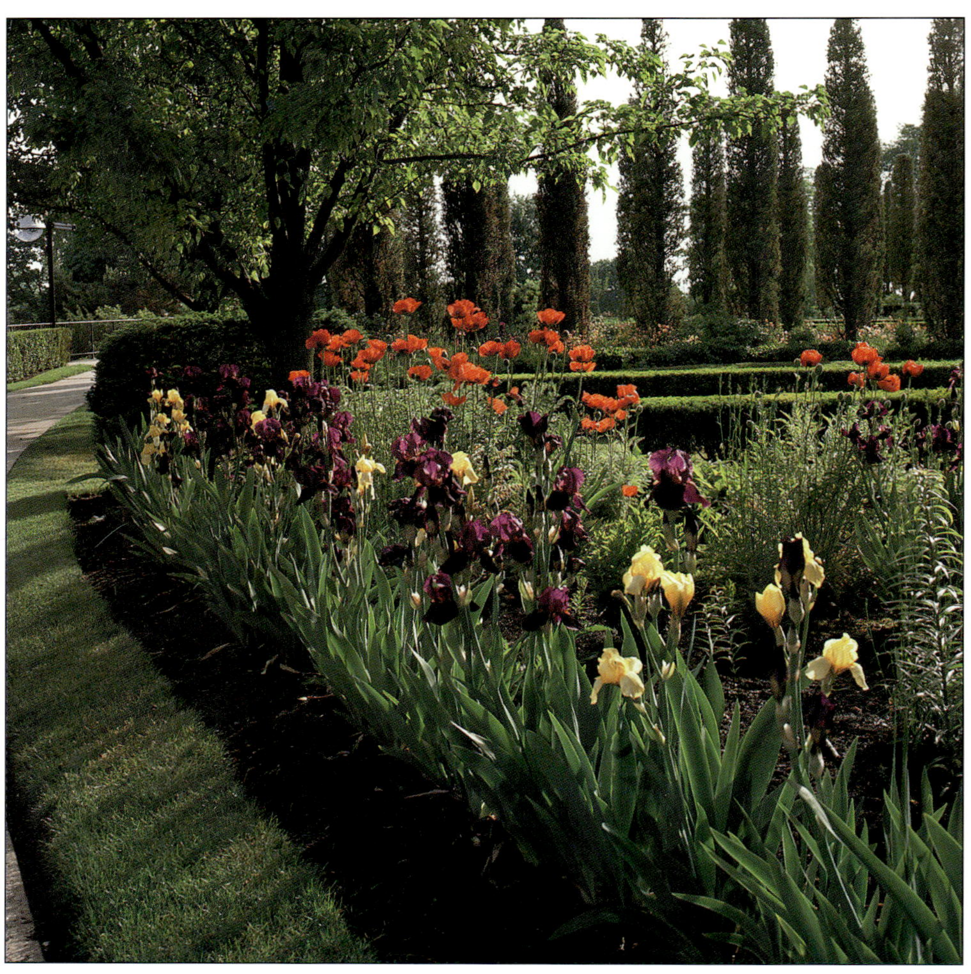

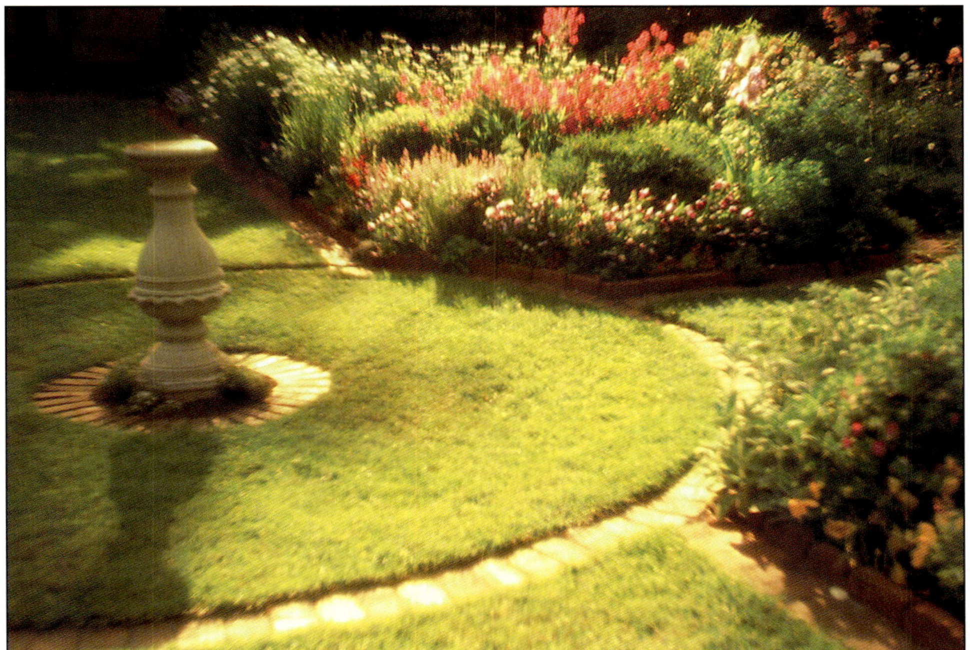

A soft-focus filter and slight overexposure muted the bright sunlight and subdued the harsh contrast in this Elizabethan Garden at Northwestern University in Evanston, Illinois. Shooting with a Zuiko 50-250mm lens set at 80mm, I exposed for 1/125 sec. at *f*/5.6 on Ektachrome 100 SW.

LIGHT INTENSITY

With artificial light, such as an ordinary light bulb, intensity is measurable and clearly identified. That is why a studio photographer can control light intensity very precisely. With natural light, while you can become good at estimating intensity or measuring it with sophisticated metering systems, you can't actually control intensity.

The best you can do is anticipate the effect of any given light intensity and try to avoid the most common pitfalls, such as images with severely overexposed or underexposed areas. Beyond that, you can learn to work with the given light intensity in ways that are imaginative and exciting. Consider the following possibilities:

Bright Sunlight. This is the kind of light you encounter on a clear, sunny day or on a partly cloudy day when the sun isn't behind a cloud. You can find it any time of year and during any part of the day, although the extremes of the day reduce intensity somewhat as the angle of the sun flattens. The more intense the light, the greater the contrast between the brightly illuminated portions of the garden and any areas in shadow. High-contrast light is hard for many films to handle because they can't expose well over a wide range of light intensities. So be especially observant about any shadows in your image.

If you notice that some parts of the subject are in bright light and others in deep shadow, meter the two areas separately with a spot meter or telephoto lens. If the difference between the two readings is more than three *f*-stops, don't expect to get the best exposure in both areas. Decide whether or not to concentrate on getting the best exposure in the bright area, even though this will sacrifice the areas in shadow. Imagine all the shadows as black shapes in your image. If you can't live with that, rethink your photograph. Either recompose to eliminate any unacceptable shadows or find a way to incorporate the shadows as elements of your design.

To achieve proper exposure in the dim light of the foreground shadows at this Washington, DC, garden, I had to sacrifice some of the background to overexposure. With a Zuiko 24mm lens, I exposed for 1/15 sec. at *f*/22 on Ektachrome 100 SW.

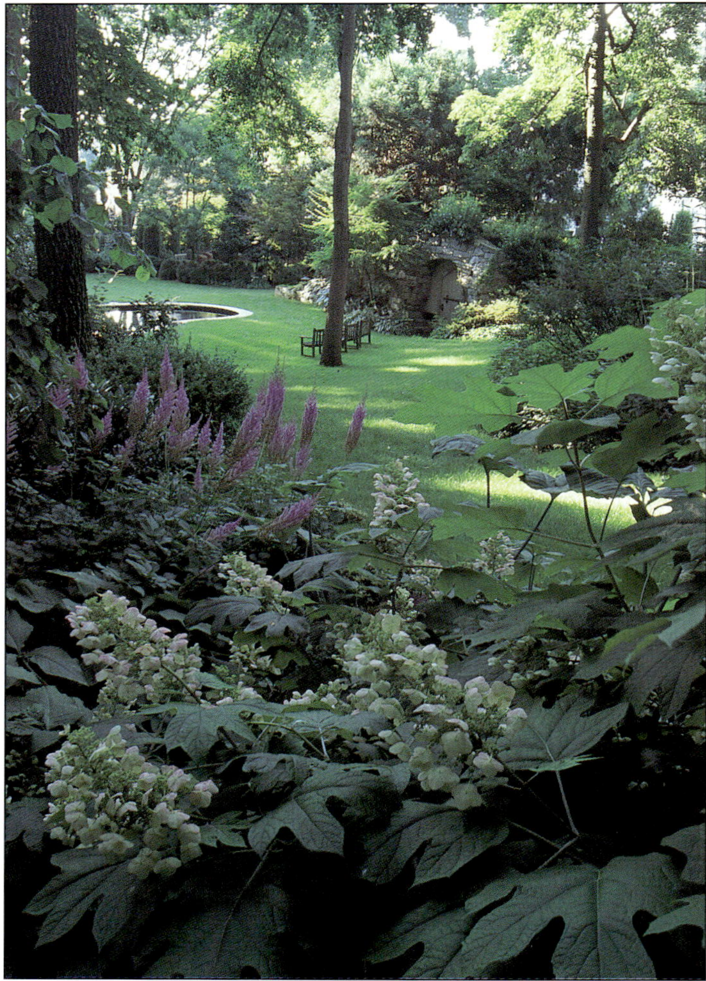

Diffused Sunlight. When sunlight passes through a translucent filter, it is diffused. The filter might be a natural object, such as a cloud, or it might be an artificial diffuser, such as a white umbrella. Diffused light softens shadows, reduces contrast, and brings out the natural colors of plants. As a result, taking photographs in diffused light is much easier than in other kinds of light because the illumination is more uniform and even. No wonder professional garden photographers often prefer shooting on an overcast day than on one that is bright and sunny. The beauty of this light is especially evident after a rain shower, when a garden glistens but the light is soft and velvety.

Dim Light. On days when the cloud cover is very thick, or in areas that are in deep shade, the light might be quite dim. This isn't a big problem, although at times this light might be too dull and lifeless to give your garden shots the sparkle you want. If you want to increase contrast so individual plants don't get lost in a wash of green, try using high-contrast film, such as Fujichrome Velvia. Another option is to push your film: underexpose by one *f*-stop, then have the film processed at +1. Also, you'll probably have to increase exposure time in dim light, so be alert to

Even the very dim light of sunrise can accumulate on film when you use a slow shutter speed, making evocative garden images, such as this one of Kentucky's Bernheim Arboretum, possible. Shooting with a Zuiko 50-250mm lens set at 100mm, I exposed at *f*/4.5 for 1/2 sec. on Fujichrome 100.

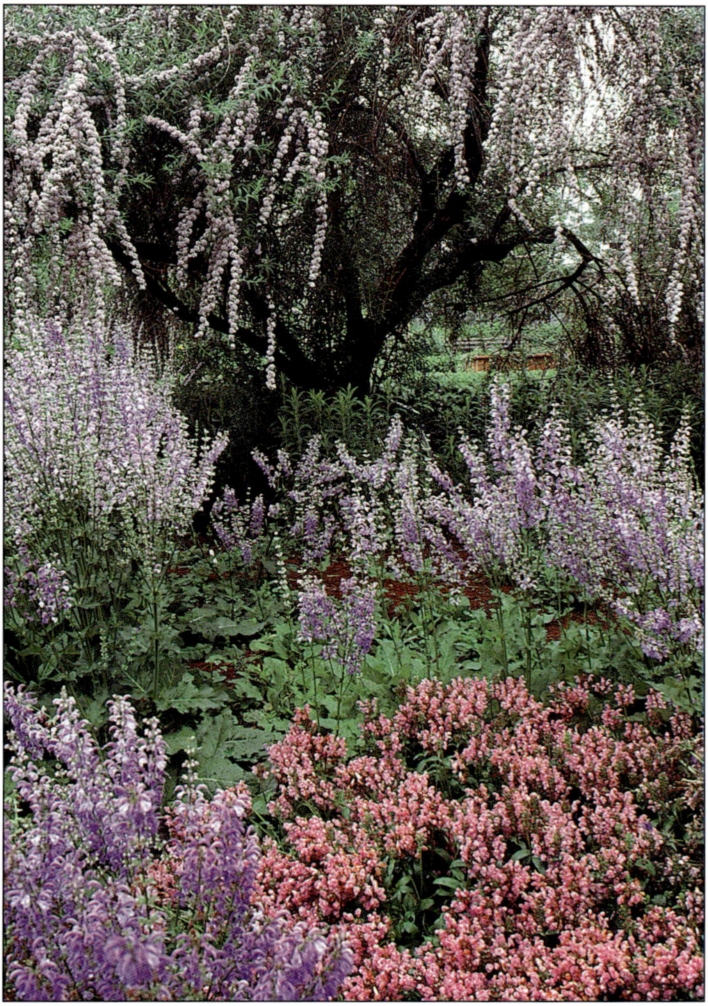

The diffused light of a bright, overcast spring day provides uniform illumination on this vignette shot with a Zuiko 50-250mm lens set at 180mm at the New York Botanical Garden in the Bronx, New York. The exposure was 1/60 sec. at *f*/5.6 on Kodachrome 25.

Diffused frontlight in a Colorado garden keeps the whites on these columbines bright and the purples rich in color. Here, I used a Zuiko 90mm macro lens, exposing for 1/30 sec. at *f*/11 on Ektachrome 100 S.

Metering the bright yellows in this garden overview at the Minnesota Landscape Arboretum helped maintain color saturation throughout despite harsh midday light. With a Zuiko 35-70mm zoom lens set at 35mm, I exposed for 1/15 sec. at *f*/22 on Ektachrome 100 SW.

windblown movement. Such movement might cause unwanted blur during a longer exposure.

DIRECTION OF LIGHT

Becoming sensitive to the direction of light can be one of the most valuable skills you develop as a garden photographer. The difference in the quality of the light and, by extension, the impact of your image can be dramatic depending on your orientation to the light. To the extent that you can move into a particular position, you can control the direction of light. You must always consider how the direction of light affects your garden photographs.

Frontlighting. This is light that comes down from above or over your shoulder and illuminates the side of the garden scene facing you. Frontlight is best for spotlighting details in the garden, often with shadows behind them. Use it, for example, for a well-lit floral closeup or vignette with a dark backdrop. Carefully meter the area in bright light, and bracket by taking several shots toward underexposure. The main disadvantages of frontlighting are its harsh flatness and tendency to produce glare. Try polarizing to eliminate or reduce the glare, and avoid taking overviews unless the frontlight is already low on the horizon.

Sidelighting. This light strikes your subject from the side at about 90 degrees, essentially illuminating one side while leaving the other in shadow. You are most likely to encounter sidelighting early in the morning or late in the afternoon, when the light is warmer and isn't as intense as at it is at midday, making it easier to work with. Sidelight is excellent for bringing out textures in individual plants, vignettes, or overviews. It also casts interesting shadows that you can incorporate in your garden images for graphic purposes. If you find many reflections or glare on the foliage, consider polarizing.

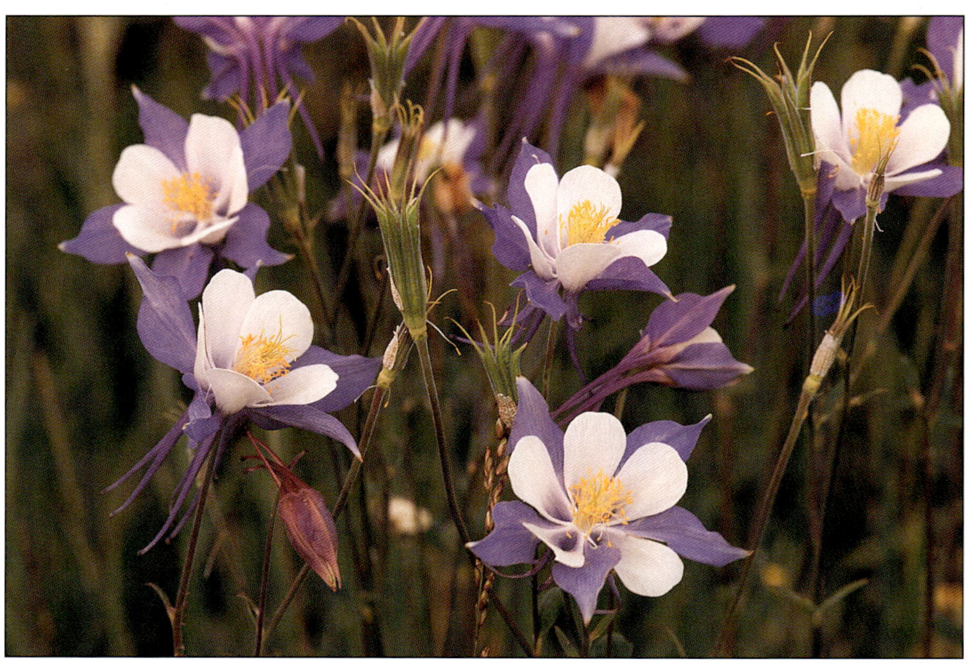

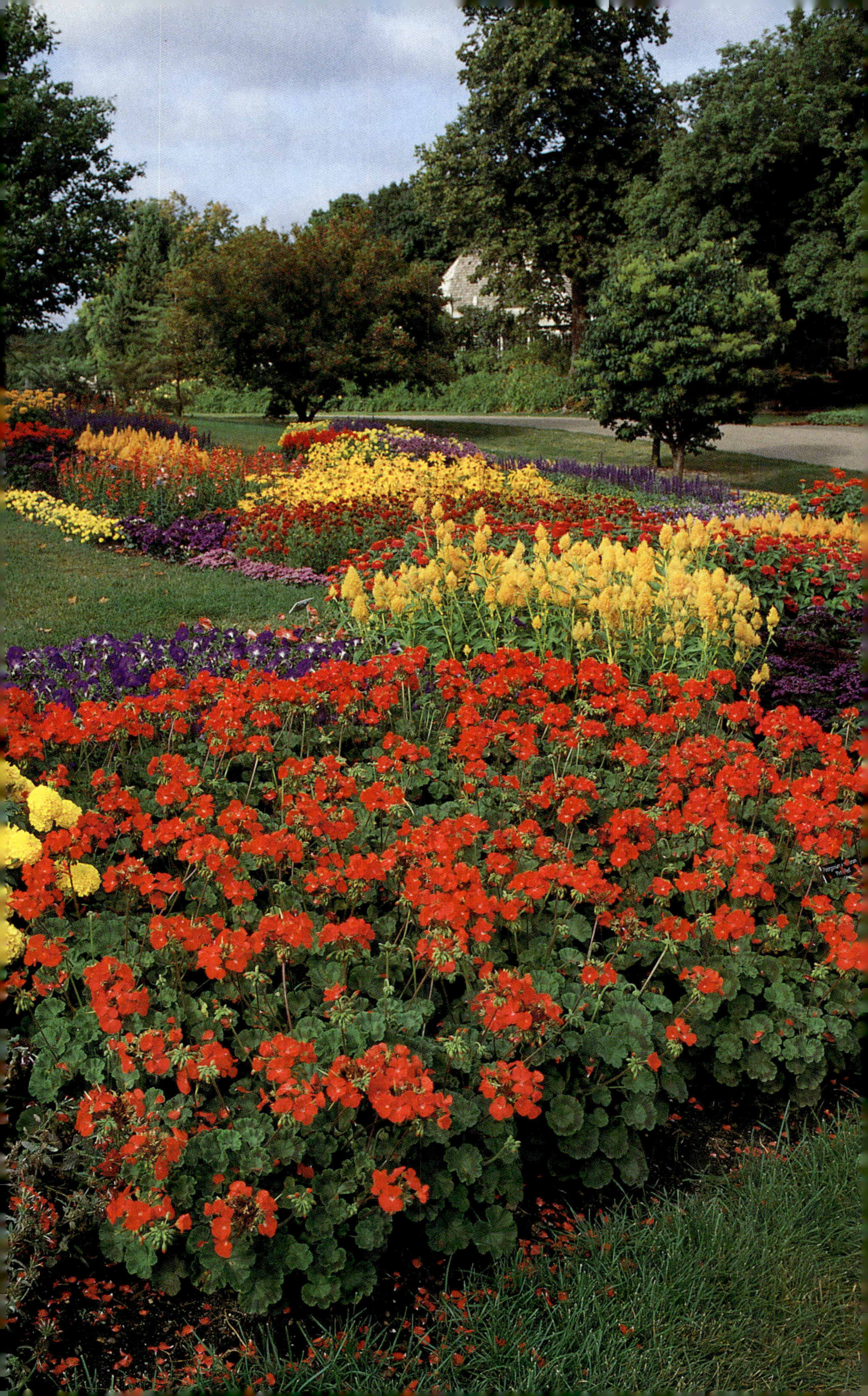

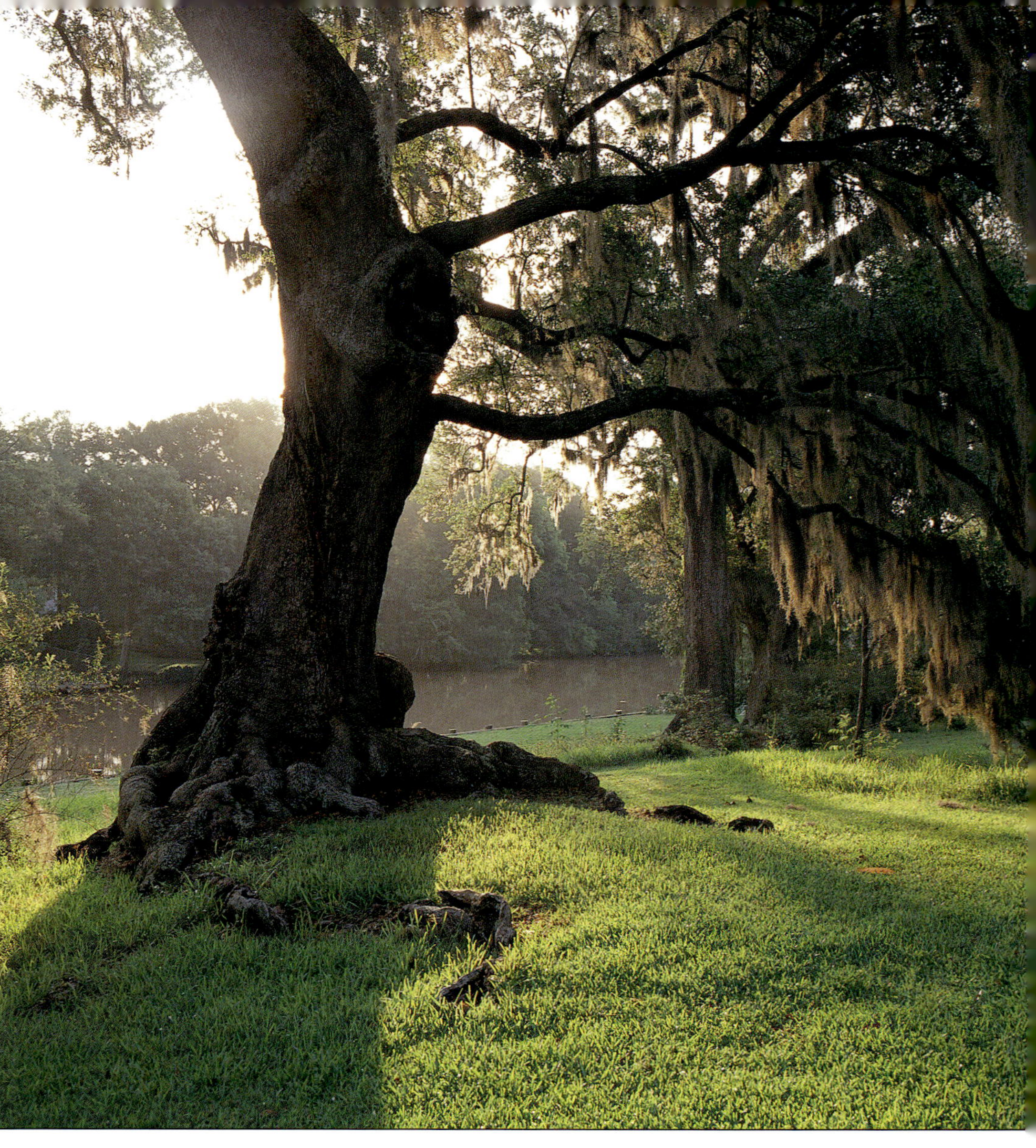

Blocking the setting sun behind a tree softens the high contrast light and produces low-angled backlight on the lawn for an atmospheric shot of Louisiana's Shadows on the Teche. Shooting with a Mamiya 65mm lens, I exposed Ektachrome 100 SW for 1/60 sec. at *f*/16.

Backlighting. This type of light faces you and passes through the vegetation from behind. Its effect is often compared to that of stained glass. In garden photographs, backlight is especially beautiful, so use it at every opportunity—even to the extent of walking around your subject.

The trickiest part of using backlight is getting good exposure. You don't want to meter the brightest area of the plant or garden—and certainly not the sun itself—because that will cause the entire image to be underexposed. Instead, spot-meter a point in your image that represents roughly the middle intensity, and use that reading for your exposure. Lock in that meter reading if you need to recompose before shooting. Also, bracket backlit shots toward overexposure (most photographers err toward underexposure with backlight, so this will give you some insurance).

Be aware that backlighting might cause sun flare. These are the spots of light that occur when the sun's rays enter the camera lens. Avoid flare by using a lens, or sun, shade and, if necessary, by further blocking the

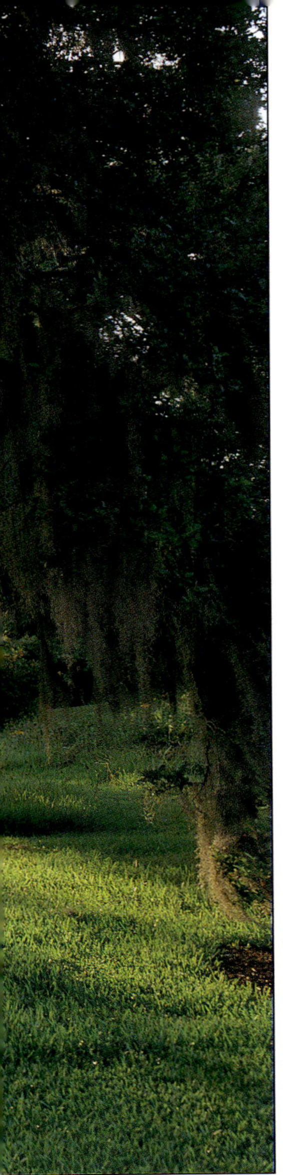

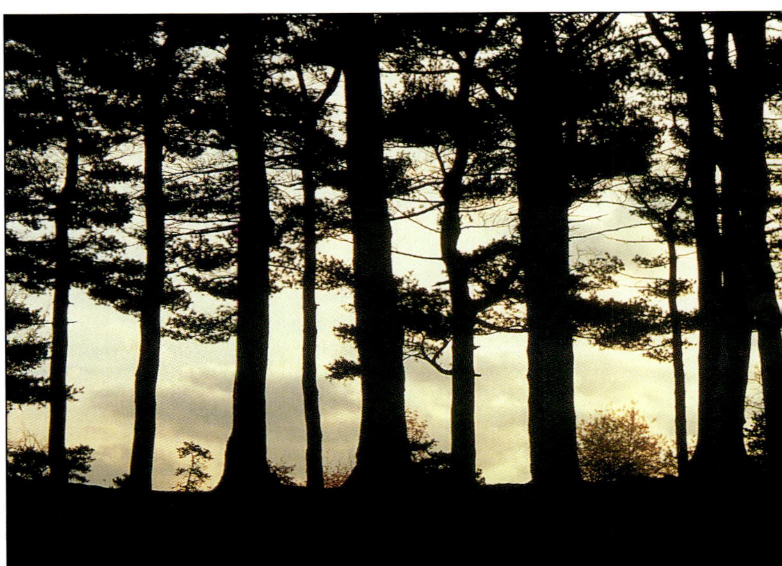

sun from above with your hand or an opaque object. As you look through the lens, check to see if the flare is gone. As you become more experienced, you might want to experiment with images that incorporate flare to soften the light and create a filmy aura.

COLOR OF LIGHT

This varies with the temperature of the light and with atmospheric conditions. Generally, the higher the temperature of the light, the cooler the appearance of its color. Midday illumination is considered cool white light and measures 5500K. Sunset light, which is much warmer than midday light, ranges from 2000K to 2800K. The old high-school mnemonic, ROYGBIV, which describes the color spectrum from red to violet, gives the range of colors in the order of low to high temperature. Paying attention to the color of light throughout the day and in different kinds of weather will help you understand how best to use the light to enhance every garden scene.

Sunrise. The soft pinks, purples, and mauves visible just before sunrise last only a short time. Once the sun is up, the light becomes harsh and hard to handle. But if you're determined and prepared, sunrise light will reward you with its delicate warmth. To enhance the warm tones, try a film such as Ektachrome 100 SW; to neutralize the warm tones, use Fuji films or Ektachrome 100 S. Avoid using color filters, which will distort the soft, natural colors.

Since sunrise light is low-angled, it also enhances pastel tones. Look particularly for backlit or sidelit flowers, such as irises or tulips. Sunrise light also adds a lovely glow to architectural and structural elements in a garden: the paths, fences, benches, and garden ornaments.

Sunset. Everyone marvels at the warm oranges, yellows, and magentas of a fiery sunset. You can use these tonalities to good effect in your garden photographs, often for quite some time after the sun has actually set. Think about creating images in which this warm light envelops every facet of the garden. You might also want to make the light itself the focus

High contrast backlight is ideal for producing silhouettes, such as this shot of the New York Botanical Garden in the Bronx, New York. Slight underexposure on the shadow side exaggerates the contrast. Working with a Zuiko 50-250mm lens set at 180mm, I exposed for 1/250 sec. at *f*/5.6 on Kodachrome 25.

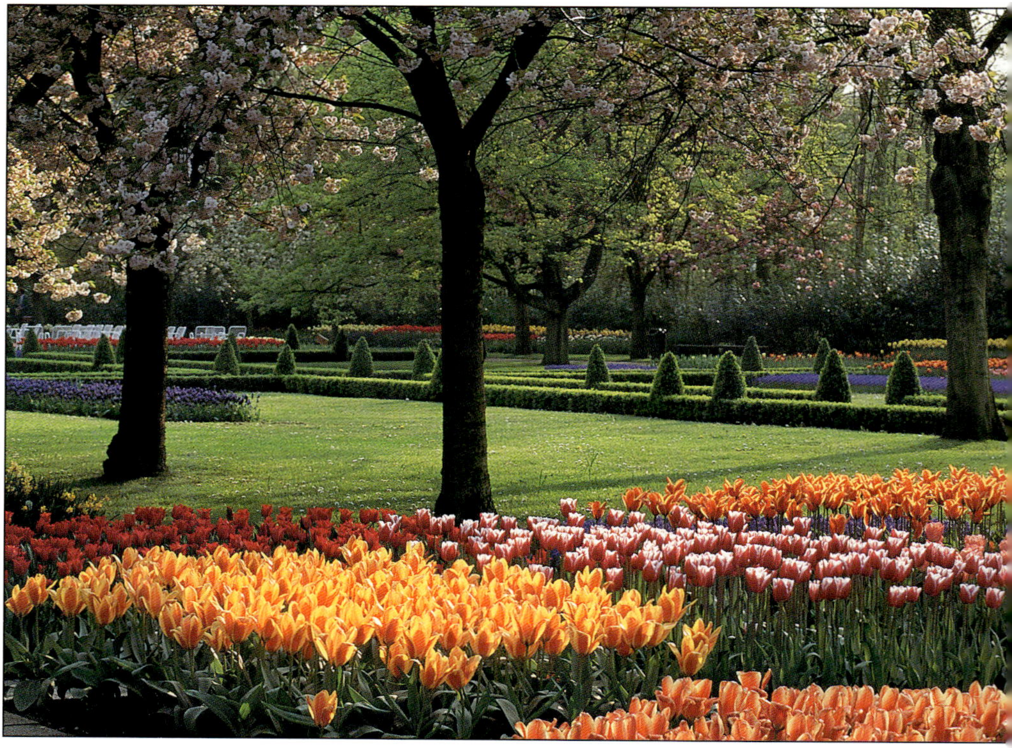

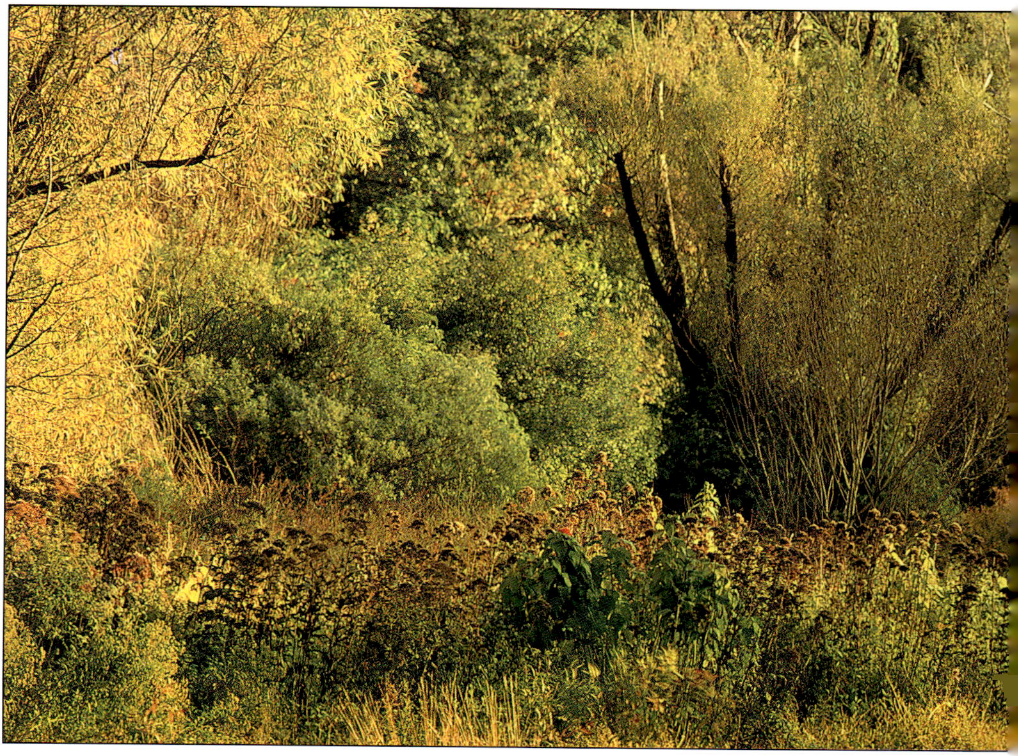

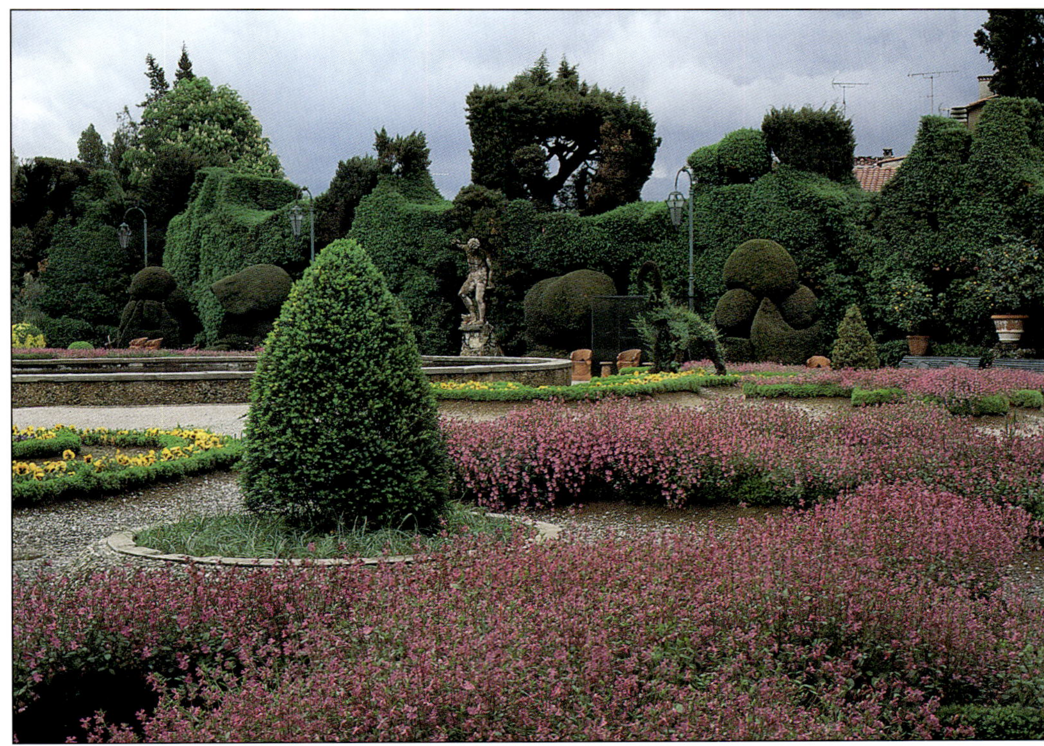

of an image by silhouetting certain aspects of the garden against a magnificent sky.

Keep in mind that sunset light is low-angled, low-intensity illumination. So you must be careful not to underexpose the plantings. Meter the middle tones, not the bright areas, especially when plants are sidelit or backlit. You should also avoid using color filters, which both destroy the subtle quality of the available light and wash the entire scene with an unnatural brazenness.

Bright Daylight. Although this is basically white light, reflections from the sky often produce a bluish cast in bright daylight. Most garden photographs aren't helped by the added blue. If your garden shots have a bluish tinge to them, experiment with filters that will neutralize the blue. Try a 1A, 1B, or 81A warming filter, which many garden photographers use routinely. Some also turn to a slightly stronger pale red CR10 filter. Some people prefer the red tonality of this filter over the magenta of the others for neutralizing blue daylight; it is simply a matter of taste. Also, the red of the CR10 filter enhances greens better than magenta filters, which is an important consideration when photographing gardens with all their green colors.

In addition, when shooting in bright daylight you'll probably want to use a polarizer—whether or not you use a warming filter—to reduce glare and remove reflections. If you piggyback two filters, check the corners of your frame for possible vignetting. This is especially important when you use wide-angle lenses.

Overcast Light. This light, found on days with a high cloud cover, is the closest thing to colorless light. As a result, it tends to reveal the true

The bluish-gray light of an overcast day enhanced the greens in this French garden. With a Zuiko 50-250mm lens set at 150mm, I exposed for 1/8 sec. at *f*/16 on Fujichrome 100.

Soft, warm-toned sunset light and Fujichrome Provia boosted the pinks and oranges in this overview taken at Holland's Keukenhof Garden. Working with a Zuiko 35-70mm lens set at 35mm, I exposed for 1/15 sec. at *f*/16.

The low-angled sunset backlight enhanced the autumn colors of these wetland grasses at the New York Botanical Garden in the Bronx, New York. Here, I used a Zuiko 50-250mm lens set at 200mm and exposed for 1/125 sec. at *f*/8 on Kodachrome 25.

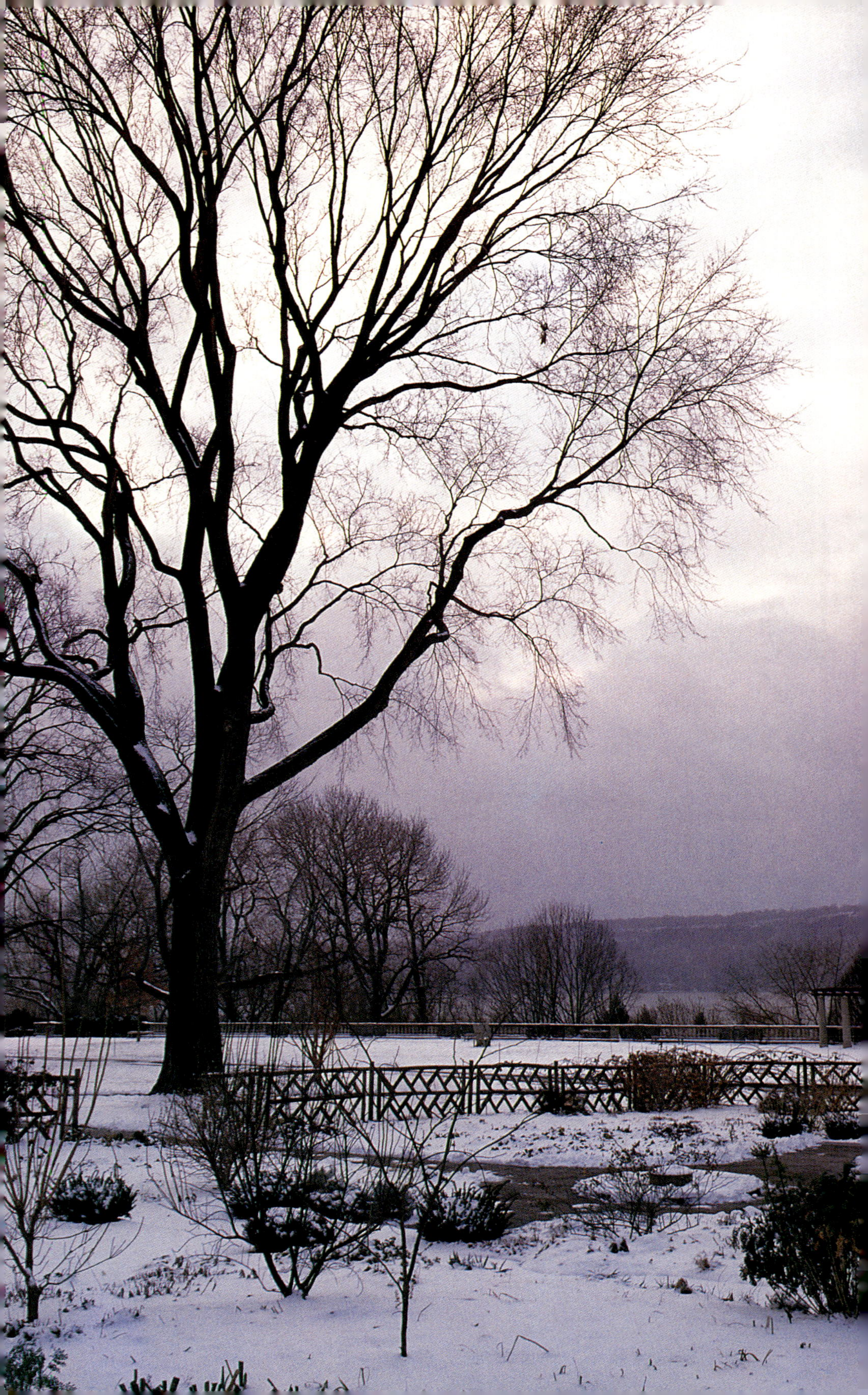

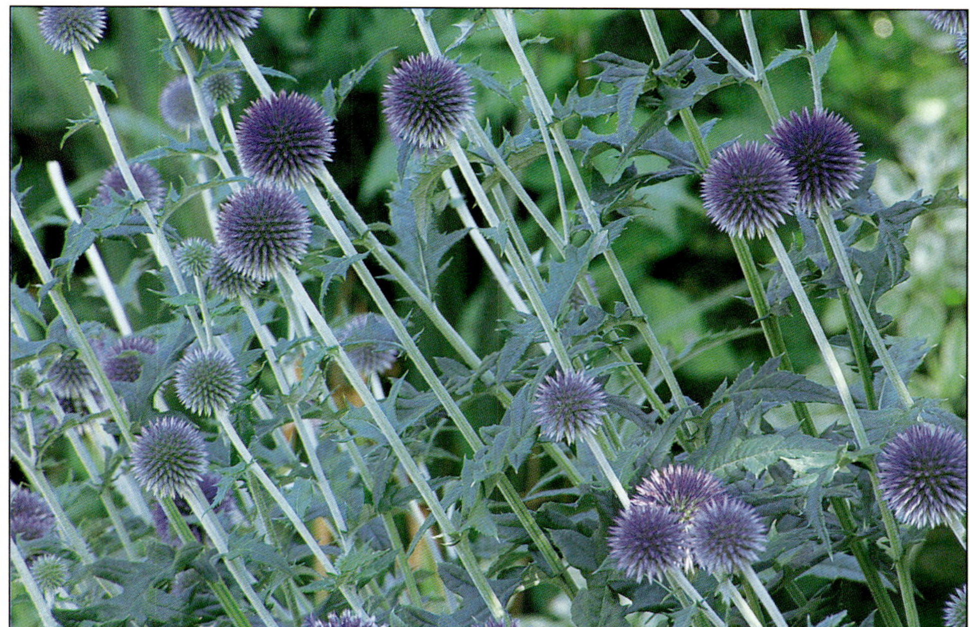

colors of the garden. This propensity is particularly advantageous for closeups and vignettes, in which the colors of the plantings play a large role. In overcast light, metering is straightforward and exposure is uncomplicated: what you see is what you get.

Bounced Light. When sunlight passes through foliage or bounces off nearby structures, it picks up their colors. To counteract the green color of light filtered through an overhead canopy of vegetation, use a warming filter, such as the 81A or CR10. In other situations, learn to notice if extraneous colors affect the garden. For example, the red color of a house might tinge the flower beds around the foundation.

As you judge each situation, determine whether the added color is intrusive. If so, the best way to counteract the color is to use film that will help neutralize its effect. Shoot a warm-tone film, such as Agfa 50 or Ektachrome SW, EPX, or LPZ, to neutralize cool colors; shoot a cool-tone film, such as Fuji Velvia or Ektachrome S, to offset warm colors.

GETTING THE BEST EXPOSURE

One of the biggest challenges garden photographers face is getting the optimal exposure. While all the factors discussed so far—the intensity, direction, and color of light—are important considerations, in the field you are likely to encounter a mixture of these conditions and/or conditions that change within a matter of moments.

Clearly, you must always keep looking before deciding what you have to do to get the best possible exposure. In addition, you'll have to give some thought to choosing the right film, and to the possibility of pushing film. The following final pointers will assist you in your pursuit of the best exposure:

- Avoid high-contrast light conditions unless the high contrast works for you, such as in silhouettes or a spotlighted foreground subject with a deep shadow backdrop. Expose for the bright area, and let the shadows go black.

The greenish light filtered through nearby foliage adds a cool touch, which was enhanced by the use of Fujichrome 100 for this detail of globe thistle taken at Monet's home in Giverny, France. I used a Zuiko 50-250 lens set at 180mm and exposed for 1/60 sec. at *f*/5.6.

A wash of pinkish gray light colors an otherwise monochromatic landscape shot at Wave Hill in New York. Working with a Zuiko 35mm lens, I exposed for 1/125 sec. at *f*/8 on Fujichrome 100.

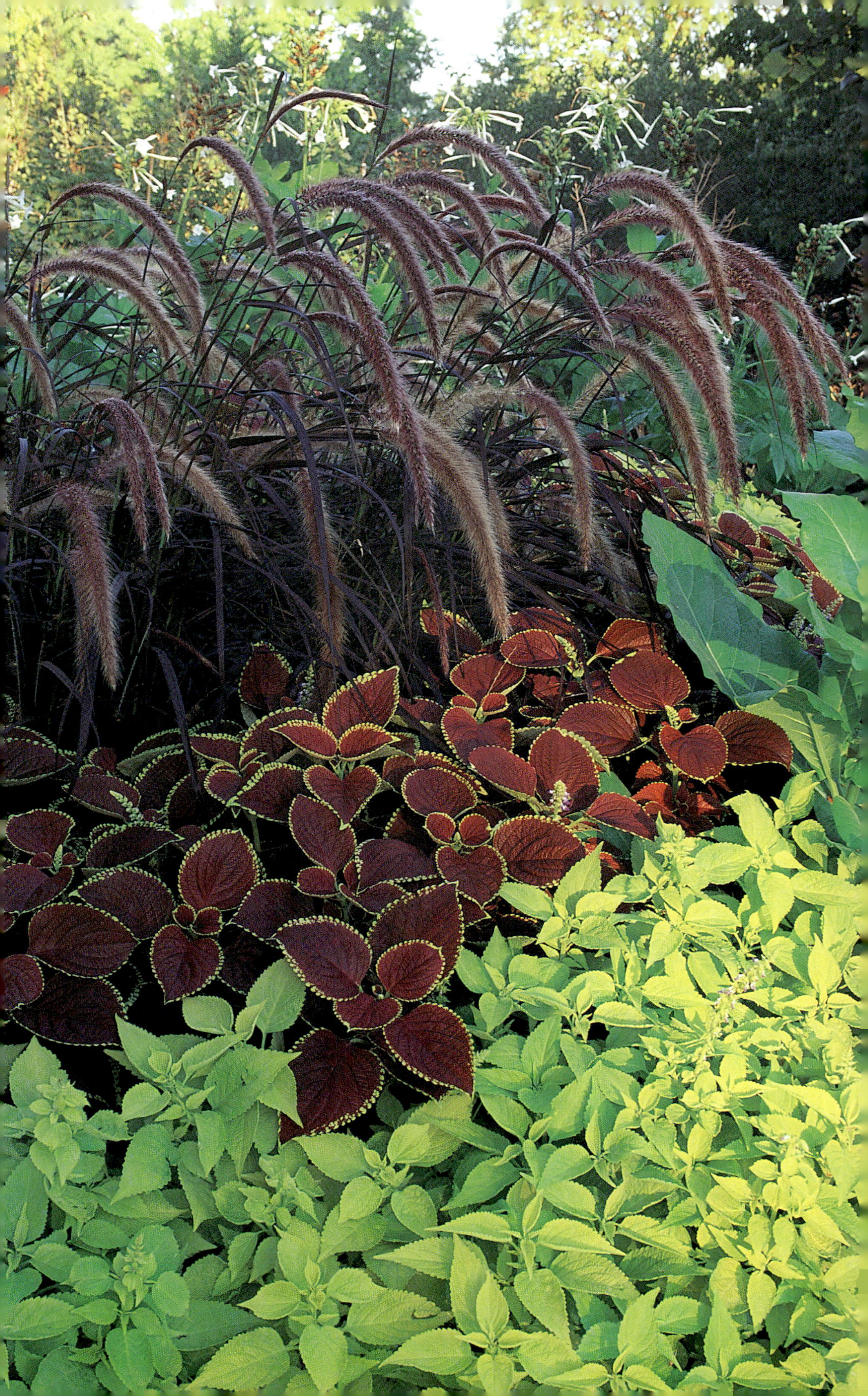

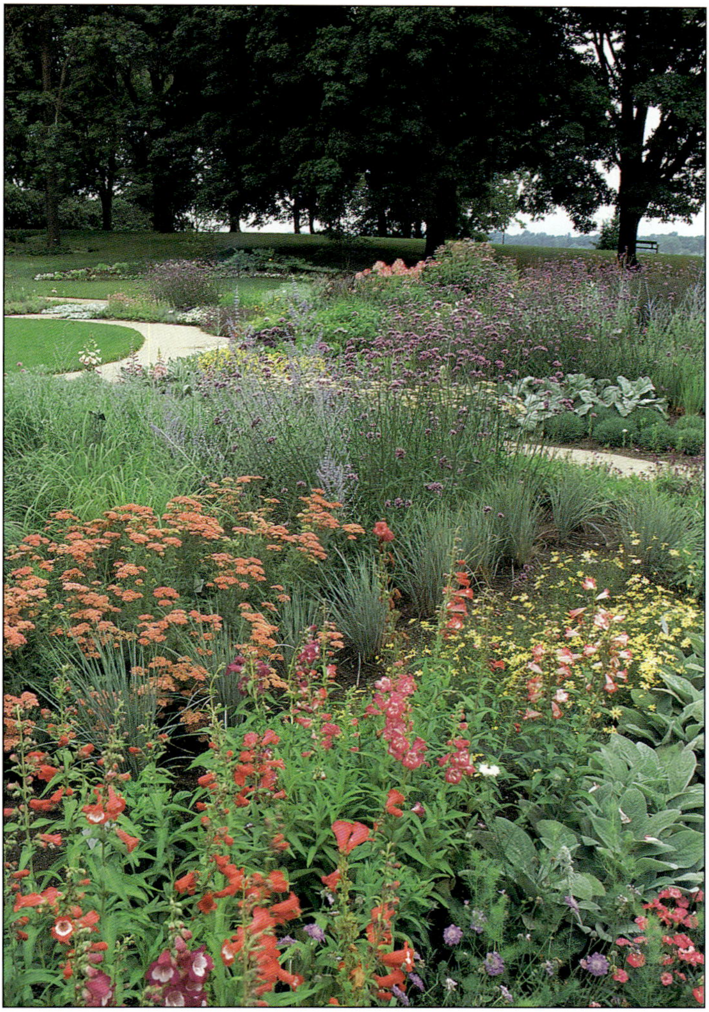

Where contrasting color values coexist, as they do in this shot of Wisconsin's Boerner Botanical Garden, you should expose for the middle range. Here, good exposure on the reddish brown coleus caused acceptable overexposure in the light greens and underexposure in the shadows. Shooting with a Zuiko 35-70mm lens set at 70mm; I exposed for 1/125 sec. at *f*/11 on Fujichrome 100.

Uniform overcast light simplified exposure for this overview of Noerenberg Garden in Lake Minnetonka, Minnesota, despite considerable color contrasts. I metered the brighter foreground plantings to render the row of trees dark. This provided an effective backdrop that also screened the dull sky. With a Zuiko 28mm lens, I exposed Ektachrome 100 SW at *f*/11 for 1/60 sec.

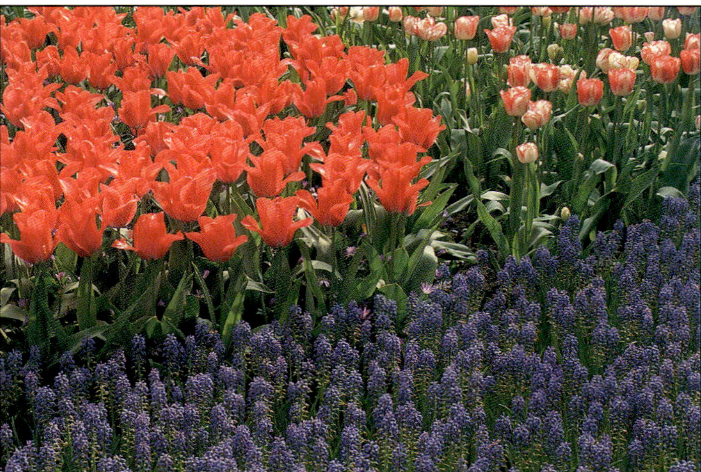

In this detail of a private garden in Holland, careful metering on the middle-toned reds kept all the colors vivid and maintained translucence on the brightly backlit flowers. Here, I used a Zuiko 50-250mm lens set at 200mm. The exposure was 1/125 sec. at *f*/16 on Fujichrome Velvia.

Metering the gray stone simplified exposure on this water garden at Courrances in France. And the dim, late day light was ideal for using a slow shutter speed to render the flowing waters of the fountain a milky white. With a Sonnar 80mm lens, I exposed for 1/8 sec. at *f*/16 on Ektachrome EPN.

Instead of aiming for perfectly white snow, which would have reduced detail in this bright sunlight, I overexposed the tree by only half a stop. This kept the snow acceptably white and maintained crispness in the textures on this winter scene at the New York Botanical Garden in the Bronx, New York. Shooting with a Zuiko 50-250mm lens set at 100mm, I exposed for 1/250 sec. at *f*/11 on Fujichrome 50.

Metering the steel gray sky, which was roughly equal to an 18 percent gray card, properly exposed the green of the grass and yellow of the forsythia in this dramatic prestorm image shot at the New York Botanical Garden in the Bronx, New York. To be on the safe side, check that all colors fall within 1 1/2 *f*-stops of the meter reading and bracket accordingly. Working with a Zuiko 35-70mm lens set at 40mm, I exposed at *f*/5.6 for 1/60 sec. on Fujichrome 50.

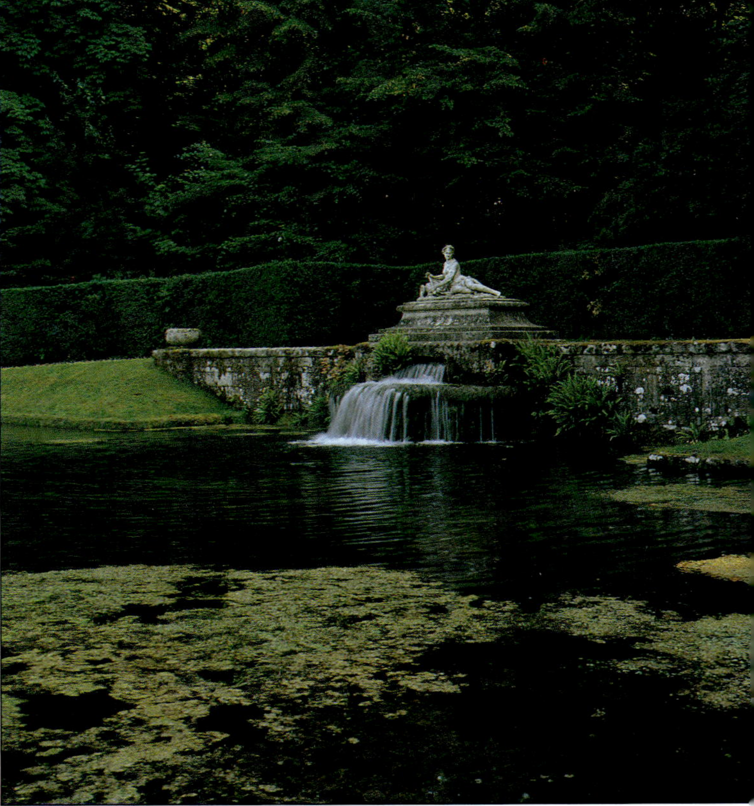

- Photograph gardens in low-contrast illumination, which is present on overcast days, early in the morning, and late in the afternoon. Meter the middle intensities in the scene to avoid the pitfall of underexposure.
- Within a given light intensity, expose for light plant colors, even though dark colors will be a bit underexposed. Such color saturation often enriches the colors in a garden and makes them more lush.
- Use a polarizer to reduce or eliminate glare in bright light; this will reduce contrast and make metering easier.
- Meter from as close to your main subject as possible. Otherwise, use a spot meter or telephoto lens to pinpoint meter readings with accuracy, especially in high-contrast light.
- In extreme low-contrast light and in a garden with plants of similar color, increase contrast by pushing the film one *f*-stop. This procedure works best with high-contrast film, such as Fujichrome Velvia.

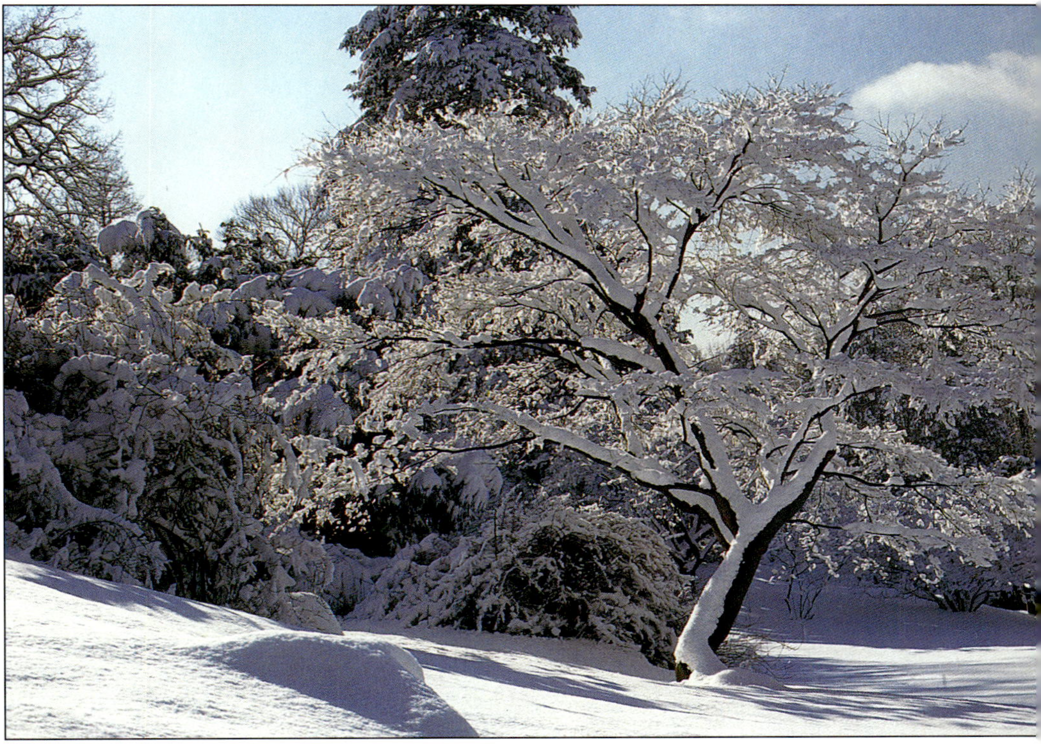

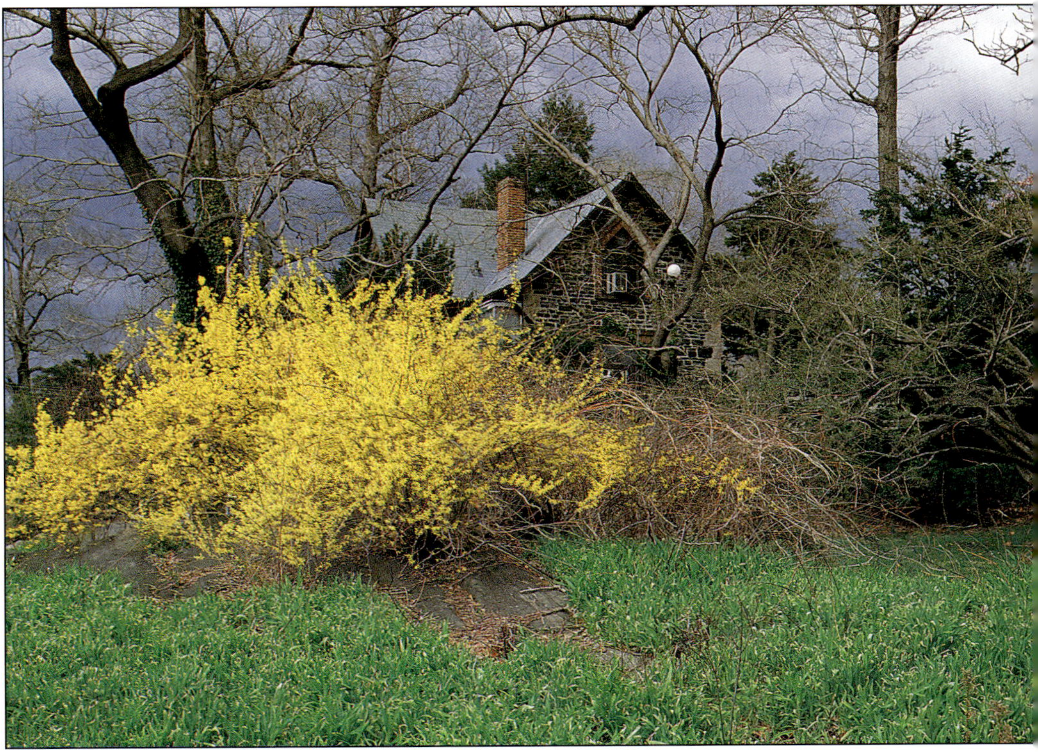

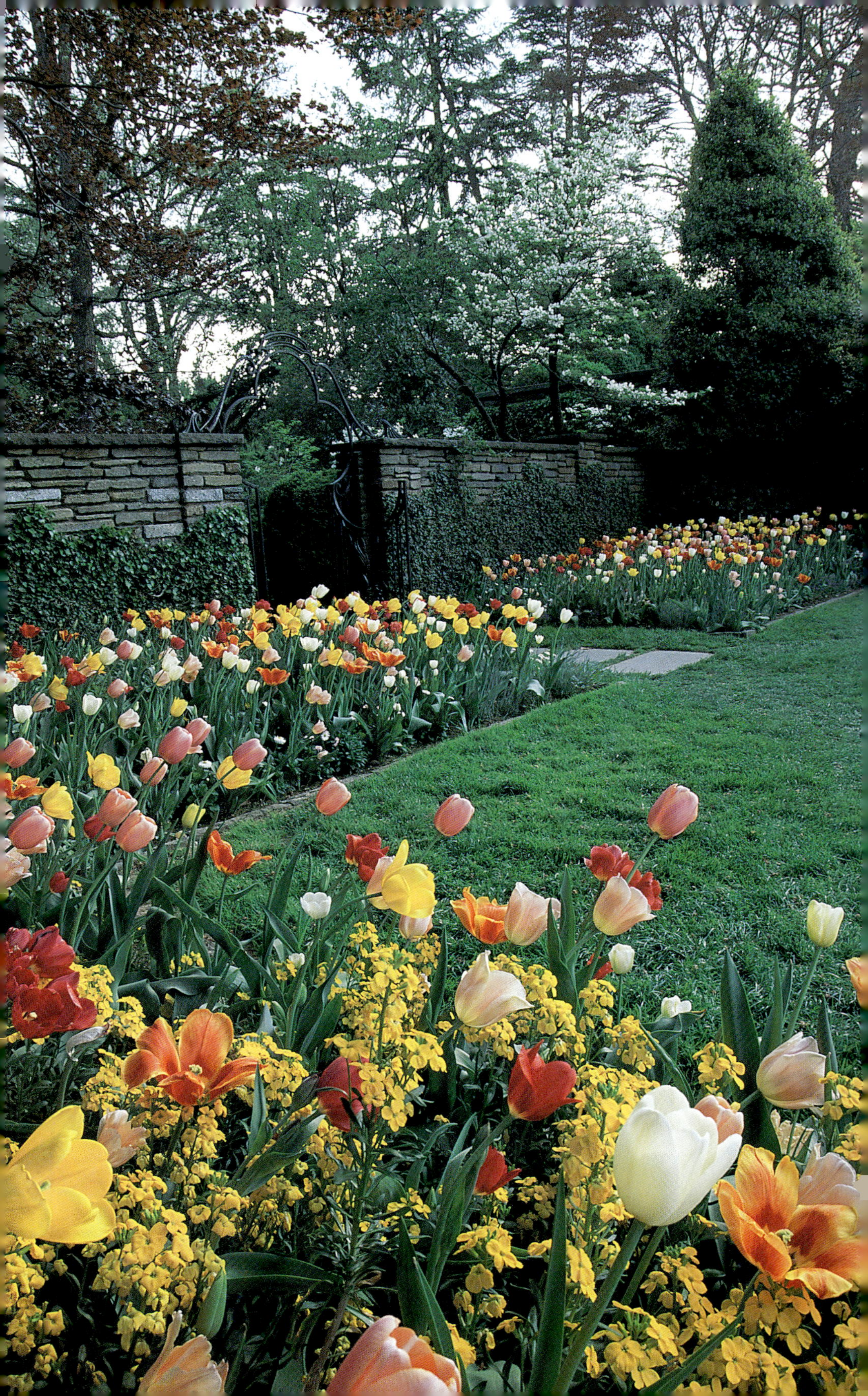

CHAPTER 5

Mastering Camera Techniques

The extreme sharpness of this overview of Washington, DC's Dumbarton Oaks comes from my maximizing depth of field with a very small aperture, precise focusing 1/3 of the way into the frame, and waiting for the wind to stop before shooting. With a Zuiko 35-70mm lens set at 35mm, I exposed Fujichrome Velvia at *f*/16-22 for 1/15 sec.

In this vignette of Milwaukee, Wisconsin's Mitchell Park Conservatory, I achieved maximum sharpness by stopping down the lens to *f*/11, focusing on the yellow coreopsis in the center, and waiting for the wind to stop before releasing the shutter. Here, I used a Zuiko 35-70mm lens set at 50mm and exposed Fujichrome Velvia for 1/15 sec.

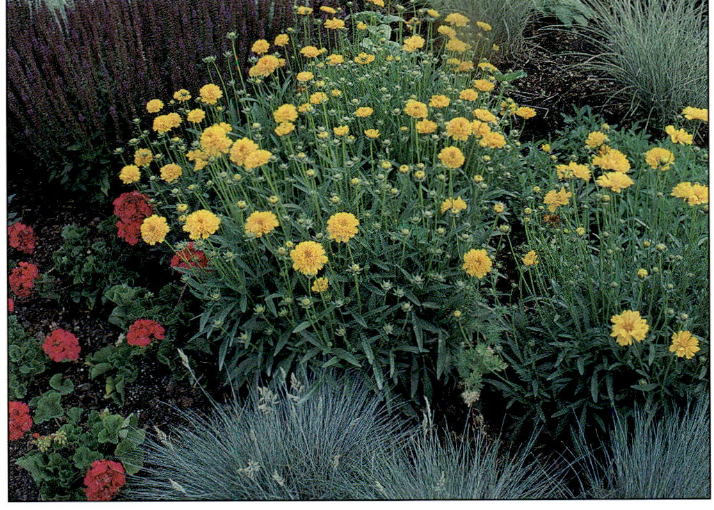

What techniques do you need to know in order to take outstanding garden photographs? Essentially, they boil down to a few. First, you must know which lens to choose for the kind of image you want to create. You also have to be able to recognize the quality of the available light, as well as to make it work for you in terms of good exposure and excellent atmosphere. And you must understand how to get the degree of sharpness you want in your shot.

Moving back for a high vantage point and choosing a wide-angle lens to encompass this overview of Mansfield, Ohio's Kingwood Center also served to increase depth of field and sharpness. Working with a Zuiko 21mm lens, I exposed Ektachrome 100 S for 1/15 sec. at *f*/16.

Separating the foreground roses from the backdrop while keeping this Villandry, France, setting identifiable required selective sharpness. To achieve this, I moved close to the roses and limited depth of field via a wide aperture. With a Zuiko 24mm lens, I exposed for 1/125 sec. at *f*/4-5.6 on Fujichrome 100.

This chapter looks closely and carefully at the issue of sharpness because it is so central to effective garden photography. Whether you're shooting an overview of a garden scene, a vignette of a group of plantings, or a detail of a flower, you must be in control of what is sharp.

This isn't to suggest, however, that all garden photographs must be ultra-sharp. You might want a perfectly sharp garden overview but a partial blur for your vignette. You might prefer a razor-sharp floral closeup but only be able to keep a portion of the flower in sharp focus. So it is especially important that you are clear in your own mind about what has to be sharp and what doesn't.

Your decision might be based on an aesthetic preference. For example, you might want a slightly blurred background so that the foreground roses stand out better. Alternately, your decision might reflect practical considerations. For example, you might not be able to shoot at a fast enough shutter speed to prevent some blurring of the windblown grasses you're photographing in relatively dim light. The point is to come to these decisions about image sharpness with knowledge and an ability to previsualize the outcome.

Image sharpness depends on a number of interrelated factors that are at the heart of the concept of "photographic seeing." As you master these technical aspects of photography, you'll learn how to control one of the keys to its creative possibilities. To maintain the highest possible degree of control over sharpness in your garden photographs, use a tripod whenever possible, especially when you shoot in low-intensity light. (Some gardens restrict the use of a tripod or require prior arrangements, so check in advance if you're planning to photograph in an unfamiliar garden.)

FINDING THE RIGHT DEPTH OF FIELD

One of the chief differences between the way the human eye sees and the way the camera sees has to do with sharpness. The eye is quite resilient and has the ability to shift quickly back and forth, focusing on a

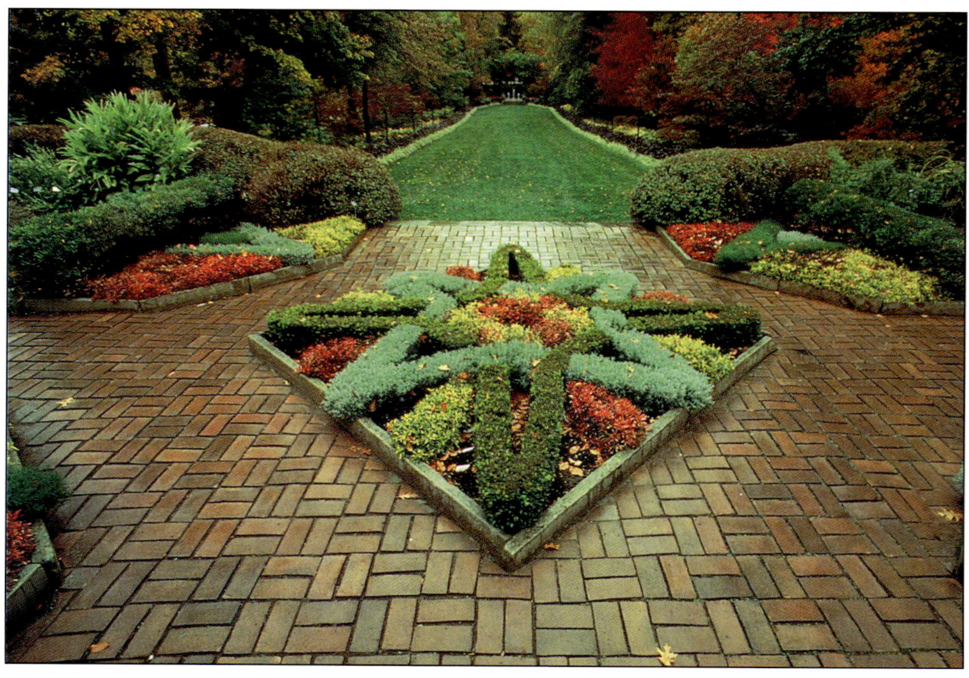

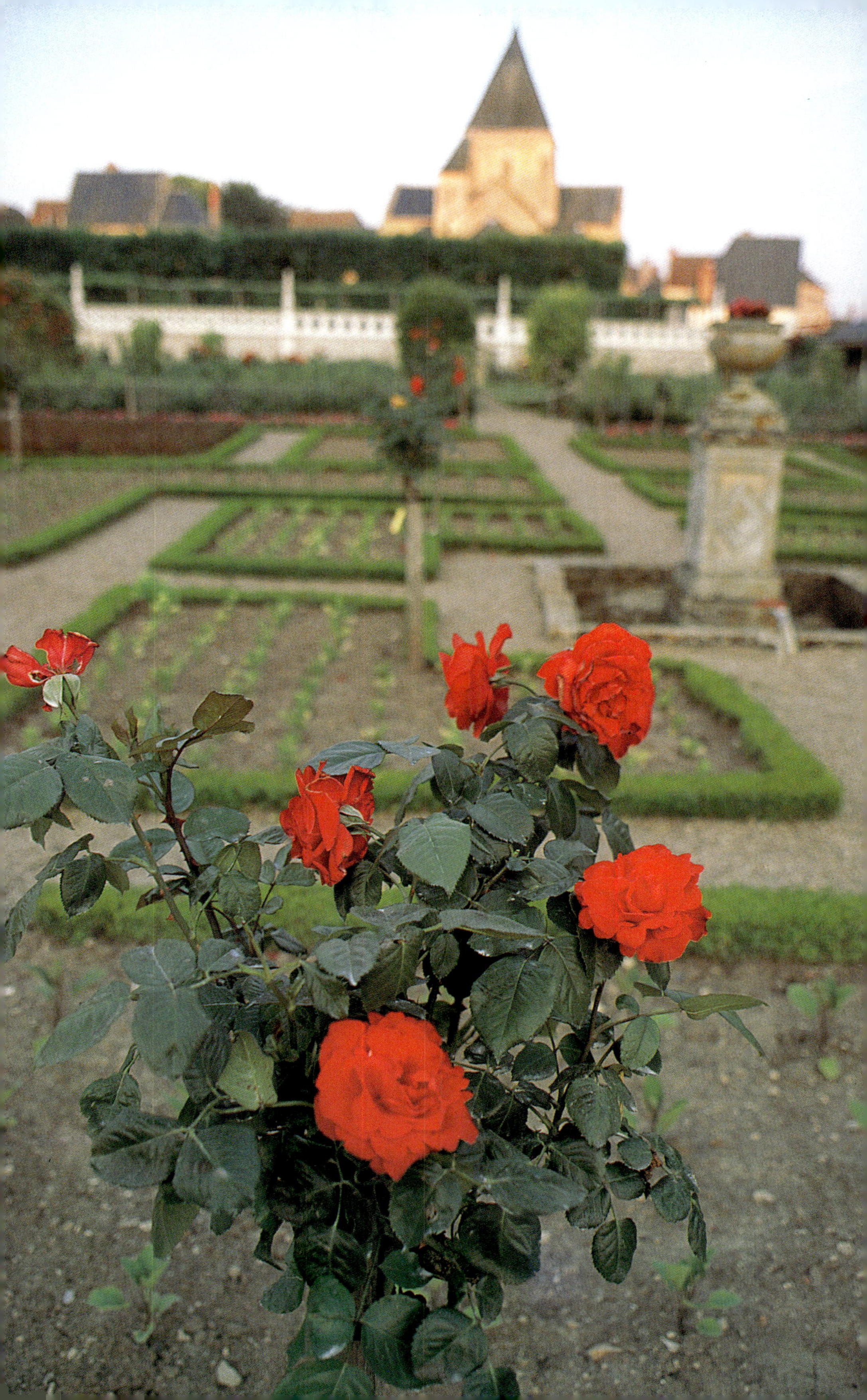

Floral closeups often work well against a soft, blurry background. To obtain that effect in this detail of pansies in a private Alabama garden, I used a small aperture to maintain sharpness and a telephoto macro lens close in to limit depth of field. Shooting with a Zuiko 90mm macro lens, I exposed Ektachrome 100 SW for 1/30 sec. at *f*/11.

close subject one moment and a more distant one the next. Of course, when you focus on something close, the surroundings are out of focus. But you don't really notice this because as soon as you glance upward, your eyes adjust to the new focal distance. You see a blur only if you have bad eyesight, but it is a blur you can't control.

Photographic seeing is quite different. A defined area of sharpness forward and back from the focal point—the exact point on which you're focusing—exists. This area of sharpness is referred to as depth of field. It varies with the size of the aperture, the distance between you and your subject, and the type of lens you're using. Keep in mind the following points about depth of field as you shoot.

- The smaller the aperture, the greater the depth of field.
- The farther away the subject is, the greater the depth of field.
- The wider the lens, the greater the depth of field.

So, to maximize the range of sharpness, whether in garden or general photography, select a small aperture, move back from your subject, and use a wide-angle lens. Keep these points in mind whenever you're shooting a broad garden expanse or if you want to be sure that a foreground

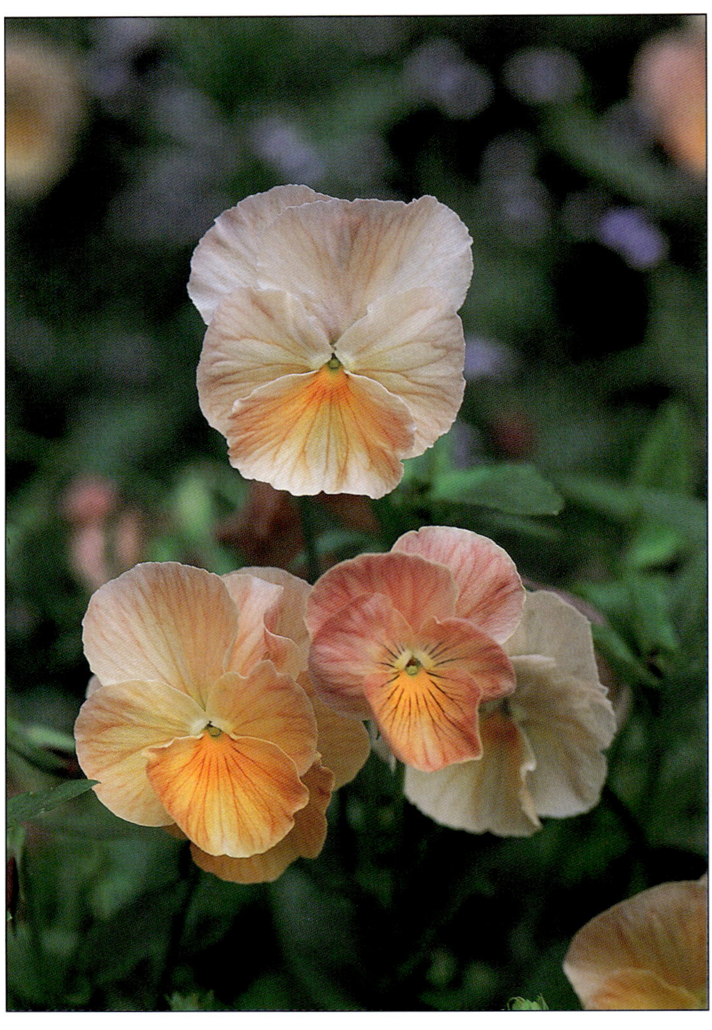

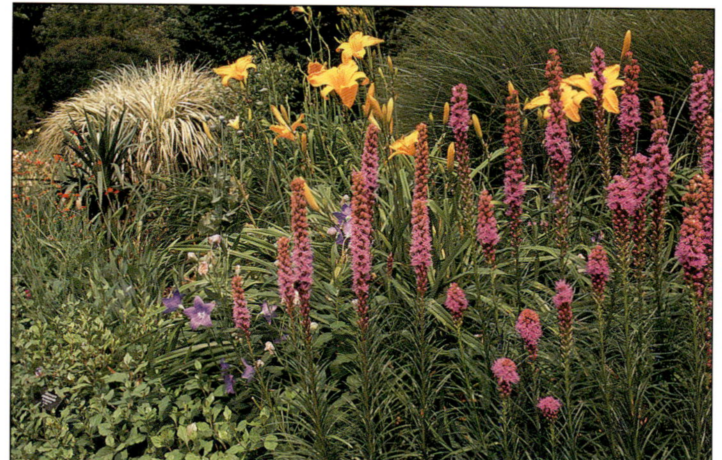

To maximize depth of field, I photographed this telephoto vignette of New York's Wave Hill with a small aperture. Precise focusing on the day lilies, about 1/3 of the way into the frame, also helped extend the range of sharpness. Here, I used a Zuiko 35-70mm lens set at 70mm and exposed Ektachrome 100 SW at *f*/16 for 1/60 sec.

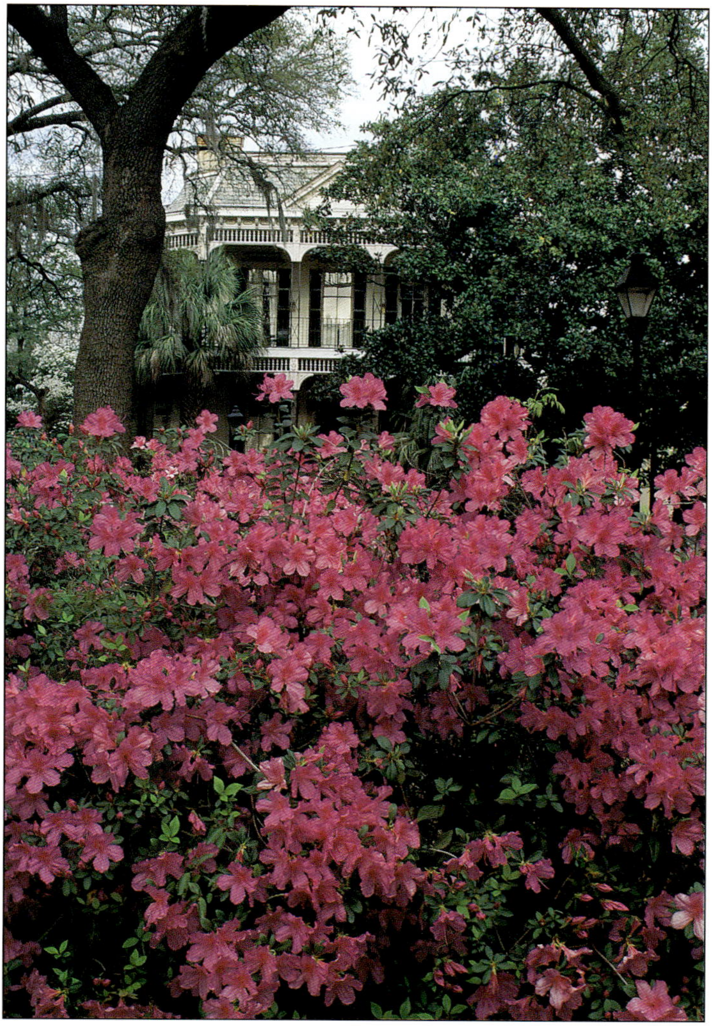

I wanted to get both the foreground azaleas and the Savannah, Georgia, setting sharp, so I had to use a small aperture and a wide-angle lens. Shooting with a Zuiko 35-70mm lens set at 35mm, I exposed at *f*/16 for 1/60 sec. on Ektachrome 100 SW.

With a point-and-shoot camera with automatic exposure, control over sharpness depends on careful focusing and using a tripod. In this photograph taken at Florida's Epcot Center, my locking the focus on the tree increased the range of sharpness while the shaded, uniformly illuminated setting rendered the automatic exposure reliable. Here, I used an Olympus Stylus Zoom 115 and Ektachrome 100 SW.

floral display and the building some distance behind it are both sharp. If you can't utilize all three factors, use as many as you can to increase the depth of field. Suppose you are in a conservatory or on a narrow path where you can't move back. Just use your aperture setting and a wide-angle lens to extend the range of sharpness.

Conversely, to restrict the range of sharpness to a narrow "slice of the scene," select a wide-open aperture, move close to your subject, and use a telephoto lens. The camera's ability to narrow the range of focus is particularly handy when you want to blur the area behind a group of flowers to help them stand out in sharp relief or to camouflage an unappealing backdrop. It also enhances shots that isolate a cross section of plantings in what looks like a slice of the scene, where both foreground and background vegetation are blurred, and only the essential subject remains sharp. Keep in mind that the areas of greatest sharpness aren't equal in both directions from the focal point. As a rule of thumb, the area of sharpness in an image extends 1/3 forward and 2/3 back from the focal point.

For most garden photographs—certainly for documentary-style overviews, vignettes, and details—you'll want the greatest sharpness

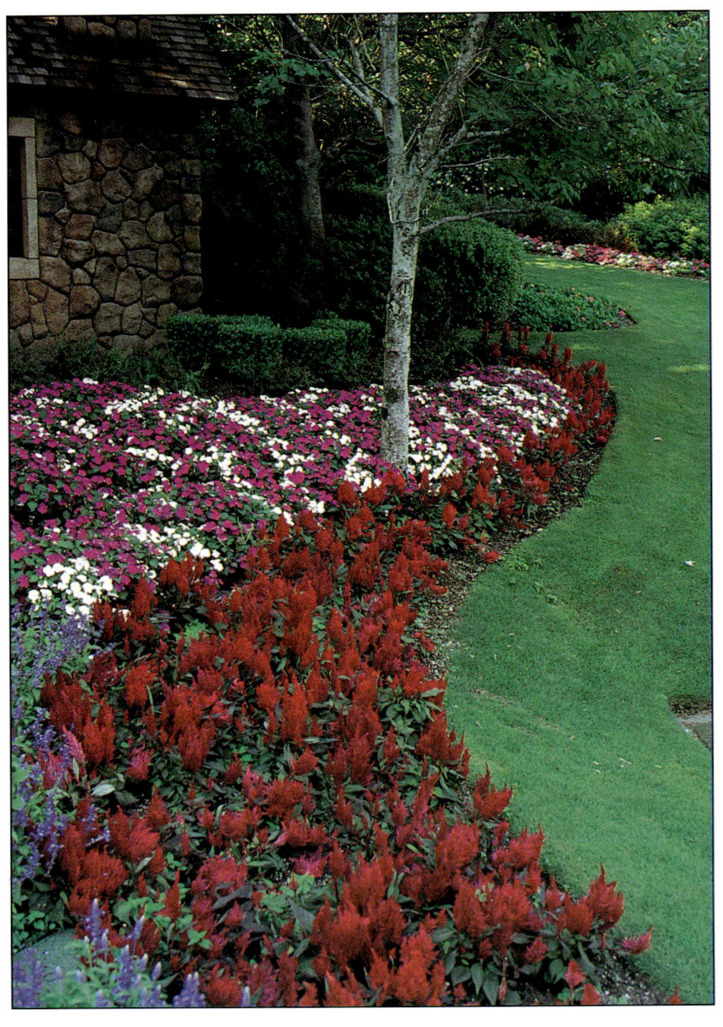

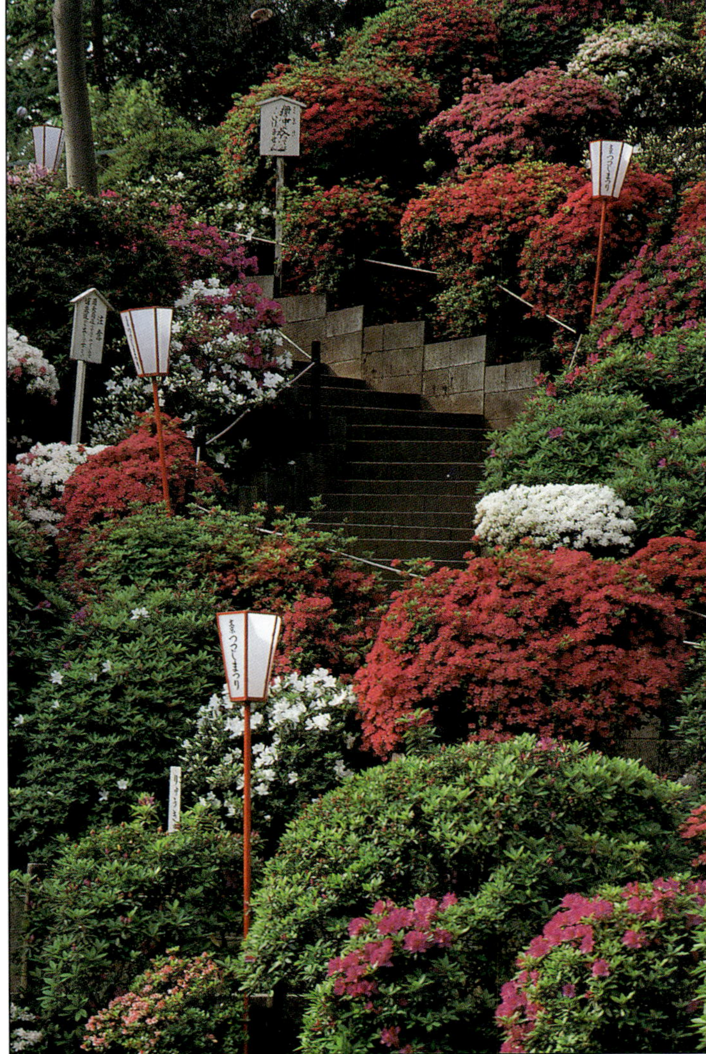

Even though this telephoto shot of an azalea garden in Tokyo, Japan, was made at an aperture setting of *f*/5.6, it is fairly sharp because it was taken from a distance of 200-300 feet. Windy conditions required a fast shutter speed of 1/125 sec. and precluded using a smaller aperture. Here, I used a Zuiko 50-250mm lens set at 200mm and Fujichrome 100.

throughout the frame and, therefore, the greatest depth of field. However, impressionistic images of gardens should be part of your visual repertoire, and one way to create them is by limiting the depth of field. For example, through selective and deliberate blurring, you can transform unsightly background distractions into a wash of glorious color as a backdrop for a floral closeup.

Of course, your distance from the subject and lens choice aren't dictated only by considerations of sharpness. These decisions should suit your sense of composition—what you want to include and how much of the frame it should occupy. So you should concentrate on aperture settings and see how they affect sharpness.

SETTING THE APERTURE

If you care only about sharpness and maximum depth of field, what aperture setting should you use? As a rule of thumb, a small aperture setting, such as *f*/11, will give you the sharpest image possible, whether you're

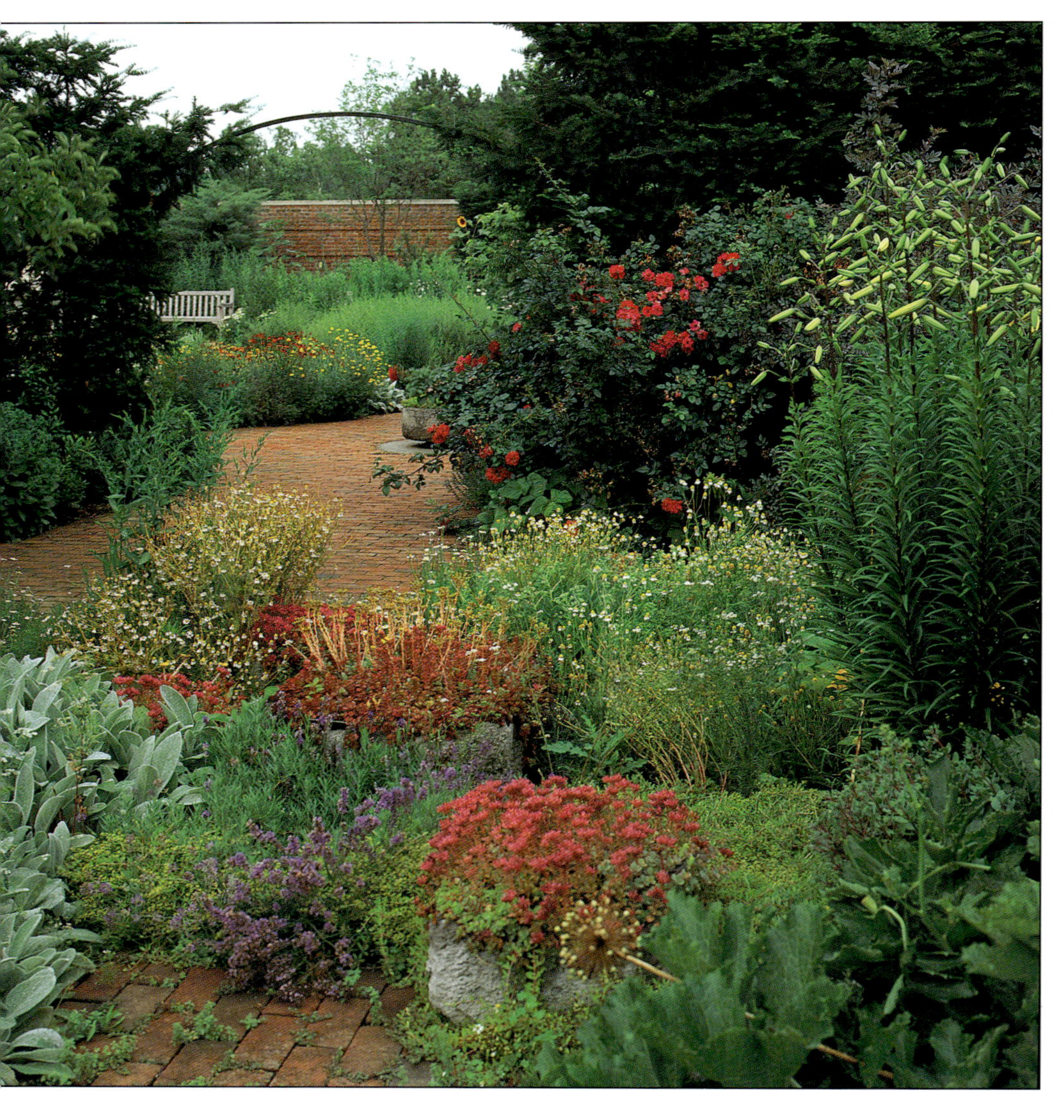

Despite my using a very small aperture and a wide-angle, medium-format lens for this vignette at the Chicago Botanic Garden in Glencoe, Illinois, some sharpness had to go to create this composition, with its close foreground plants. Working with a Distagon 50mm lens, I exposed for 1/30 sec. at *f*/16 on Fujichrome Velvia.

A bright day enabled me to use a small aperture (although a smaller setting would have been preferable) and a fast shutter speed to achieve sharpness, despite windy conditions at this iris garden in New Jersey. With a Zuiko 35-70mm lens set at 50mm, I exposed at *f*/11 for 1/125 sec. on Kodachrome 25.

From a distance of 30-40 feet, a point-and-shoot camera was far enough away from the subject at the New York Botanical Garden in the Bronx, New York, to achieve reasonable sharpness even at automatic aperture and shutter-speed settings. Here, I used an Olympus Stylus Zoom 115 and Kodachrome 25.

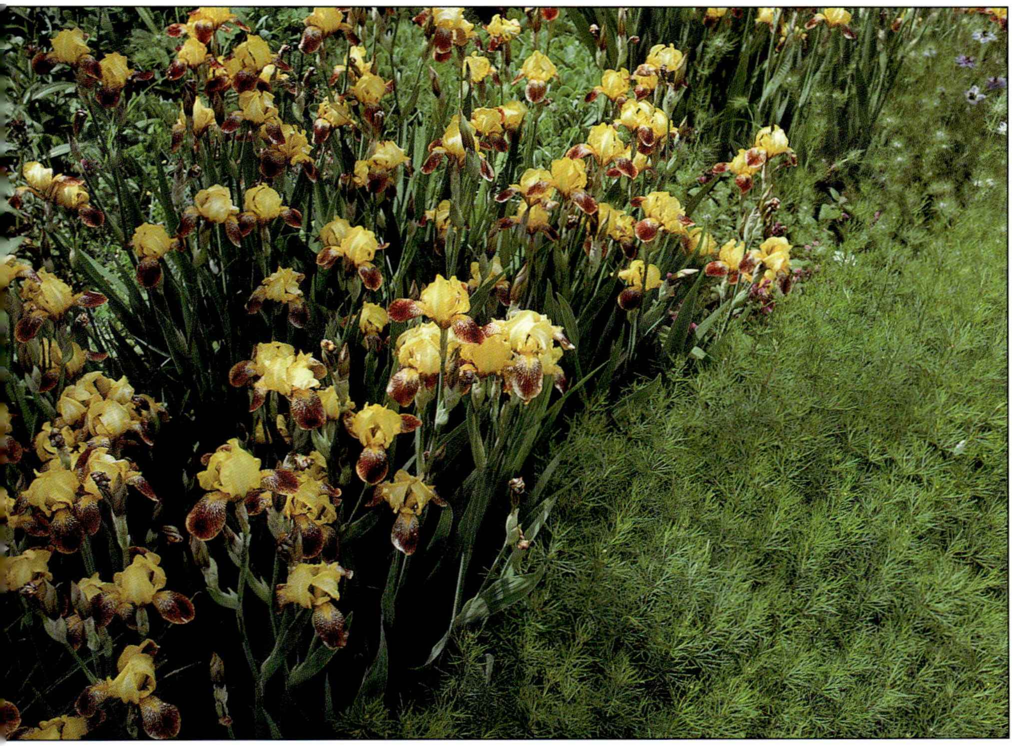

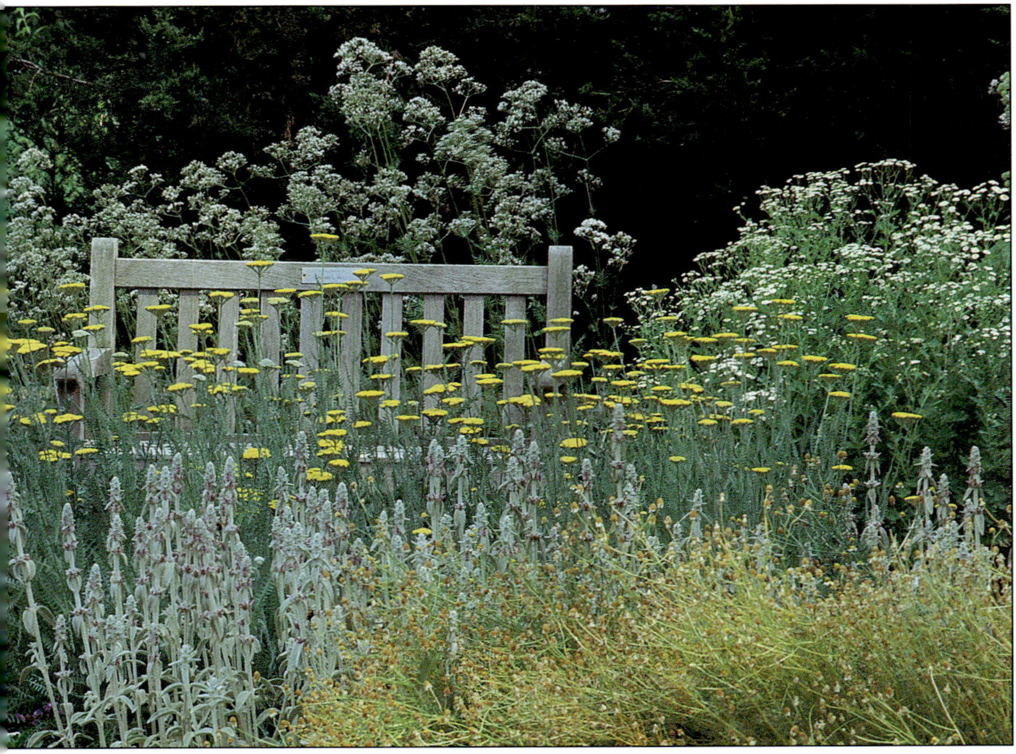

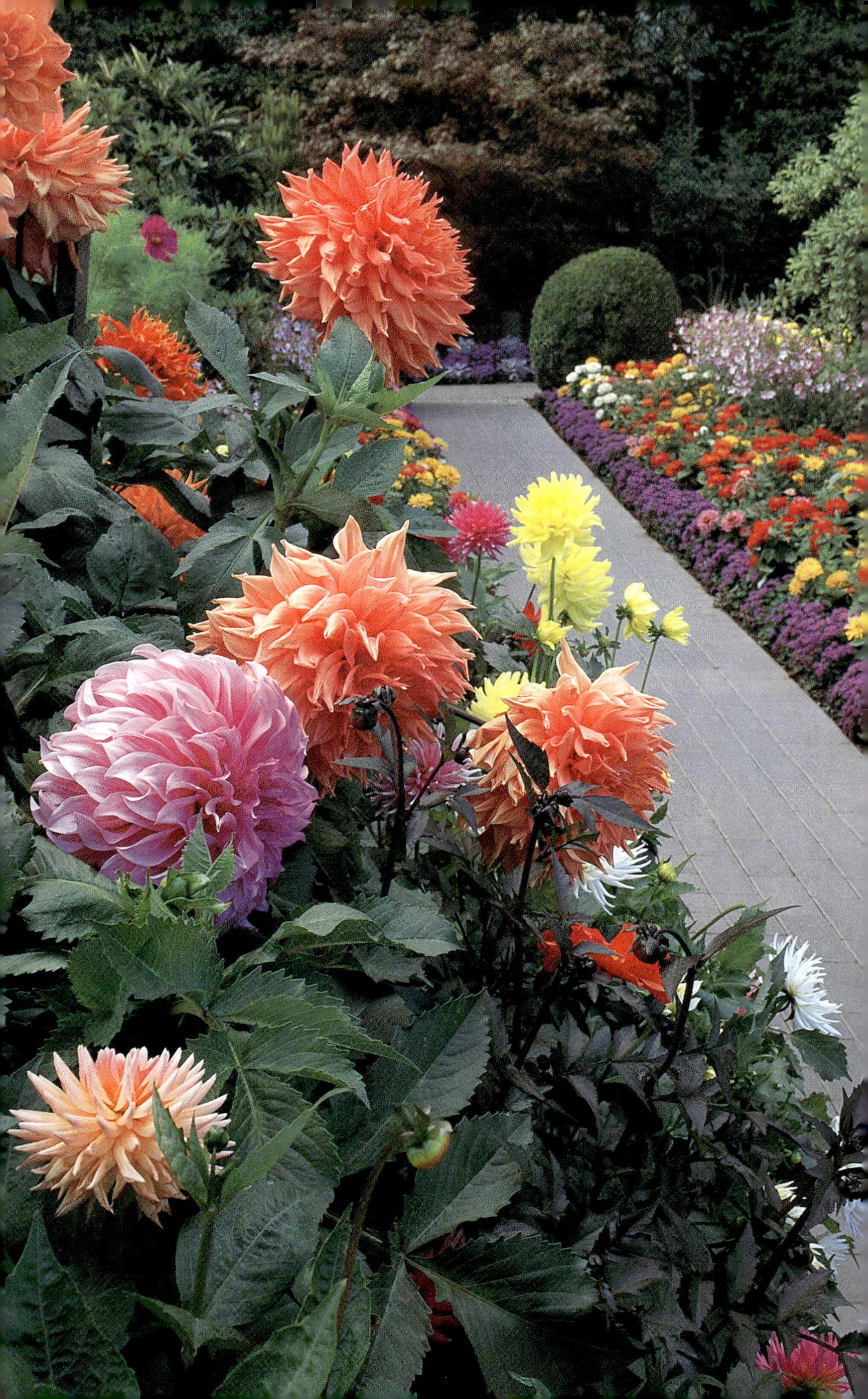

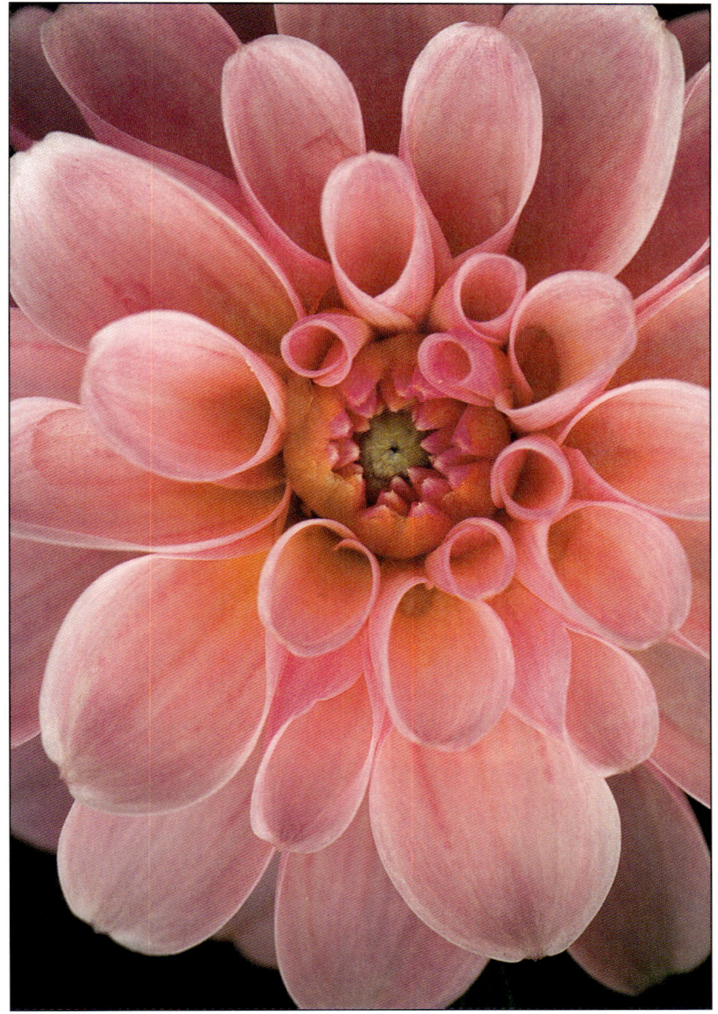

A windy day at Buchart Gardens in Victoria, British Columbia, required a fast shutter speed to freeze the movement of the dahlias. The moderate aperture setting, together with careful focusing on the foreground orange dahlias, maintained sharpness in the foreground, although the background is slightly blurred because of the limited depth of field. Shooting with a Zuiko 35-70mm lens set at 35mm, I exposed Fujichrome Velvia for 1/125 sec. at *f*/5.6.

By waiting for this wind-tossed dahlia in an Anchorage, Alaska, garden to come to a stop, I was able to use a slow shutter speed and a reasonably small aperture. A smaller aperture would have required a slower shutter speed, which wasn't acceptable for stopping movement. Working with a Zuiko 90mm macro lens, I exposed for 1/8 sec. at *f*/11 on Ektachrome 64 EPX.

shooting overviews, vignettes, or details. (Most professionals don't recommend using the camera's smallest aperture because the lens isn't sharpest at that setting; one *f*-stop below the highest *f*-stop is considered the optimum setting for getting maximum depth of field. For example, on an *f*/22 lens, *f*/16 produces maximum depth of field.)

But the aperture setting, working together with the shutter speed, also controls exposure by varying the amount of light that hits the film. If you're photographing on a bright, sunny, wind-less day, you shouldn't have any problem. And if your camera is on a tripod, as it should be, you can easily afford to use the optimal aperture.

However, your best aperture setting for sharpness might not be an option if the prevailing light is dim and you're contending with windy conditions. If the wind is blowing in occasional gusts with calm periods in between or in a fairly constant stream, you might be able to shoot those wind-tossed grasses or flowers with the best aperture setting, provided you can anticipate those moments of calm. Otherwise, you might have to give priority to using a fast shutter speed to freeze movement. And that would force you to use a wider aperture to maintain proper

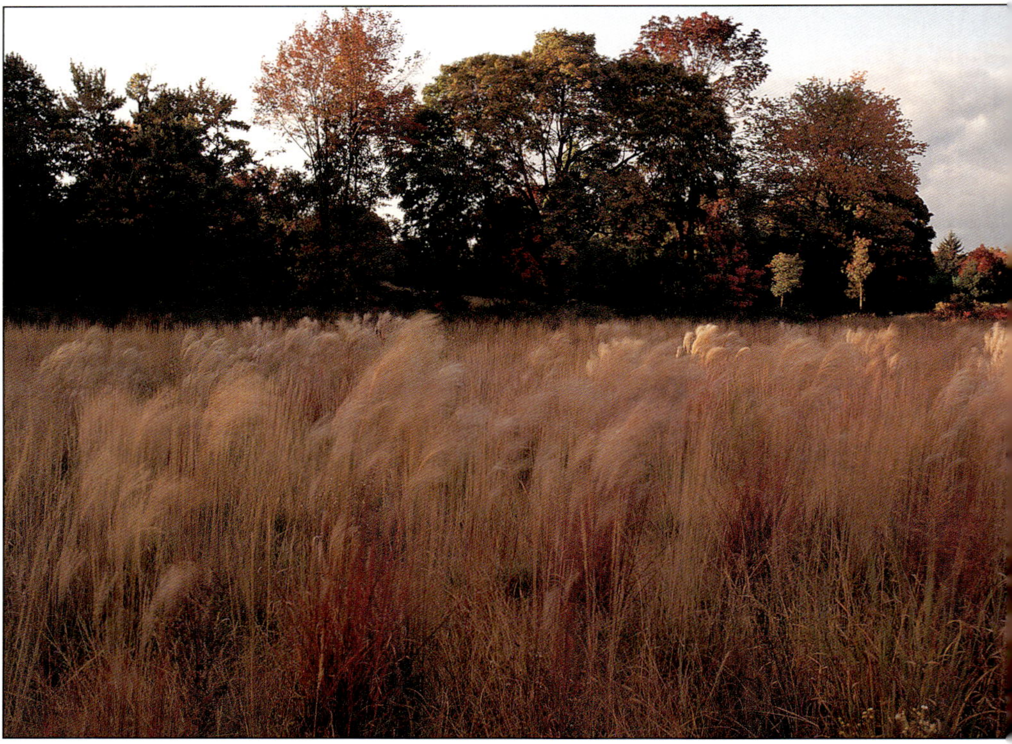

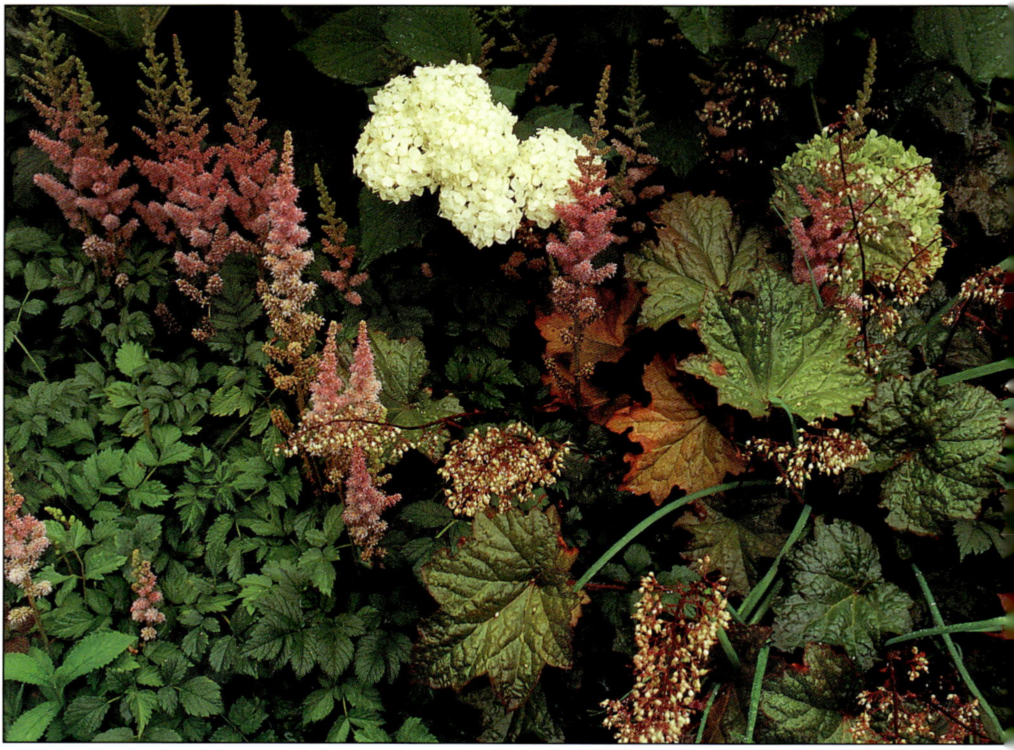

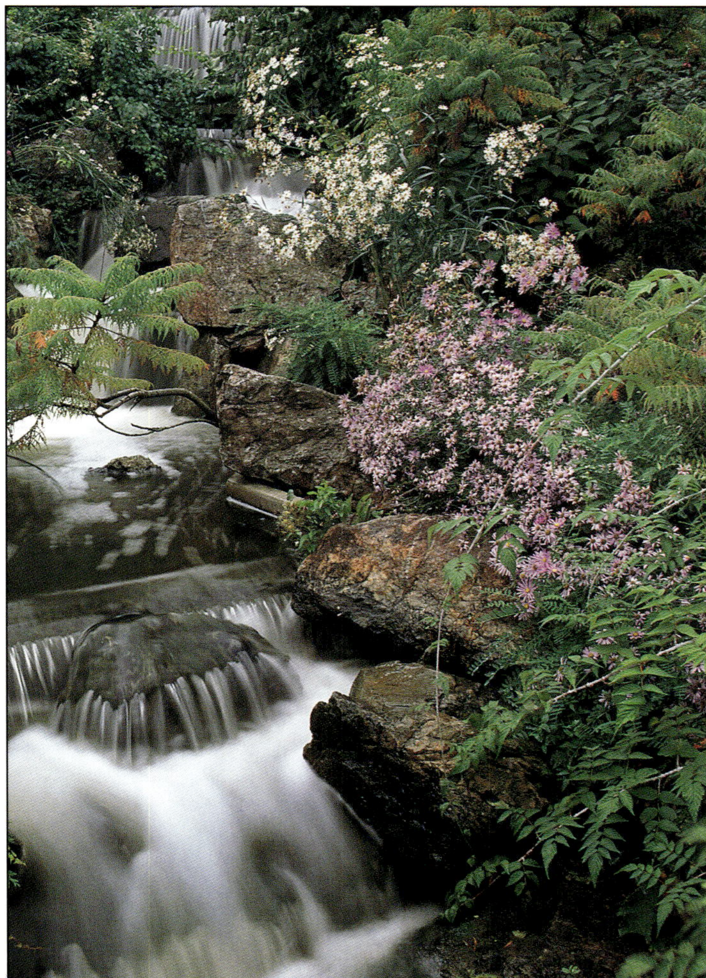

A deliberately slow shutter speed caught the movement of these swaying grasses at Becton Dickinson World Headquarters in New Jersey and permitted the use of a small aperture despite the dim light. With a Zuiko 35-70mm lens set at 35mm, I exposed for 1/4 sec. at *f*/16 on Fujichrome 100.

Cameras with automatic-exposure features are generally programmed to select the fastest possible shutter speed for the available light. Here, in dim light, the shutter speed would be slow, so sharpness depended on waiting until the breeze stopped blowing the astilbes at New York City's Conservatory Garden. Here, I used an Olympus Stylus Zoom 115 and Ektachrome 100 SW.

Even with a two-stop neutral-density filter and a very small aperture setting, a shutter speed of 1/8 sec. was the slowest possible to record the flow of water in this stream at the Chicago Botanic Garden in Glencoe, Illinois, given the bright light conditions. Here, I used a Zuiko 35-70mm lens set at 35mm and exposed Ektachrome 64 EPX at *f*/22.

exposure, sacrificing some sharpness based on depth of field in the process.

COMING UP TO SHUTTER SPEED

Remember, sharpness is the product of several factors. The shutter speed affects image sharpness when you're working with a moving subject. So if you're shooting a garden on a perfectly still day, give priority to your aperture setting, even if this means using a slower shutter speed. You might be able to get a sharp image with slower exposures down to 1 sec., provided your camera is mounted on a tripod. But if the wind is blowing, you'll probably want to use a fast shutter speed.

As a rule of thumb, select a shutter speed of no less than 1/30 sec. for a sharp image in general garden photography. But suppose that you want to shoot closeups or shoot without a tripod. Here, you would set the shutter speed at 1/60 sec. or faster.

Of course, you can create wonderful effects with slow shutter speeds even if the wind is blowing. You have no hard and fast rules to adhere to, so experiment with shutter speeds of 1/2 sec. or more. Vary the speed according to the light and wind conditions. Bracket liberally.

For sharp reflections, such as this one shot at the Donald M. Kendall Sculpture Garden at PepsiCo World Headquarters in Purchase, New York, focus on the most important element in the reflection and use a small aperture to extend depth of field. Working with a Zuiko 35mm lens, I exposed at *f*/11 for 1/60 sec. on Kodachrome 25.

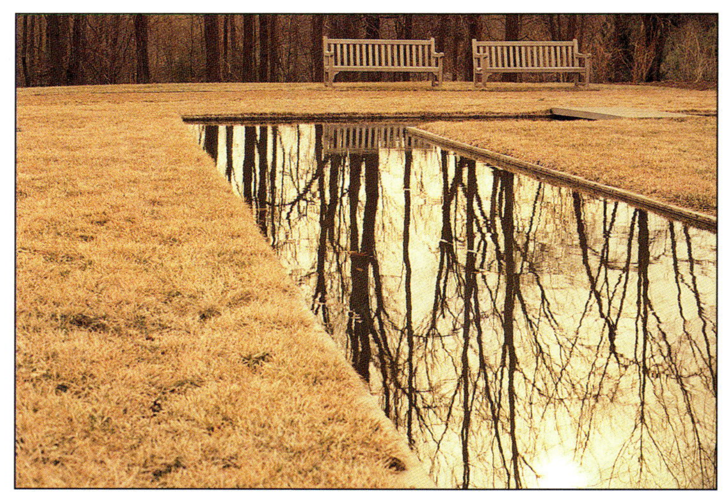

It is more important to focus on a prominent foreground subject than on distant background elements. In this LaGrange, Georgia, garden, the background mansion creates a sense of place without being sharp. Shooting with a Zuiko 21mm lens, I exposed Fujichrome Velvia at *f*/8 for 1/30 sec.

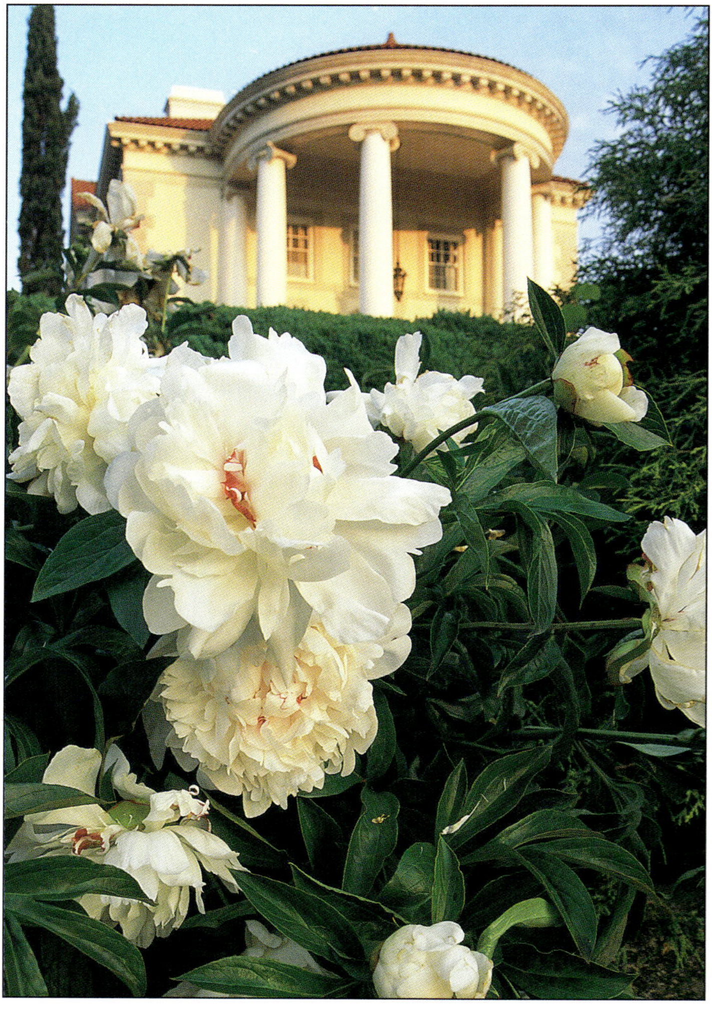

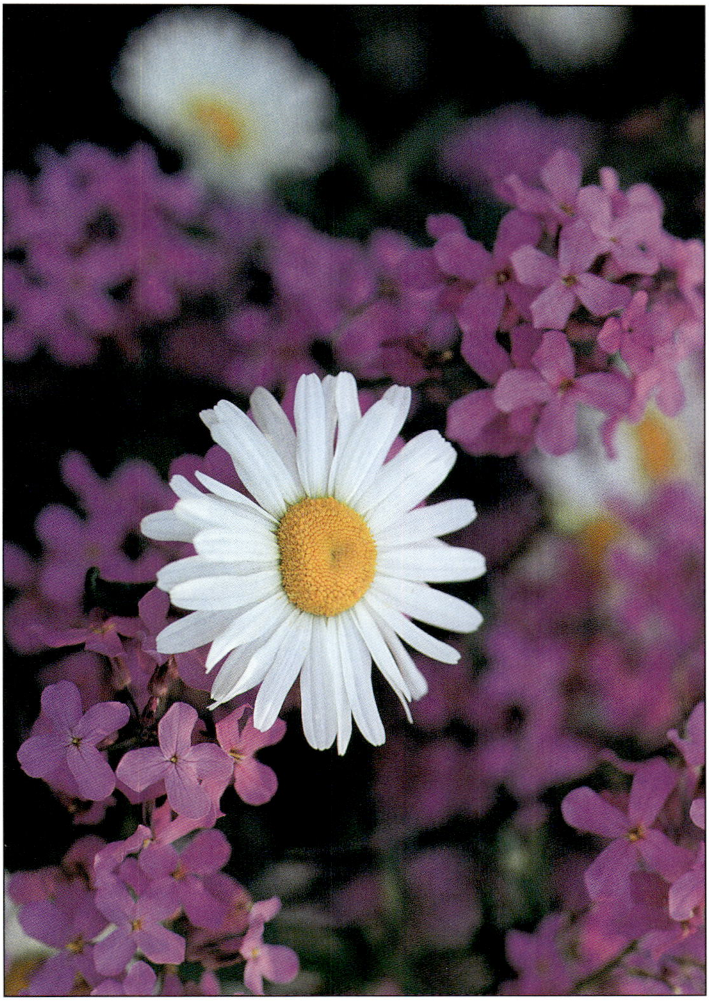

Only the daisy in this closeup of the Shakespeare Garden at Northwestern University in Evanston, Illinois, had to be sharp. Careful focusing provided that sharpness, while a wide-open aperture and a macro lens limited the depth of field for a fuzzy backdrop. With a Zuiko 90mm macro lens, I exposed for 1/60 sec. at *f*/4.5 on Ektachrome 64 EPX.

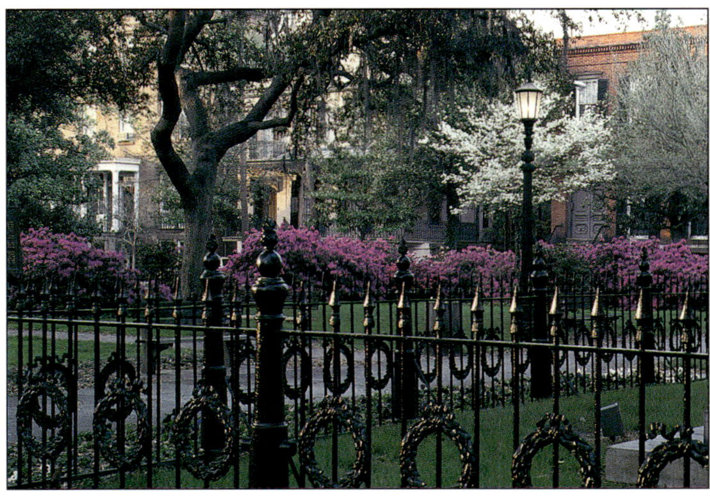

By moving back, focusing on the iron railing, and using a small aperture, I was able to achieve enough depth of field to maintain sharpness throughout this image of a Savannah, Georgia, mansion. Shooting with a Zuiko 35mm lens, I exposed Fujichrome 50 for 1/30 sec. at *f*/11.

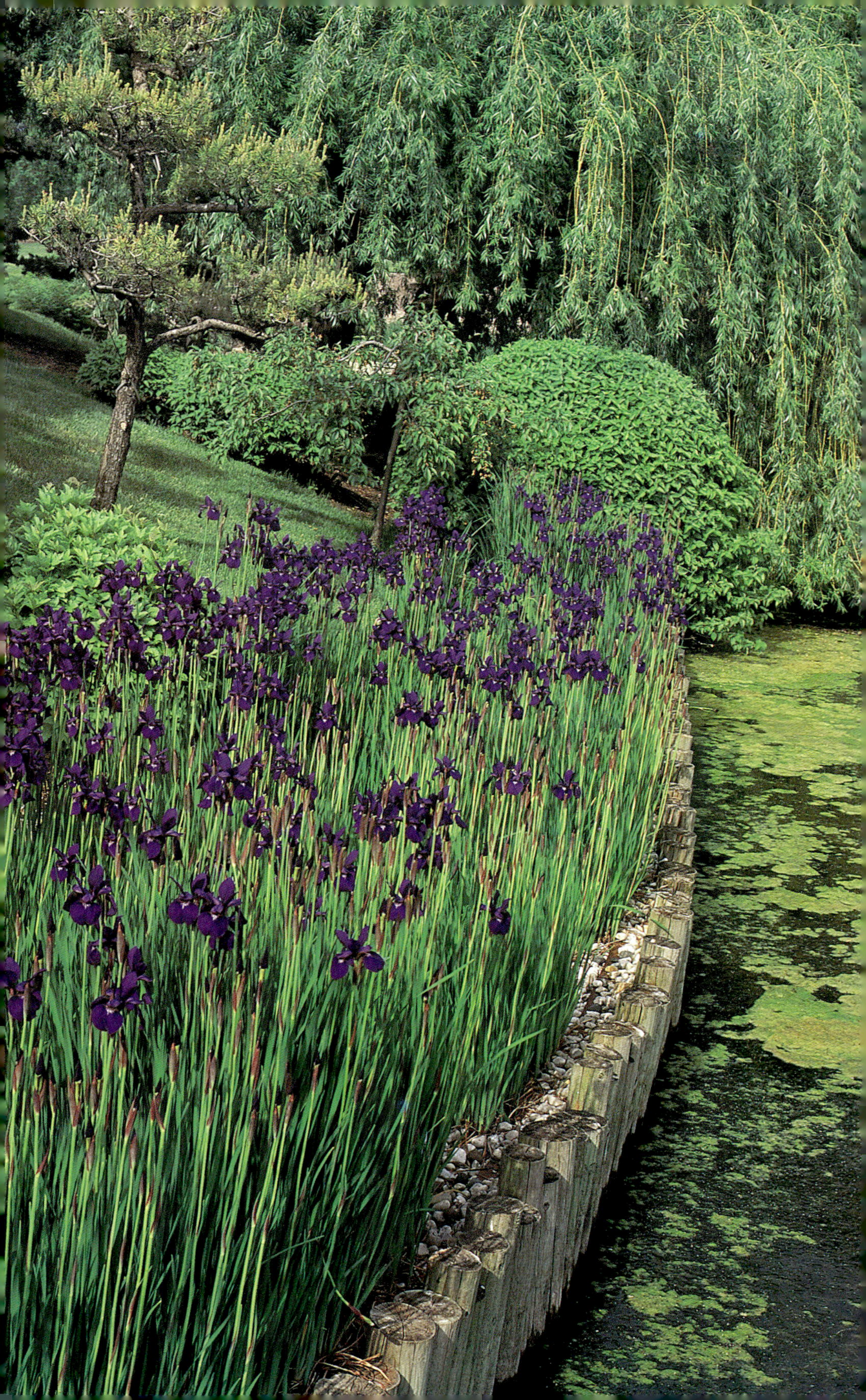

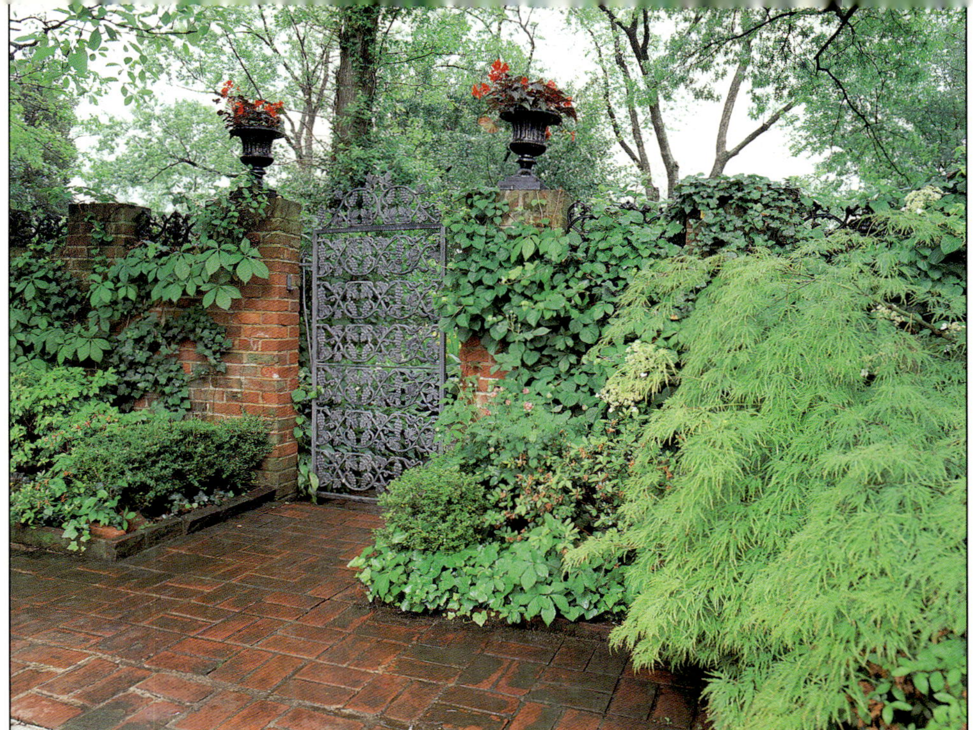

FINE-TUNING THE FOCUS

Once you've worked out the best combination of aperture setting and shutter speed for a sharp image, your next task is to focus on the most important element in the frame. Keep in mind that the depth of field determines the area of greatest sharpness, and that area goes forward and backward from the focal point. For optimal sharpness throughout the image, focus 1/3 into the frame. If you're using a fairly wide aperture setting (*f*/5.6 or wider), give priority to rendering the foreground plants sharp, even if this means the background goes slightly out of focus. If you find the backdrop distracting, narrow the depth of field even more and focus on the foreground.

On the other hand, you might want to deliberately throw the foreground out of focus to frame the scene interestingly or to isolate a slice of the scene. In this situation, narrow the depth of field and focus farther into the frame. Remember also that the depth of field decreases the closer you get to your subject and the narrower the scope of the lens.

Focusing is most critical in floral closeups because you are likely to be close and working with a macro or telephoto lens. Furthermore, movement is magnified at close range. So be especially precise about your focal point, choosing a particular feature within the flower to focus on. If the stamens and pistils are out of focus, the image will suffer much more than if the outer petals aren't quite sharp.

Cameras have a variety of focusing systems, and you should become familiar with yours. The easiest to use is a through-the-lens system with a preview button that shows you exactly what is in focus throughout the frame. However, a small aperture setting means that the preview image will be rather dark and difficult to decipher. Accurate, precise focusing takes patience and practice. Don't rush at this point after you've taken so much care with all the other techniques.

Since the gate was the most essential element of this vignette of a private garden in St. Louis, Missouri, I kept it in sharpest focus, even though this made the plants less sharp. Working with a Mamiya 65mm lens, I exposed Fujichrome Velvia for 1/15 sec. at *f*/22.

Focusing 1/3 of the way into the frame and shooting from a distance of 100 feet with a small aperture maximized sharpness on the many textures in this overview of the Chicago Botanic Garden in Glencoe, Illinois. Here, I used a Zuiko 50-250mm lens set at 150mm and exposed at *f*/11 for 1/60 sec. on Fujichrome 100.

CHAPTER 6

Seasonal Changes

Your own garden is a good place to start seasonal picture-taking. The overcast light of a cloudy day and my film choice enabled me to bring out the rich colors in this detail of spring pansies in a private garden in Greensboro, North Carolina. With a Zuiko 90mm macro lens, I exposed at *f*/5.6 for 1/2 sec. on Ektachrome 100 SW.

I carefully composed this vignette to capture the various shapes, colors, and textures of spring flowers in a private garden in New York. Here, I used an Olympus Stylus Zoom 115, autoexposure settings, and Ektachrome 100.

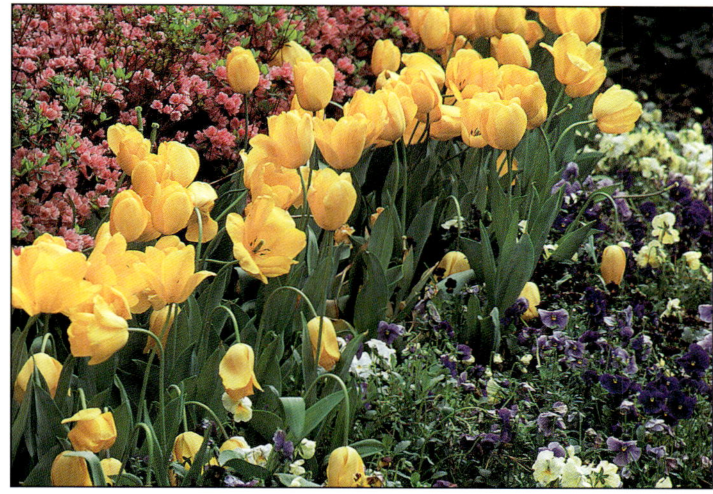

A garden is truly a place for all seasons when it comes to creating stunning photographs. And the more often you visit a particular garden—whether it is your own or a public one in your area—the more you'll become aware of the subtle changes that occur as one season flows into the next. You'll notice new shoots and buds as they emerge, witness blooms at their peak, and marvel as changes in light and weather transform familiar terrain.

Flowering dogwoods enliven this dimly illuminated spring woodland scene made at the New York Botanical Garden in the Bronx, New York. Shooting with an Olympus Stylus Zoom 115, autoexposure settings, and Fujichrome 100 kept the rich greens and bright whites in proper contrast.

Late spring blooms spill over the flower beds at Mount Vernon outside Washington, DC. The wide-angle perspective encompasses an overview that includes both garden and setting. I slightly overexposed to brighten the overcast scene. Working with a Zuiko 35-70mm lens set at 35mm, I exposed at *f*/16 for 1/30 sec. on Fujichrome Provia.

Of course, photographers familiar with the cycle of seasonal plants will be well-prepared for the kinds of images that are possible. Don't bother looking for tulips in August or chrysanthemums in May. This kind of seasonal awareness will be especially important if you're traveling to gardens famous for particular collections. Nothing is as disappointing as finding that the flowers you expected to photograph aren't in season.

This chapter will alert you to some of the typical photographic finds of each season, although exact dates will vary with your location and the weather conditions from one year to the next. But don't always set out with a specific notion of what you hope to photograph. A plan shouldn't become a straightjacket. Instead, leave room to approach each garden visit with a sense of discovery and finding the unexpected.

Remember to notice not only the individual plants, but also the entire arrangement of the garden and how it comes to life in a different way as the year progresses. And always keep your eye on the special qualities of light. Light changes as the days wax and wane, and the sun's position in the sky differs from one season to the next.

THE SIGNS OF SPRING

Spring doesn't so much burst into bloom as test to see if the time is right for a full floral eruption. Shrubs, such as forsythia, witch hazel, and rosebud, are early harbingers of spring. You can effectively photograph them on a cloudy day. The overcast illumination brings out their radiant color, especially if they're set against a background of dark foliage or a nearby building.

Certain bulbs, such as crocuses, narcissus, grape hyacinths, and tulips, also herald spring's arrival. Capture them in vignettes using any kind of low-angled light—front-, side-, or backlight—to help define the shape of each individual flower in the grouping. Later spring bulbs, such as irises, look best in subdued, diffused light. For a more dramatic effect, try photographing them in backlight. Soon after, you'll find flowering trees—

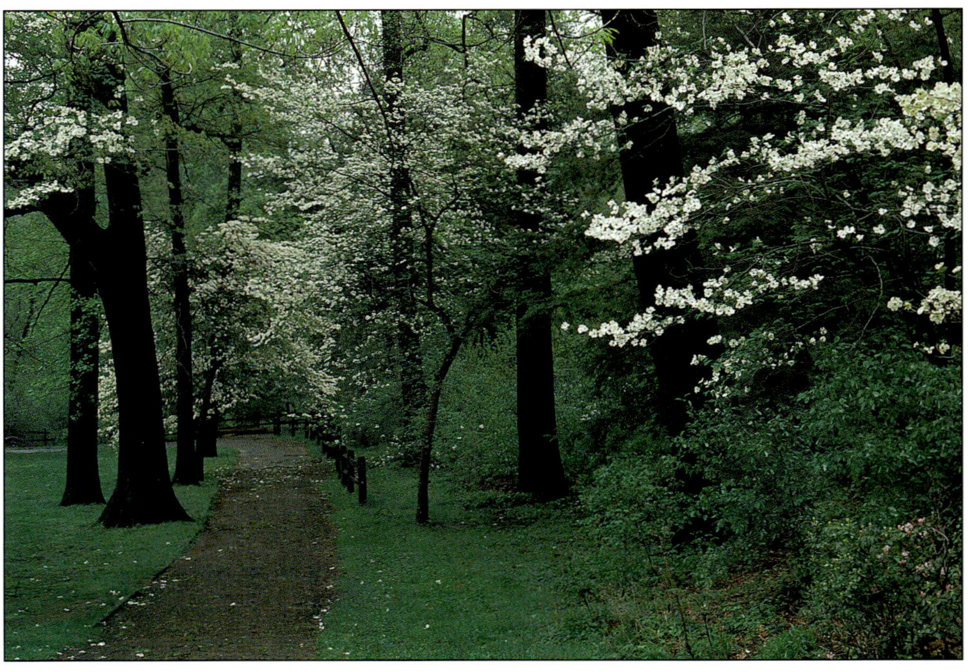

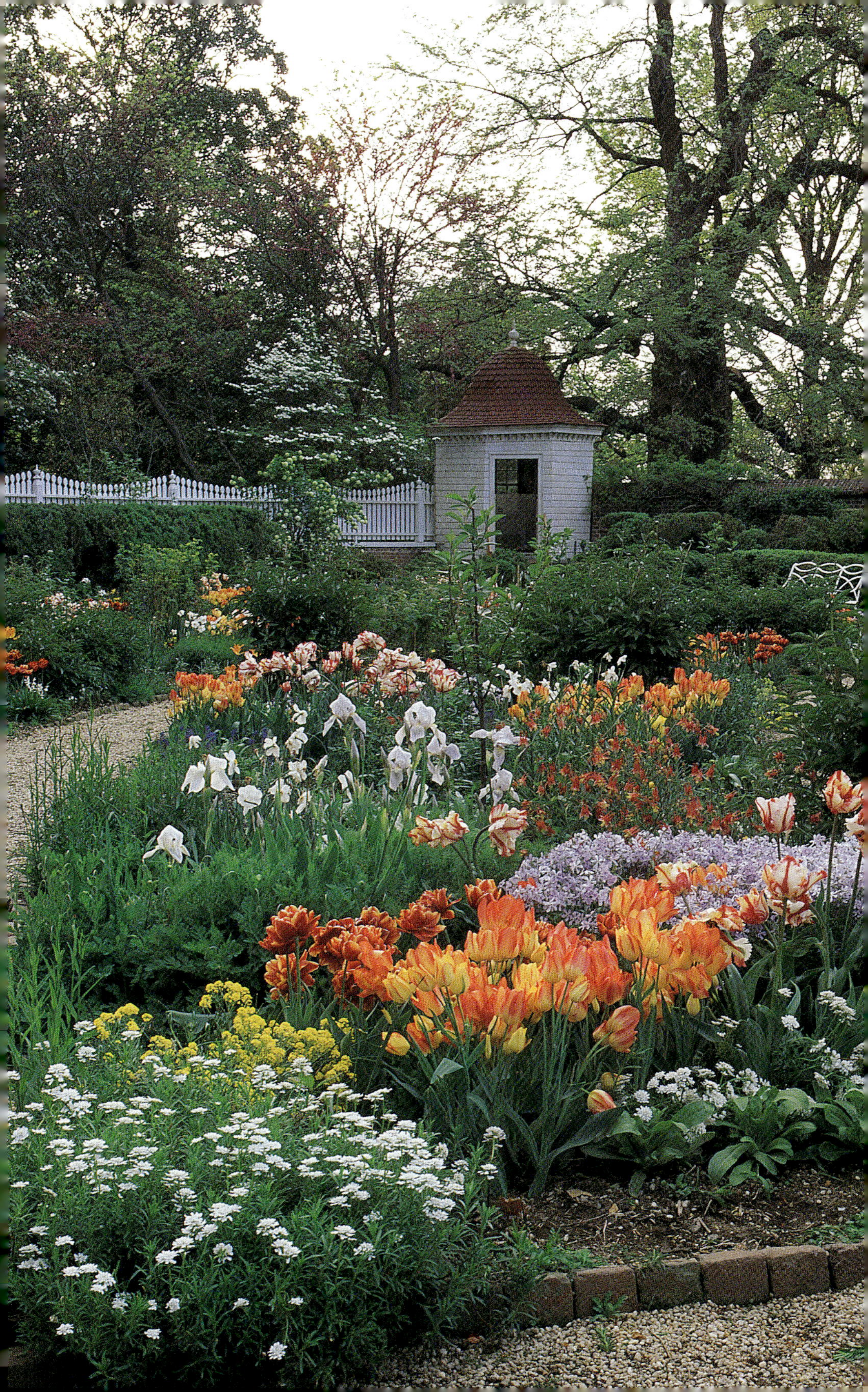

I recorded this summer mix of brilliant annuals and perennials at Buchart Gardens in Victoria, British Columbia, on an overcast day. A moderate telephoto setting compresses the space between the flowers, and the relatively fast shutter speed and small aperture kept the image sharp. Shooting with a Zuiko 50-250mm lens set at 130mm, I exposed Fujichrome Provia for 1/125 sec. at *f*/16.

magnolia, dogwood, cherry, and crabapple trees. If you can, shoot them against a contrasting dark backdrop or from a distance using a telephoto lens in order to concentrate on their flowers.

Throughout the early spring, try to capture the delicate young green of budding leaves. To bring out the soft pastel colors of trees, shoot them on overcast days or in diffused light, preferably low-angled front- or sidelight, not backlight. Both spring mist and rain enhance their fresh tonalities, which might also benefit from slight overexposure from the meter reading. As you continue to photograph through the spring, watch for dead spots and try to avoid them. If that is impossible, camouflage them by hiding them behind other plants or structures.

SUMMER PERSPECTIVES

Summer gardens offer a gaudy profusion of annuals and perennials to photograph, from roses and hydrangeas to dahlias and zinnias. While their colors beckon you into the garden with your camera, keep in mind that the summer sun can wilt the brightest floral image. If possible, avoid photographing in bright sunlight and in the middle of the day. If you

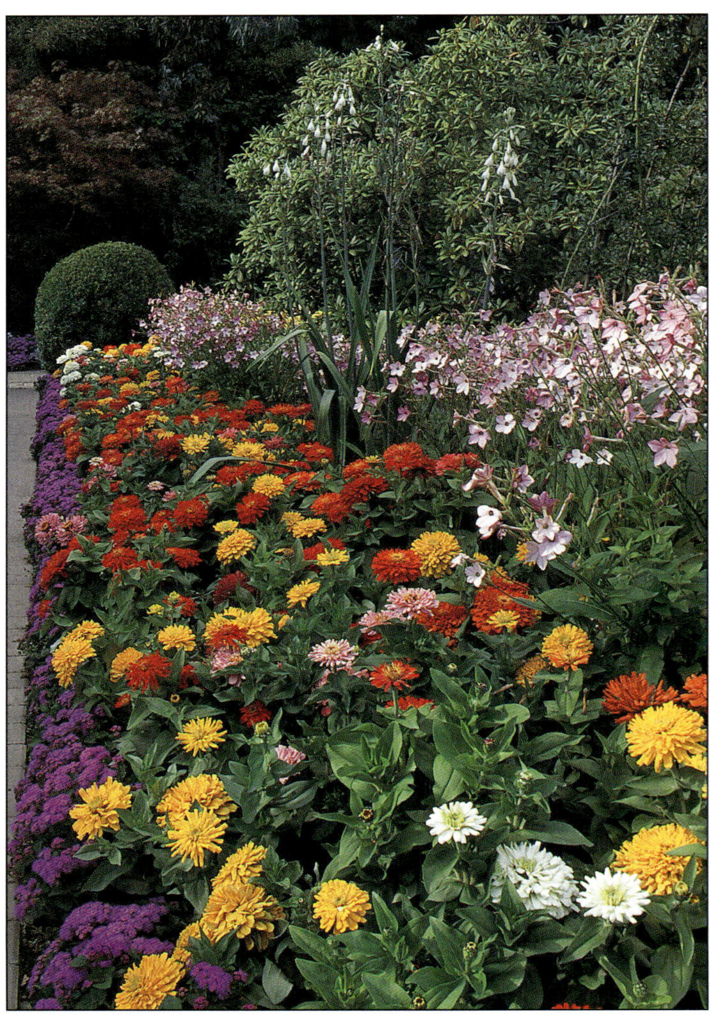

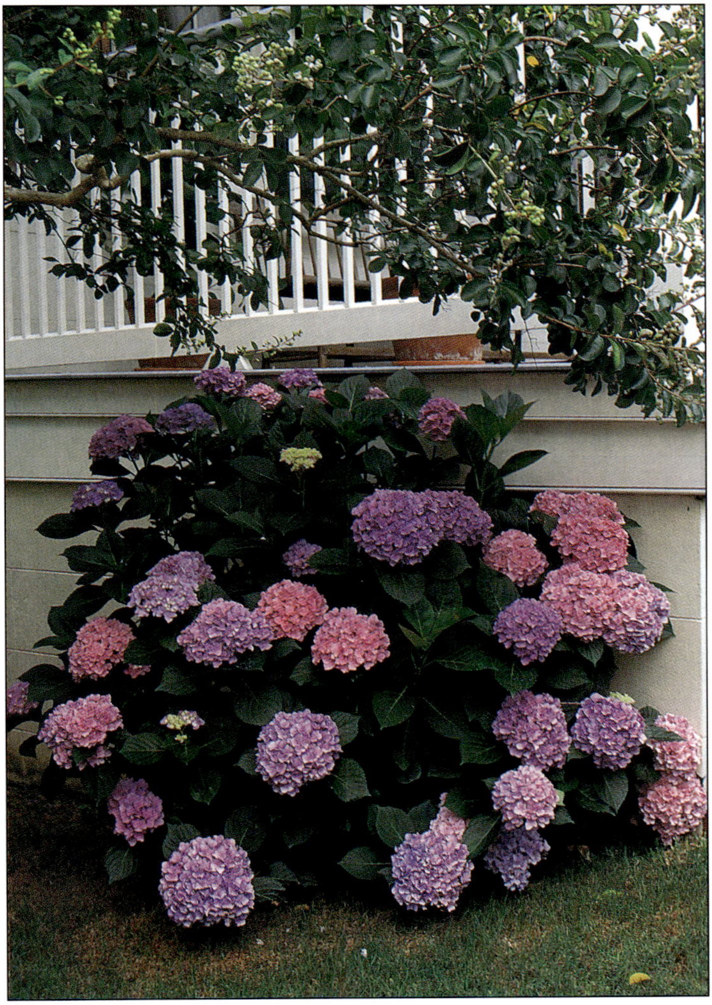

A hydrangea shrub in a private garden in Natchez, Mississippi, makes a fine focal point for this shot, taken with a slightly wide-angle setting to frame the porch above. The film and exposure settings enlivened the colors on this overcast day. With a Zuiko 35-70mm lens set at 40mm, I exposed Fujichrome Provia at *f*/8 for 1/60 sec.

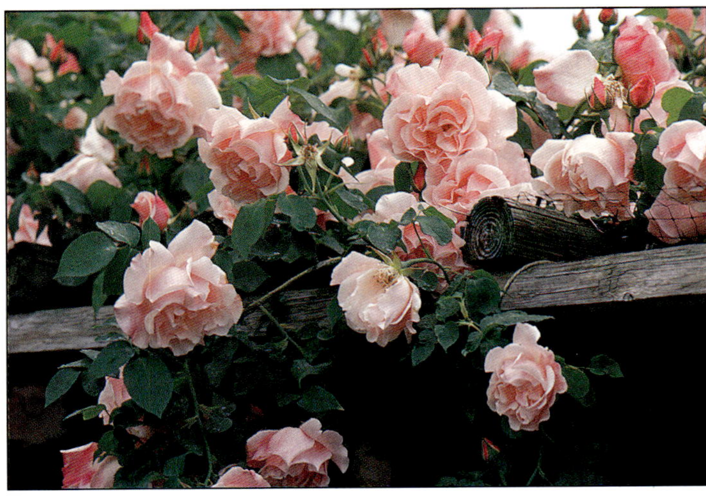

Moving to the right spot and using a telephoto zoom lens helped me frame this tight, upward shot of summer roses cascading over a trellis at Wave Hill in New York. I wanted to block the bright overcast light in the background and to maintain the delicate pinks. Working with a Zuiko 50-250mm lens set at 200mm, I exposed Fujichrome 100 at *f*/8 for 1/30 sec.

This telephoto shot masses the summer flowers at Villa Garzoni in Italy, thereby enhancing the impact of their colors within the formal garden setting. Slight overexposure and my film choice brightened the dull light. Here, I used a Zuiko 50-250mm lens set at 180mm and exposed at *f*/5.6 for 1/60 sec. on Fujichrome 100.

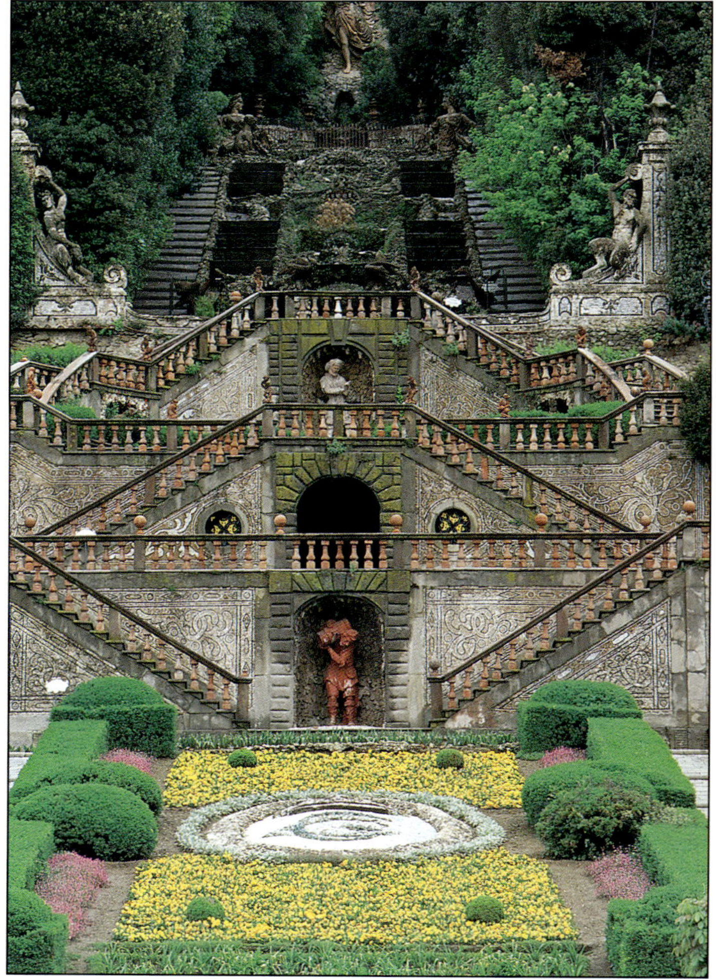

must take some summer garden shots in harsh sunlight, see if polarizing helps remove glare and bright spots. Another option is to use your fill-flash, which is the low-intensity flash setting that many cameras with dedicated flash units provide, to even out the light and possibly darken the background so your floral subjects stand out better.

Roses are particularly problematic in this regard. A summer favorite, roses are often a disappointment for photographers. Unless you're shooting closeups, you need to pay close attention to bright areas that might dominate your image and spoil it. Also, notice distractions, such as people, paths, and signs in the background. Use a wide-angle lens to get close to a good arrangement of roses in the foreground. Then check that the rest of the rose garden creates a supportive backdrop.

Summer is also the time to focus on natural gardens. In recent years, more gardeners and landscapers have turned to plantings of native wildflowers both to reduce garden maintenance and to work more closely with nature. Such natural gardens often include a variety of grasses and meadow plants with great textures. Photograph these in the late afternoon using the low sun for sidelighting or backlighting to achieve the most dramatic results.

As perennials emerge throughout the summer months, find ways of grouping or massing them to maximize their impact. Try a handful of peonies, a border of day lilies, or an expanse of lupines or lavender. Alternatively, you can juxtapose different floral neighbors into interesting vignettes that contrast their shapes, colors, and textures.

Move as needed to improve your composition and to get a flattering light on your garden subjects. Work around dead flowers or find unusual ways to make them appear interesting. For example, portray the scattered on the ground, show them as interesting forms, focus on the remaining stems and internal structures, or integrate them into fall foliage and textures. And remember to vary your vantage point, including shots from below toward the sky. This helps eliminate a confusing background, especially if the sky polarizes well.

AUTUMN VISTAS

Because everyone knows about the beauty of fall foliage, the question for garden photographers is how best to portray that foliage in such a way that it radiates a special luminosity and richness of colors. In general, the warm yellows, reds, oranges, and browns in a garden scene photograph best when the sun is low, so try to incorporate sunrise or sunset light to make fall colors glow. Use backlighting and sidelighting to bring out textures and enrich colors still more. On occasion, you might want to use warming filters to enhance colors. For example, warming filters help if you're photographing at high noon on a bright, clear day or shooting closeups of foliage on a dull, overcast day when the light is grayish.

Keep in mind that the peak foliage time is fairly short and that some specimens are at peak color for only a few days. So if you want to capture fall color, get outdoors often to shoot the best color in your vicinity. Each time you venture forth, think of the kinds of plantings to feature. Check the grass gardens, which should be their most lush at this time of year and photograph beautifully in backlight or sidelight. Look for

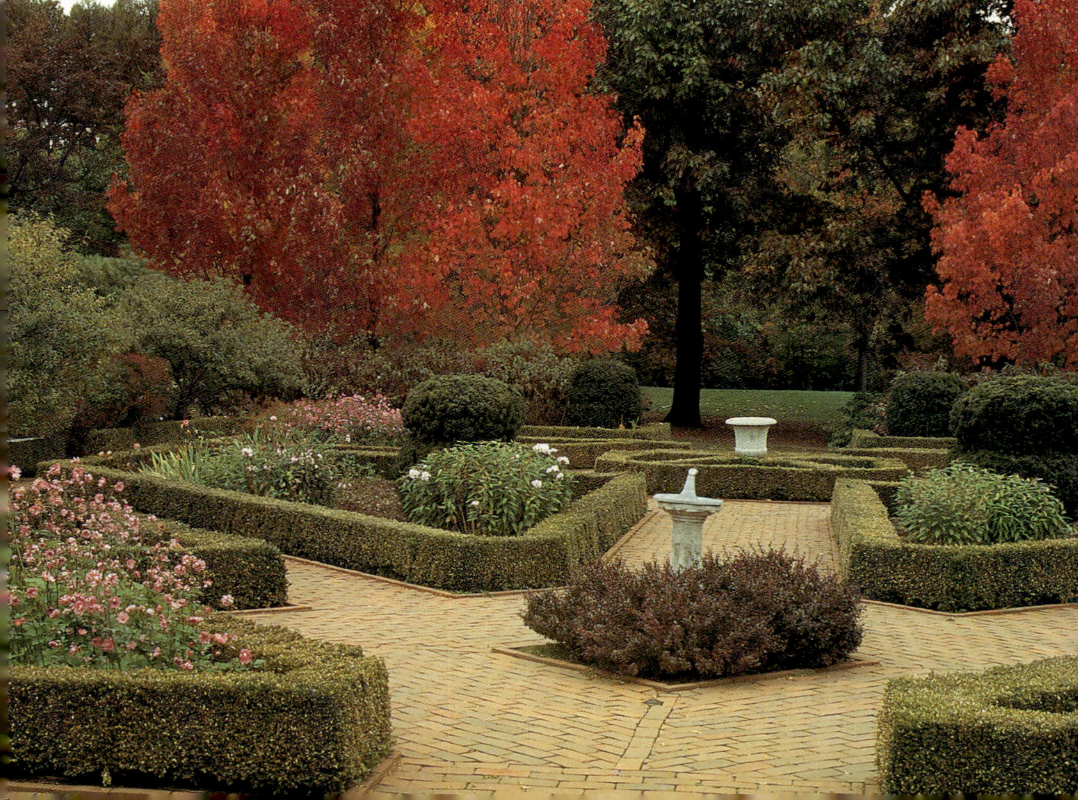

A wide-angle setting was just wide enough to frame this overview and to include some of the brilliant fall foliage at the Kingwood Center in Mansfield, Ohio. The warm tones benefit from my choice of film, and the exposure settings provided the necessary depth of field on a windless day. Shooting with a Zuiko 35-70mm lens set at 35mm, I exposed for 1/15 sec. at *f*/11 on Ektachrome 64 EPX.

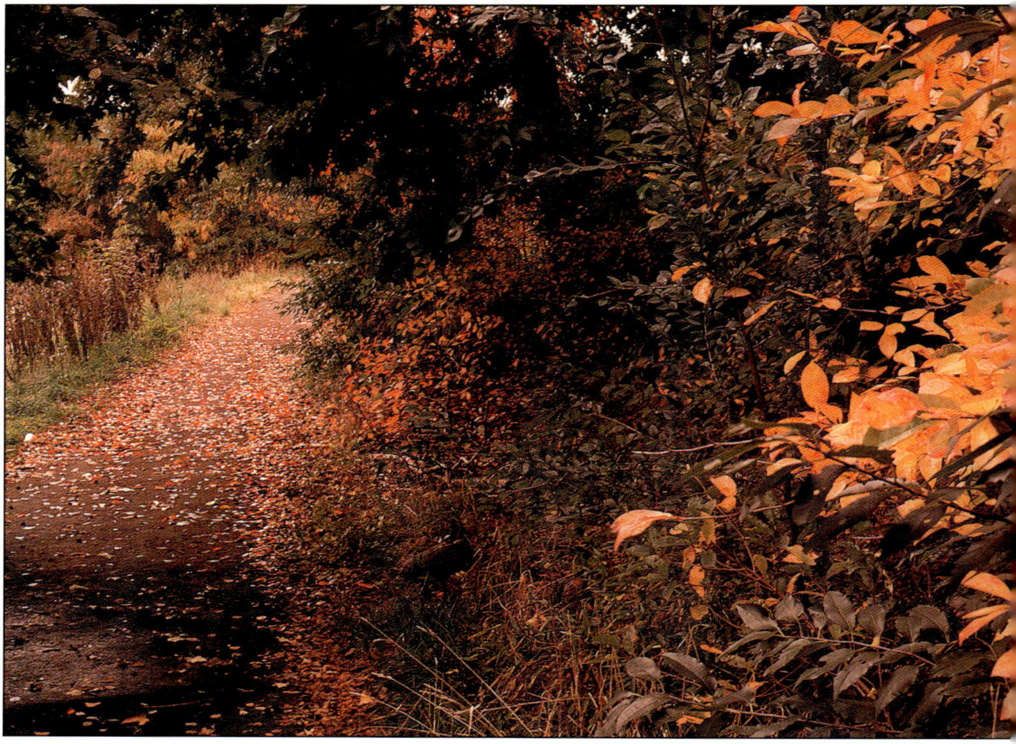

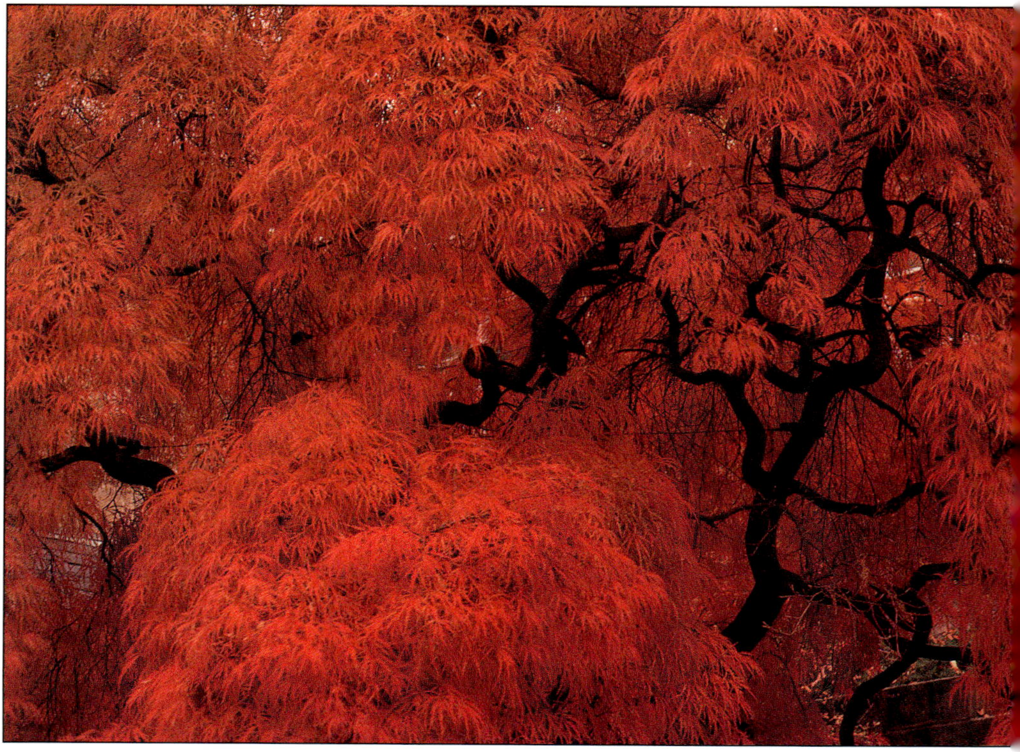

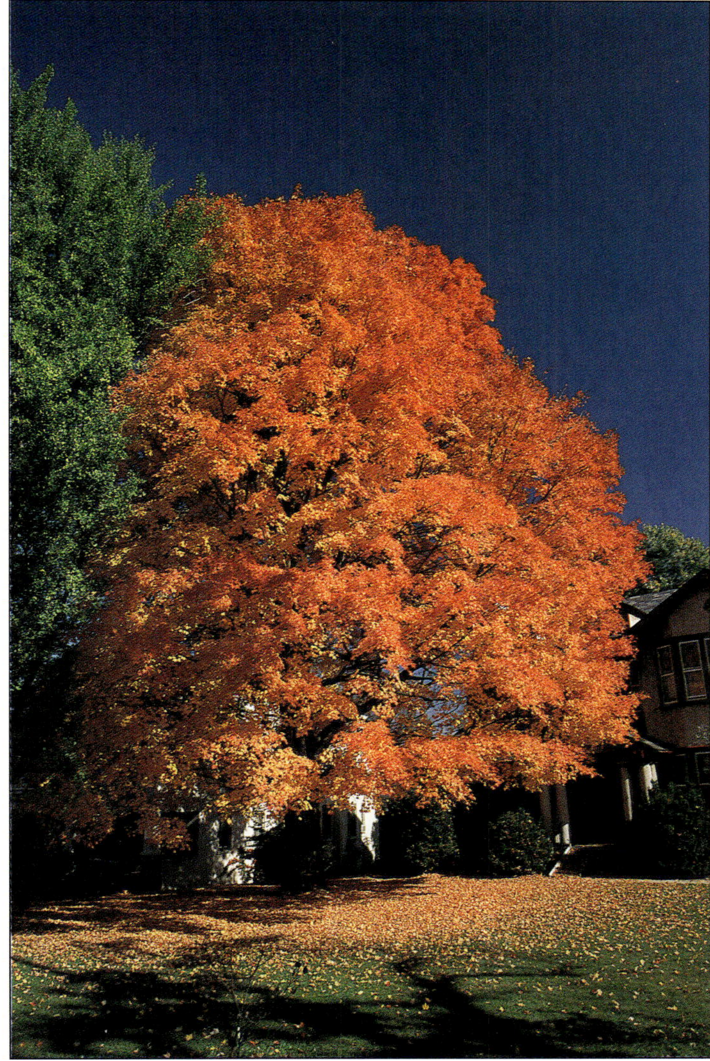

An unusual vantage point captures the leaves strewn on a path at the New York Botanical Garden in the Bronx, New York. A wide-angle lens framed the vignette, while my film choice, exposure settings, and a filter kept the colors warm and saturated. With a Zuiko 35mm lens and an 81B warming filter, I exposed Kodachrome 25 for 1/8 sec. at *f*/8.

This detail of a split-leaf Japanese maple shot in a private garden in Yonkers, New York, emphasizes the rich red color of the fall foliage. Working with a Zuiko 90mm macro lens, I exposed Fujichrome 100 at *f*/11 for 1/30 sec.

A polarizing filter deepened the blue sky and cut glare to bring out the fall-foliage colors in this wide-angle shot of a private garden in Virginia. My film choice dramatized the colors even further. With a Zuiko 35-70mm lens set at 35mm, I exposed at *f*/8 for 1/125 sec. on Fujichrome Provia.

chrysanthemums and coneflowers for interesting vignettes and details. And, of course, feature trees when they are at peak color.

Work with paths to help organize your compositions. This is particularly important when flowers are past their prime and become subsidiary subjects. And camouflage dead areas by repositioning yourself for a better perspective before you release the shutter.

WINTER VIEWS

Unfortunately, many photographers don't consider gardens appropriate subjects during the winter months. Although gardens are bereft of their bright colors and luxuriant foliage, they present fascinating graphic and textural possibilities to astute photographers. Consider the formal design elements: line, shape, pattern, and contrast. Keep your images simple and spare so their focal point is self-evident.

Continue to think in terms of the overview, vignette, and detail. For example, develop a garden landscape scene around a river or stream. In a

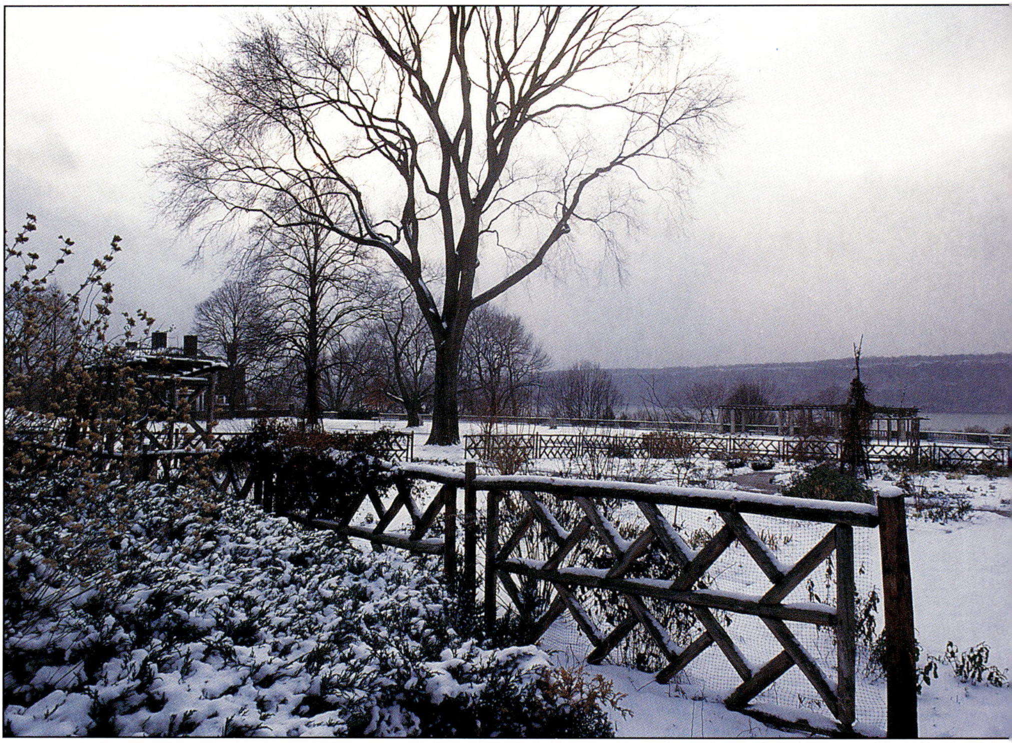

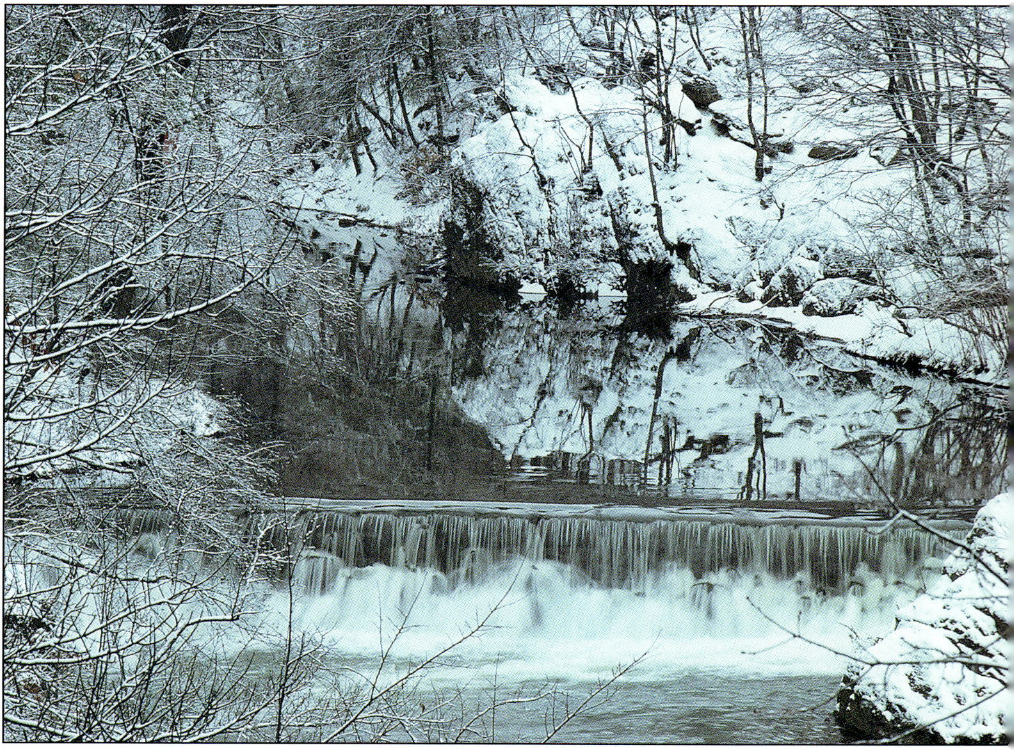

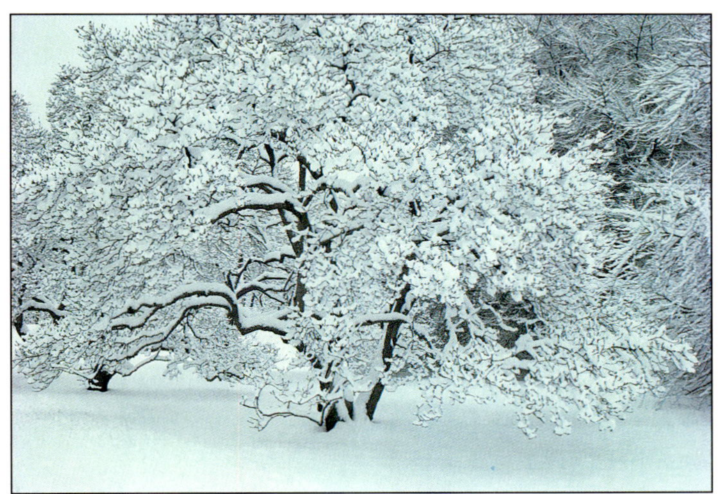

This basically monochromatic image of the garden at Wave Hill in New York emphasizes the contrast of lines created by the fencing and tree against snow and an overcast sky. I deliberately exploited the bluish cast via my choice of film and slight underexposure. Shooting with a Zuiko 35mm lens, I exposed Fujichrome 100 at *f*/8 for 1/60 sec.

A small cascade on the Bronx River makes a fine focal point for this winter portrayal photographed at the New York Botanical Garden in the Bronx, New York. A telephoto lens setting framed the overview. My choice of film and the very small aperture maximized image sharpness, while a moderately slow shutter speed made the water milky white. Here, I used a Zuiko 50-250mm lens set at 150mm and exposed Kodachrome 25 for 1/60 sec. at *f*/16.

Freshly fallen snow brings out the graceful lines of the branches and the shape of this magnolia tree at the New York Botanical Garden in the Bronx, New York. Shooting handheld with a Nikkor 80-200mm lens set at 100mm, I exposed at *f*/11 for 1/250 sec. on Kodachrome 25.

wet meadow, find interesting textures in the dried grasses and wildflowers, which you can portray differently on overcast and sunny days. Another possibility is to work with a stand of bare trees. Look closely at the pattern of their bark, imaginatively group their trunks, or focus on their snow-laden branches.

Since your images will tend to be monochromatic, you should approach a winter garden with the eye of a black-and-white photographer. What bits of color remain will tend to be subdued earth tones, so work to bring out their subtle beauty. In general, expose for the middle tones, the grays and browns of tree bark and winter grasses, rather than the extremes of contrast, such as white snow or black rock outcrops.

If you're planning to shoot after a snowfall, get out while the snow is still fresh and unsullied. Meter carefully because snow tends to underexpose and turn gray. Determining exposure is easier on overcast days than in harsh sunshine. As a rule of thumb, meter the white and then overexpose by one to two *f*-stops depending on how bright the snow is. If you're shooting on a sunny day, check to see if the sky polarizes well.

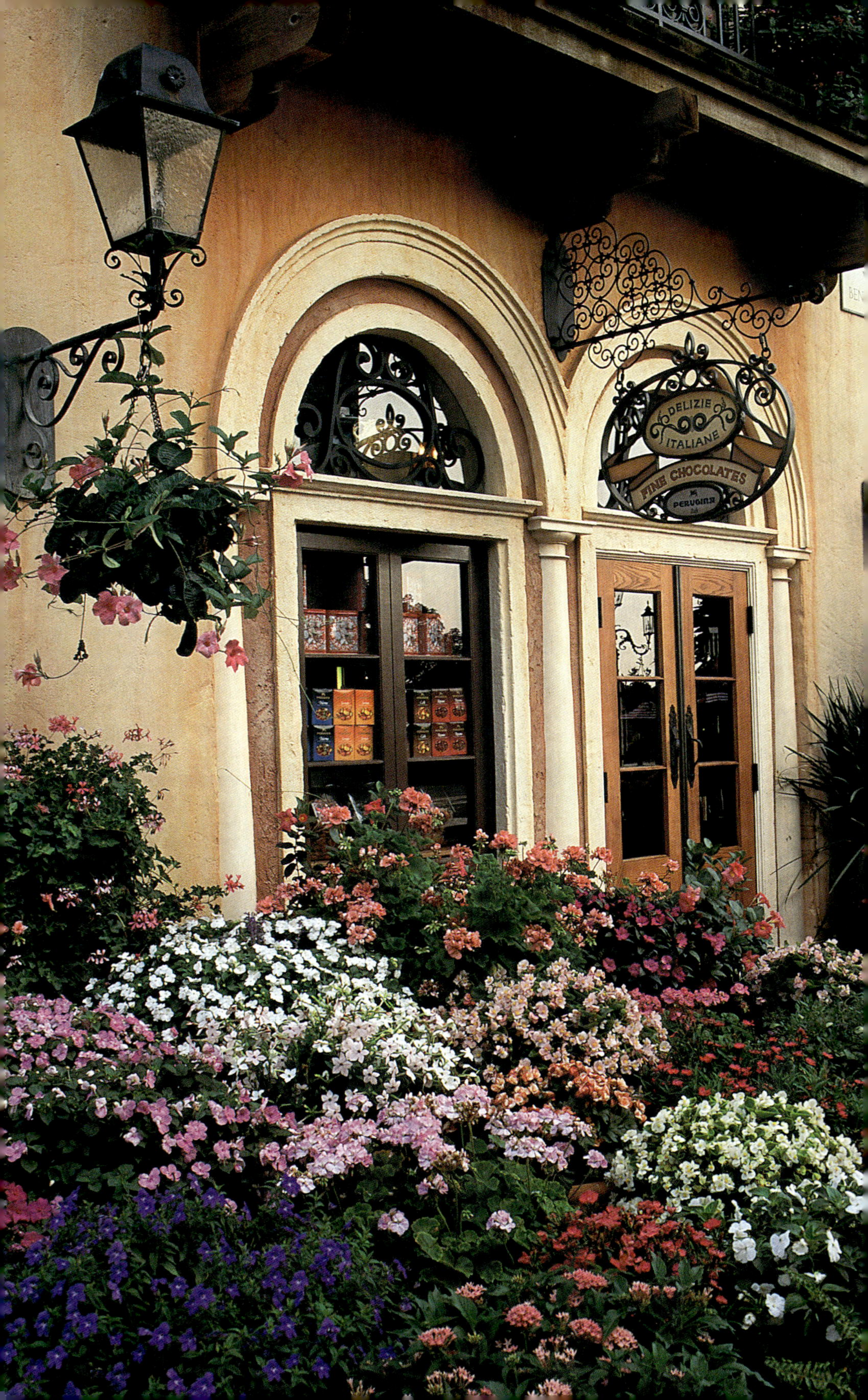
DELIZIE ITALIANE
FINE CHOCOLATES
PERUGINA

CHAPTER 7

Garden Varieties

Potted flowering plants are the mainstay of this entryway garden at the Italian Pavilion in Florida's Epcot Center. The vignette combines the plantings with their architectural backdrop. Working with a Zuiko 35-70mm lens set at 35mm, I exposed for 1/15 sec. at *f*/11 on Ektachrome 100 SW.

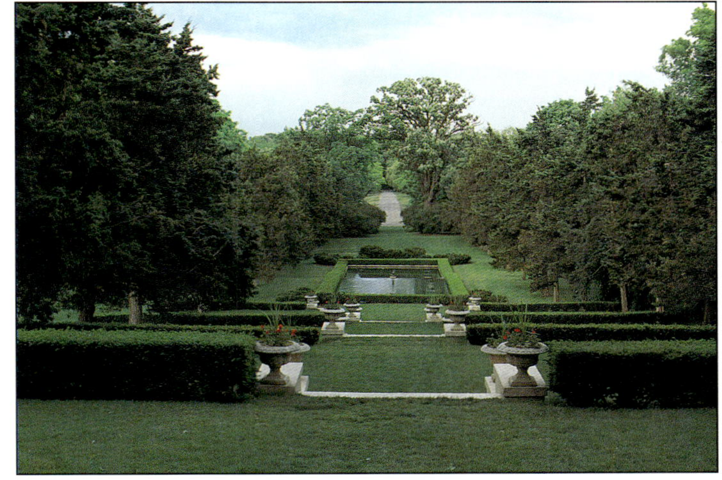

The unexpected grandeur of Cantigny Gardens in Wheaton, Illinois, is a marvelous example of garden design transforming the midwestern landscape. Here, I used a Zuiko 35-70mm lens set at 35mm and exposed at *f*/8 for 1/60 sec. on Fujichrome 100.

While each garden is unique, design styles are recognizable. Some of these are particular to a country, region, or period in history. They often reflect deeply held beliefs and attitudes embedded in the culture of the time and place. In this sense, gardens are living testaments, not only to those individuals who designed them but to the people who were meant to use and enjoy them.

Well-defined paths, rectilinear flower beds, and curved rose arbors, such as these at the Missouri Botanic Garden in St. Louis, are signs of a formal garden design. With a Zuiko 35-70mm lens set at 35mm, I exposed Ektachrome 100 SW for 1/30 sec. at *f*/16.

As a photographer, you need to understand the ideas behind various types of gardens so you can look more carefully and organize what you see into more revealing images. In a somewhat oversimplified approach, the many varieties of gardens are divided into four convenient categories in this chapter: formal, natural, home, and water gardens. These divisions are too broad for any garden historian, but they serve as a guide to the visual perspectives you'll want to capture as you explore each kind with your camera.

FORMAL GARDENS

These gardens place a great deal of emphasis on the human role in creating a garden. Formal gardens reveal rather than hide a great deal of planning. Fine historic examples are the magnificent estate gardens of England, France, and Italy, with their architectural and decorative ornaments and extensive system of paths, steps, and even canals. Look for symmetry in the layout, but don't feel that every image must be perfectly balanced. Incorporate paths, stairs, walls, and statuary to help guide the eye in your compositions.

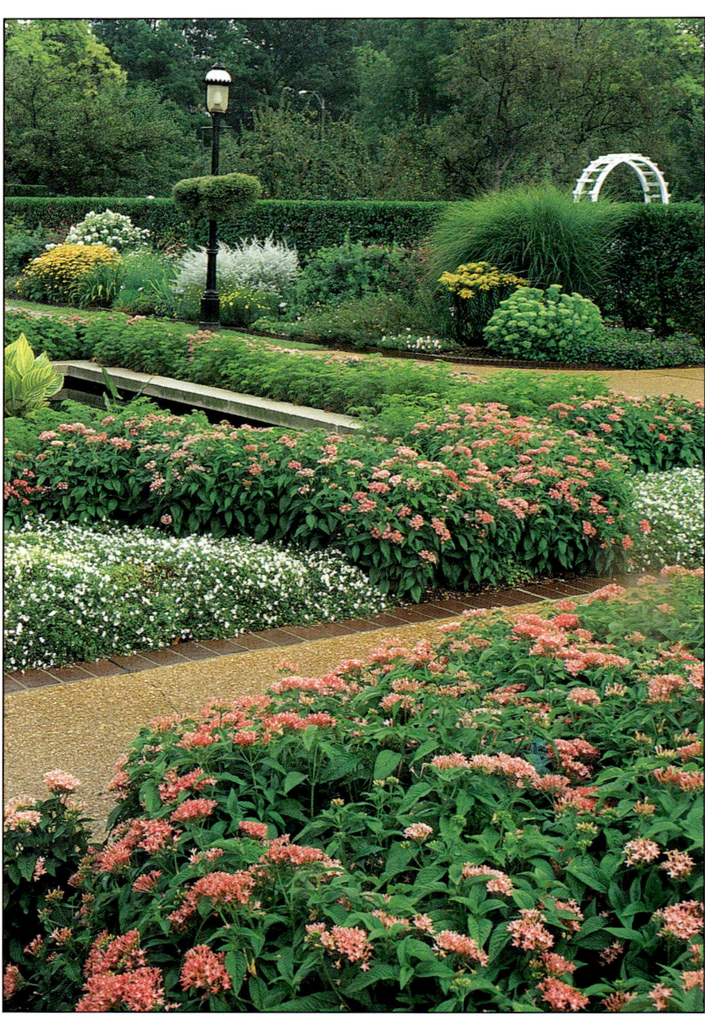

Emphasize overviews to show the precision of the design, and plan your image in terms of shapes, textures, and colors. This strategy is especially important when you photograph large rose or vegetable gardens. For topiary, be sure the shapes are well-defined against a simple backdrop. For large expanses of bulbs, walk around to see the best presentation for the color display. Perennial borders work well when seen in relation to a path, wall, or architectural structure and when shot in low-angled or diffused light that brings out textural nuances.

Think, too, about unusual juxtapositions that an individual garden might present or techniques that might go against the formal nature of these gardens. For example, you might want to soften the stark symmetry of a formal garden by shooting in soft, early morning light and using a diffusing filter. An alternative is to portray straight paths as strong diagonal lines in your composition. Experiment to find new, untraditional ways to depict these most traditional kinds of gardens.

NATURAL GARDENS

Unlike formal gardens, natural gardens attempt to create a sense of spontaneity in their design. The better planned they are, the less visible the human hand and mind are. Traditional Japanese gardens, English home gardens, rock gardens, seaside gardens, grass gardens, woodland gardens, and meadow gardens—all of these are examples of the trend toward natural presentations.

To photograph such gardens most effectively, emphasize vignettes that show a combinations of plants. Focus on the textures of the foliage, which are often more interesting and central to the effect than color. Use your medium telephoto lenses to juxtapose flowers with foliage, grasses, rocks, and other diverse elements. In addition, work with overviews that show the architectural or natural settings. Find an interesting perspective since you aren't as confined to a formal design: crouch down low or look down from above.

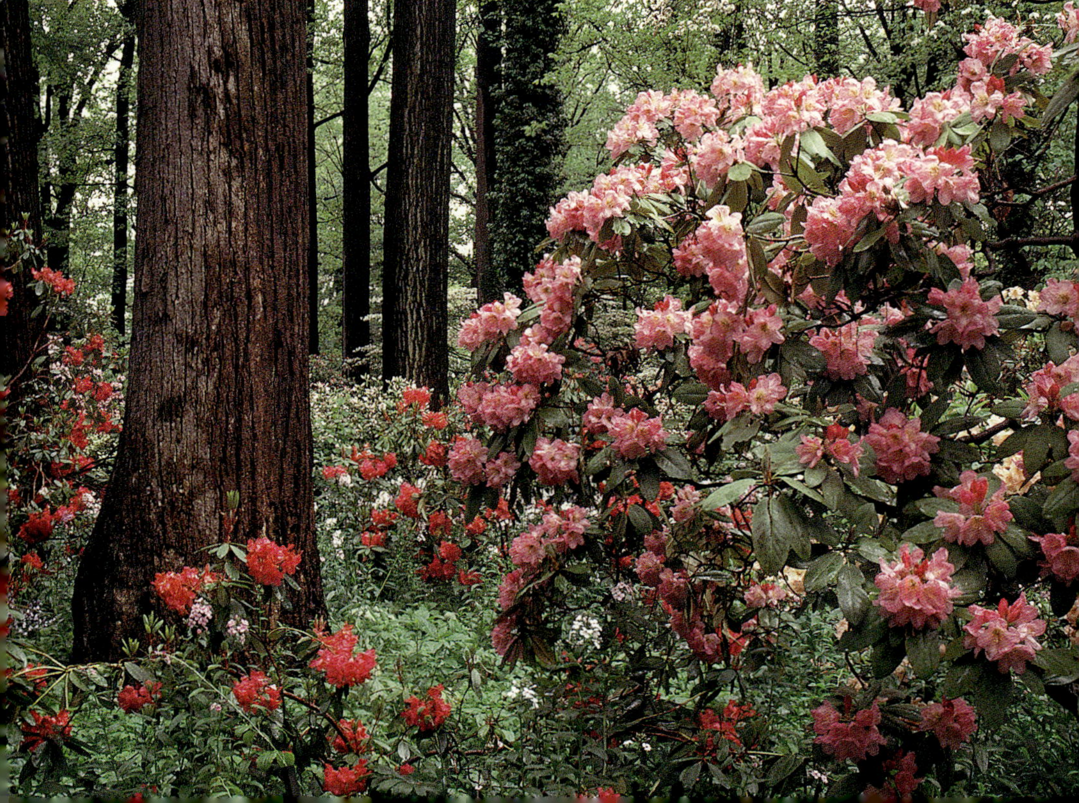

Natural gardens emphasize native plants in casual or restored environments. This Winterthur garden in Wilmington, Delaware, combines native woodlands with plantings of azaleas and rhododendrons. Shooting with a Zuiko 35-70mm lens set at 50mm, I exposed at *f*/16 for 1/15 sec. on Kodachrome 25.

Light plays a key role in portraying the distinctive textures and muted colors of most natural gardens. Analyze the light carefully to create a mood, especially a soft, romantic quality. Use backlighting liberally to highlight the plantings, and experiment with soft focus or deliberate blurring due to movement.

HOME GARDENS

Obviously, home gardens don't have the breadth and expansiveness of estate or public gardens, but their charm and character can more than make up for those deficits. Of course, gardeners who want to record the fruits of their labors will want their photographs to do justice to their efforts. You can bring out the character of home gardens by showing them in relation to the house they're meant to complement. After all, a well-planned, well-maintained home garden is often the setting that helps display the special features of the home. While you might not be able to do much about the garden plan at the last minute, you should always check for grooming and maintenance before you begin to shoot. You might even

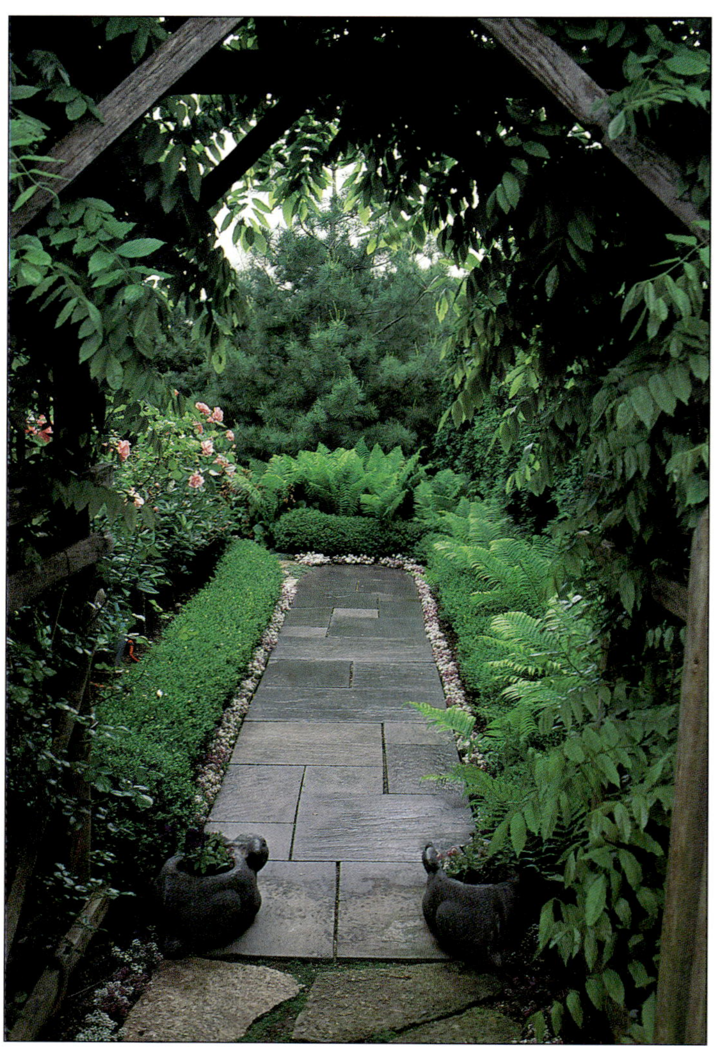

Even in private home gardens, such as this one in Highland Park, Illinois, which is outside Chicago, enticing entryways and other distinctive traits are worth exploring with your camera. Working with a Zuiko 35-70mm lens set at 50mm, I exposed Fujichrome Velvia at *f*/11 for 1/8 sec.

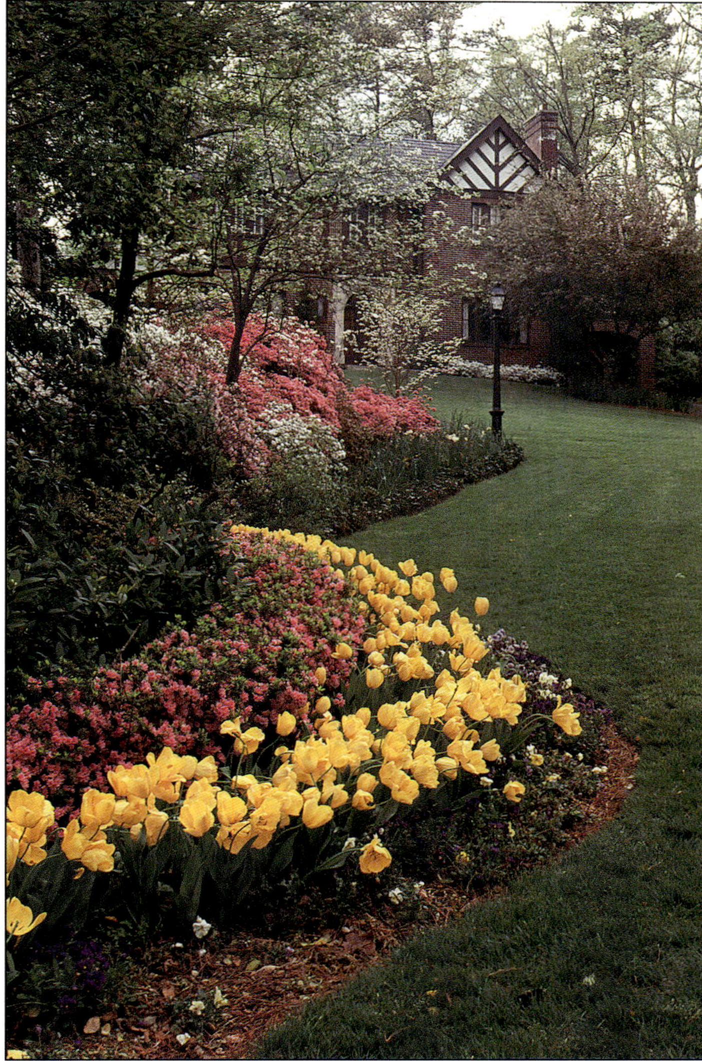

Many Southerners take great pride in embellishing their home lawns with flowering borders. This extravagant display of spring bulbs graced a home in Atlanta, Georgia. Here, I used an Olympus Stylus Zoom 115, autoexposure, and Fujichrome 100.

get ideas for better planning as you photograph in your own garden and realize what is missing or needed.

Concentrate on vignettes and closeups, though overviews might also be appropriate. Vignettes that feature such architectural details as steps, doors, gates, and windows, work particularly well. You don't have to include the home in every shot, but it helps to incorporate at least a hint of the building in order to show the relationship of the plantings to the home. Look for new perspectives and vary your angle so you don't get into a rut, especially if you're shooting in your own garden. Use your wide-angle lens in confined spaces or to get overviews that make your foreground plantings more prominent.

You might not be able to get ideal lighting conditions, especially if other homes are nearby. Analyze the lighting options carefully, and be sure to do your shooting at the best times of day for each part of the garden. And remember that overcast days are often the best for garden photography, bringing out colors and reducing glare and hot spots.

This overhead view, shot from the roof of PepsiCo World Headquarters in Purchase, New York, reveals the delicate geometry of the water gardens in the Donald M. Kendall Sculpture Garden. Shooting with a Zuiko 50-250mm lens set at 150mm, I exposed for 1/125 sec. at *f*/8 on Kodachrome 25.

Careful composition and no polarization made the reflections possible in this image of Monet's waterlily garden in Giverny, France. Working with a Zuiko 35-70mm lens set at 50mm, I exposed Fujichrome 100 for 1/60 sec. at *f*/8.

WATER GARDENS

Even gardens that aren't primarily planned around a body of water often contain pools and ponds that enhance their overall design. No doubt, the element of water adds a wonderful dimension to any garden. This is either because of the water's movement and gentle sounds or because of its reflective surface.

When photographing water gardens, you'll find yourself grappling particularly with the issues of motion and reflection, as well as how best to incorporate the water's edge as part of the composition. First, you need to decide how best to incorporate reflections. You can eliminate or minimize reflective surfaces if they have too much glare or if the reflections compete with other elements in the image. You might also try incorporating reflections as active parts of your image. To control glare and reflections so that they play the role you want them to, work with your polarizer, turning it on your lens until you see the result you want.

Next, if your water garden includes a fountain, waterfall, or cascade, decide whether you want to stop the motion with a fast shutter speed of at least 1/60 sec. or want to capture the sense of movement by using a slow shutter speed. Experiment with long exposures up to 1/2 sec. long to create the milky effect of moving water.

In terms of composition, portray the water's edge if the line adds to the dynamics of your image. As a rule, avoid overviews because they tend to be too bright and washed out. However, if you can find a high vantage point that enables you to depict the lines and shapes of a water garden, give it a try; it might be worth doing. Include interesting ornaments, such as bridges, rocks, or sculpture, to enhance these overviews.

Conversely, low vantage points can be quite effective, especially if you depict plants along the water's edge, such as irises, weeping willows, grasses, and trees, possibly with their reflections. Emphasize the beauty of individual plants or vignettes taken at close range or with a telephoto lens if you can't get close enough for details. Floating plants, such as waterlilies and lotuses, are especially lovely from a low vantage point when backlit.

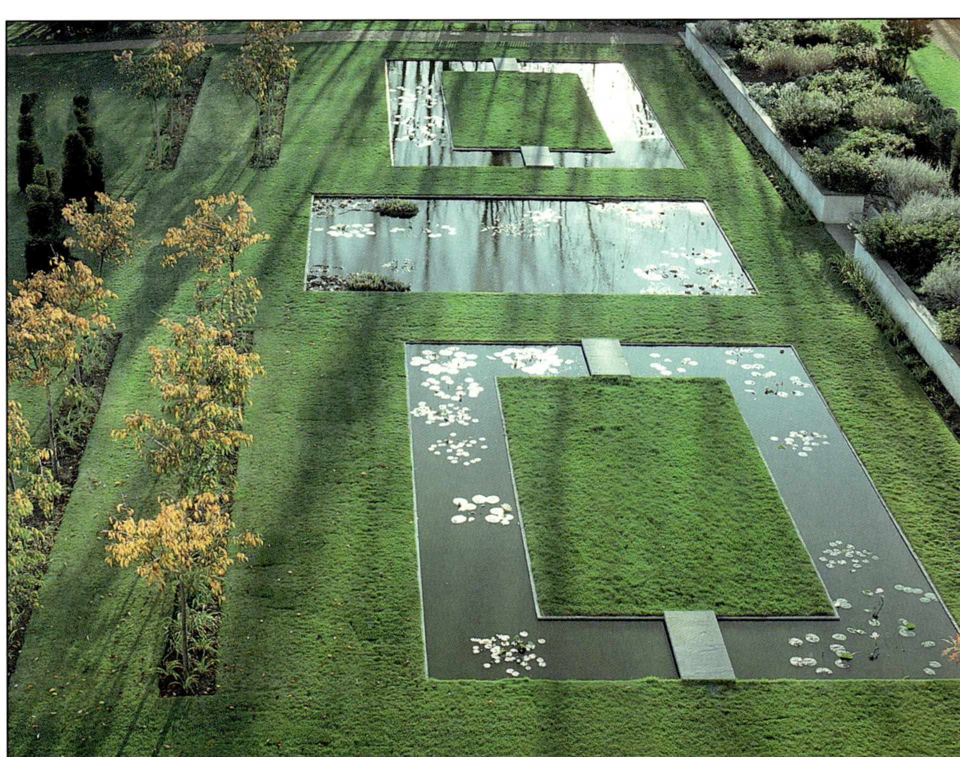

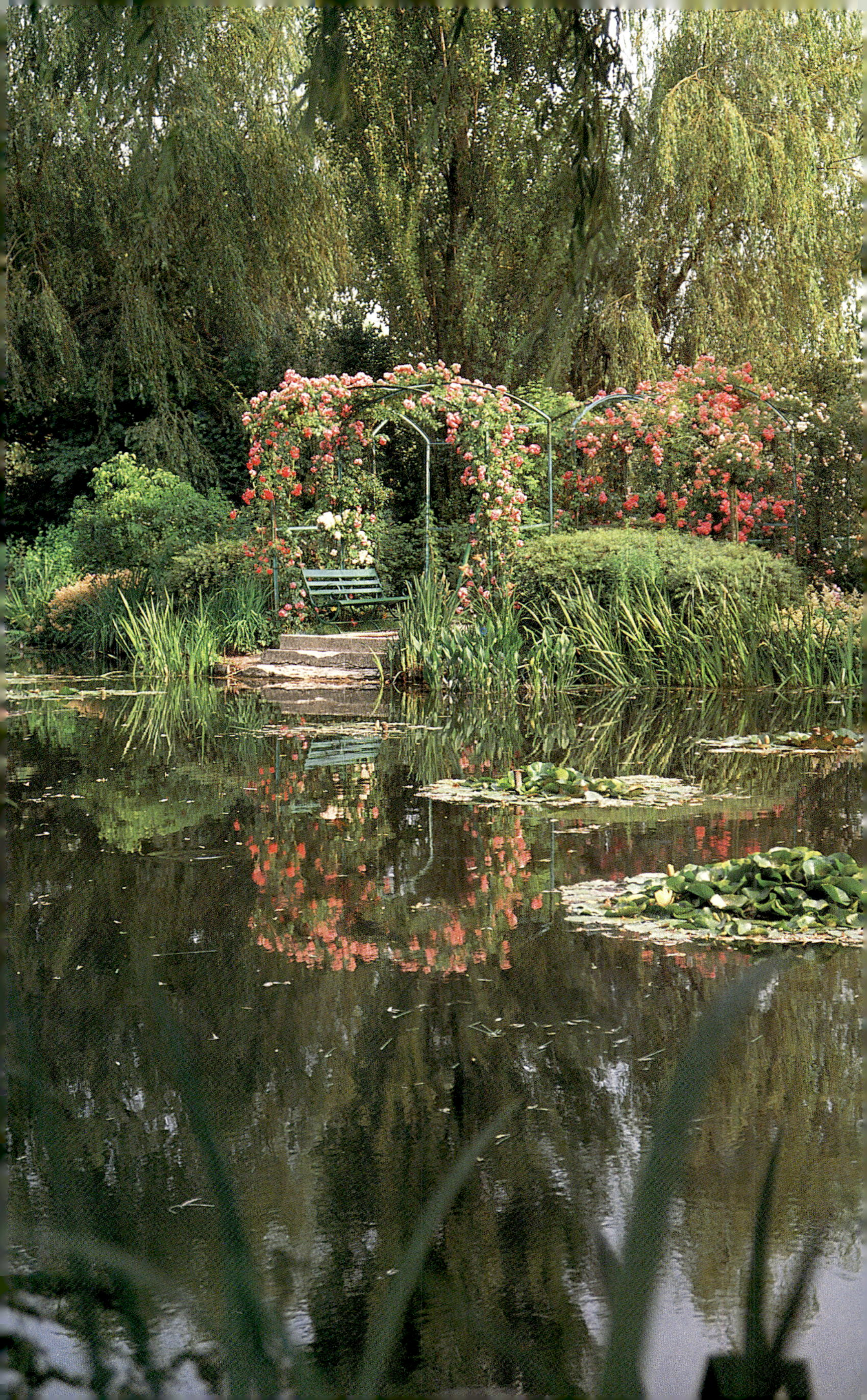

Index